Playing House

Women in German Literature

Helen Watanabe-O'Kelly, University of Oxford
Series Editor

Volume 14

PETER LANG

Oxford · Bern · Berlin · Bruxelles · Frankfurt am Main · New York · Wien

Alexandra Merley Hill

Playing House

Motherhood, Intimacy, and Domestic Spaces
in Julia Franck's Fiction

PETER LANG

Oxford · Bern · Berlin · Bruxelles · Frankfurt am Main · New York · Wien

Bibliographic information published by Die Deutsche Nationalbibliothek
Die Deutsche Nationalbibliothek lists this publication in the Deutsche
Nationalbibliografie; detailed bibliographic data is available on the
Internet at http://dnb.d-nb.de.

A catalogue record for this book is available from the British Library.

Library of Congress Cataloging-in-Publication Data:

Hill, Alexandra Merley.
 Playing house : motherhood, intimacy, and domestic spaces in Julia
Franck's fiction / Alexandra Merley Hill.
    p. cm. -- (Women in German literature ; 14)
 Includes bibliographical references and index.
 ISBN 978-3-0343-0767-3 (alk. paper)
 1. Franck, Julia--Criticism and interpretation. 2. Motherhood in
literature. 3. Intimacy (Psychology) in literature. 4. Domestic space
in literature. I. Title.
 PT2666.R264Z65 2012
 833'.92--dc23
                                2012027895

Cover image: 'Untitled' (2004) by Samantha Merley. Reprinted with permission.

ISSN 1094-6233
ISBN 978-3-0343-0767-3

© Peter Lang AG, International Academic Publishers, Bern 2012
Hochfeldstrasse 32, CH-3012 Bern, Switzerland
info@peterlang.com, www.peterlang.com, www.peterlang.net

Printed in Germany

Maria Cisyk

Contents

Acknowledgements   ix

INTRODUCTION
The 'Fräuleinwunder' and Feminism   1

CHAPTER 1
Roles: Theorizing Performativity and Performance   15

CHAPTER 2
Lovers:
The Search for and Failure of Intimacy in Berlin Literature   33

CHAPTER 3
Daughters:
Psychoanalytic Theory, Domestic Space, and Maternal Desire   63

CHAPTER 4
Mothers:
Psychoanalytic Models, the Bad Mother, and 'Maternal Drag'   111

CHAPTER 5
Fathers and Sons:
Absent Fathers, Sisters and Siblings, and Looking for Home   149

Bibliography   165

Index   179

Acknowledgements

Heartfelt thanks to everyone at Peter Lang who contributed to the shaping and publication of this book, especially Helen Watanabe-O'Kelly, Laurel Plapp and Holly Catling. Thanks also to Samantha Merley for use of her painting for the book's cover. And thanks to Father Stephen Rowan for the willing financial assistance of the Dean's Office of the College of Arts and Sciences at the University of Portland.

Thanks to current and past faculty of University of Massachusetts Amherst who provided food for thought (and sometimes food): Barton Byg, James Cathey, Sarah McGaughey and Robert Sullivan. Thanks to friends in the profession who energize and inspire me: Hester Baer, Brenda Bethman, Florence Feiereisen, Corinna Kahnke, Beret Norman, Maria Stehle and Laurie Taylor. And thanks to colleagues at Williams College and the University of Portland for their support and encouragement: Helga Druxes and Gail Newman; Trudie Booth, Maria Echenique, Lora Looney, Kate Regan and Matthew Warshawsky. Of the many wonderful people with whom I have worked (and this list is by no means comprehensive), I owe a special debt of gratitude to my partner in crime Kyle Frackman, my academic spouse Laurie McLary and our *Doktormutter* extraordinaire Susan Cocalis.

Julia Franck's *Liebediener* was the first German book that I read for fun, while in Berlin as a student in 2000. Both the author and her books have shaped my scholarly life and my personal thinking. Many thanks to Julia Franck for the pleasure and privilege of over six years of open and thought-provoking correspondence, not to mention a willingness to talk about dogs, farms, children, motherhood, the media and literature.

No matter how abstract, my academic research always has personal roots. Thanks to my mother, step-mother and father for teaching me about motherhood, fatherhood, daughterhood and humanhood. Thanks to my favorite aunt, for years of letters and the invention of the walk-and-talk. Thanks to my sister, whose perspective on life is so different from – yet as familiar as – my own. And, above all, thanks to Jamie. For everything.

The 'Fräuleinwunder' and Feminism

Although she has been writing since childhood, Julia Franck's career as an author began with winning the LiteraturWERKstatt third annual Open Mike award in 1995, an event that certainly helped to secure publication of her first novel *Der neue Koch* [The New Cook] in 1997.[1] This first publication earned Franck little attention, other than a few favourable reviews. It was with her next two publications, the novel *Liebediener* [Love Servant] in 1999 and the collection of short stories *Bauchlandung: Geschichten zum Anfassen* [Belly Flop: Stories to Touch] in 2000 that her writing gained widespread recognition.[2] The publication of these two books in close succession coincided with two simultaneous developments in German literature: a notably high number of books set in Berlin in the post-unification years, commonly referred to as Berlin literature, and a wave of publications by women authors, still referred to in scholarship as the *Fräuleinwunder* [miracle of the girls].

In many ways, these two literary trends – while distinct from each other – do overlap. Berlin literature, as the name suggests, is set in the new capital and often follows characters engaging in daily, normal activities around the city. Berlin is clearly identifiable in the text, and the specific location within the city can often be determined thanks to street names, landmarks and other clues. This literature captures Berlin at a time of transition, after the initial problems and discomforts of unification, and before it became the international hotspot for wealthy celebrities. In this Berlin the shifting landscape and the alternating sense of infinite possibilities or

1   Julia Franck, *Der neue Koch* (Frankfurt am Main: Fischer Taschenbuch Verlag, 1997).
2   Julia Franck, *Liebediener* (Cologne: DuMont Buchverlag, 1999). Julia Franck, *Bauchlandung: Geschichten zum Anfassen* (Cologne: DuMont Buchverlag, 2000).

sense of post-unification disappointment allow the characters to exist in a transitory state; at a point in their lives between leaving school and starting a career or family, the characters are neither teenagers nor adults, without obligations or responsibilities. They seem to organize their lives around encounters with others, yet these encounters can be described as chance, passing or superficial. Far from being just a backdrop of these encounters, Berlin is what makes them possible: with its party scene, its anonymity and its sense of transition and instability. Two examples of the texts frequently mentioned in this category include *Spielzone* by Tanja Dückers and *Sommerhaus, später* by Judith Hermann, although Inka Parei, Juli Zeh, Katrin Röggla and others are also linked to it.[3] Unlike the *Fräuleinwunder*, this label is not defined exclusively by female authors. More broadly interpreted, Berlin literature can include works by the following authors, among others: Thomas Brussig, Wladimir Kaminer, Sven Lager, Monika Maron, Emine Sevgi Özdamar, Ingo Schulze, Benjamin von Stuckrad-Barre and Uwe Timm.[4]

The categories of *Fräuleinwunder* literature and Berlin literature overlap but are not identical. As Feiereisen points out, the *Fräuleinwunder* texts are not really about 'Berlin an sich' [Berlin itself], although the city impacts the lives of the protagonists and is a contributing factor to their alienation.[5] Strictly speaking, the 'literarisches Fräuleinwunder' [literary miracle of the girls], a term coined by literary critic Volker Hage, is nothing more than a marketing label. Writing in the news magazine *Der*

---

3   Tanja Dückers, *Spielzone* (Berlin: Aufbau-Verlag 1999). Judith Hermann, *Sommerhaus, später* (Frankfurt am Main: S. Fischer Verlag, 1998).

4   Highlights of scholarship on Berlin literature are Katharina Gerstenberger, *Writing the New Berlin: The German Capital in Post-Wall Literature* (Rochester, NY: Camden House, 2008) and Susanne Ledanff, *Hauptstadtphantasien: Berliner Stadtlektüren in der Gegenwartsliteratur 1989–2000* (Bielefeld: Aisthesis Verlag, 2009).

5   Unless otherwise noted, all translations are my own. Florence Feiereisen, 'Liebe als Utopie? Von der Unmöglichkeit menschlicher Näheräume in den Kurzgeschichten von Tanja Dückers, Julia Franck und Judith Hermann', in Lea Müller-Dannhausen, Ilse Nageschmidt and Sandy Feldbacher, *Zwischen Inszenierung und Botschaft: Zur Literatur deutschsprachiger Autorinnen ab Ende des 20. Jahrhunderts*, Literaturwissenschaft (Berlin: Frank & Timme, 2006), 179–96; here, 184.

Spiegel in 1999, Hage grouped together young female authors who write
'[ü]ber Erotik und Liebe, die Grundmelodie dieser Bücher, ... nüchtern
und ohne Illusionen' [about eroticism and love, the basic melody of these
books, ... soberly and without illusions].[6] Hage's statement that the authors
write predominantly about sex and relationships implies a lack of political engagement or social commentary by the authors (despite evidence to
the contrary). As opposed to a movement based on stylistic or thematic
concerns, the *Fräuleinwunder* was based purely on the authors' gender,
age, attractiveness and marketability.

The label was met with a strong response. Feminists debated the ori-
gins of the term as coming from either the German women who slept with
American GIs for silk stockings or from the squeaky-clean German media
darlings of the Cold War era, such as Romy Schneider and Steffi Graf – in
both cases, the term was considered offensive.[7] Scholars universally reject
the appropriateness of the term (despite continuing to use it), but the media
and publishing companies picked up on this catchphrase and used it to
market books by women in the late 1990s.[8] In addition to Franck, a number

6   Volker Hage, 'Ganz schön abgedreht', *Der Spiegel* 12 (1999), 244–6; here, 246.
7   Tanja Rauch, 'Das Fräuleinwunder', *Emma* (September/October 1999), 104–9; here,
     105. Julia Franck, 'The Wonder (of) Woman', tr. Alexandra Merley Hill, *Women in
     German Yearbook* 24 (2008), 235–40; here, 236.
8   For critiques of the *Fräuleinwunder*, see Feiereisen, 'Liebe als Utopie?' and the fol-
     lowing: Hester Baer, 'Frauenliteratur "After Feminism": Rereading Contemporary
     Women's Writing', in Mark W. Rectanus, ed., *Über Gegenwartsliteratur: Interpre-
     tationen – Kritiken – Interventionen: Festschrift für Paul Michael Lützeler zum
     65. Geburtstag* (Bielefeld: Aisthesis Verlag, 2008), 69–85; Anke S. Biendarra,
     'Gen(d)eration Next: Prose by Julia Franck and Judith Hermann', *Studies in Twentieth
     and Twenty-First Century Literature* 28/1 (2004), 211–39; Peter J. Graves, 'Karen
     Duve, Kathrin Schmidt, Judith Hermann: "Ein literarisches Fräuleinwunder"?',
     German Life and Letters 55/2 (2002), 196–207; and Christine Frisch, 'Powerfrauen
     und Frauenpower: Zur deutschsprachigen Frauenliteratur der Neunziger', in Thomas
     Jung, ed., *Alles nur Pop? Anmerkungen zur populären und Pop-Literatur seit 1990*,
     Ostoer Beiträge zur Germanistik (New York: Peter Lang, 2002), 103–16. Scholars
     are also guilty of perpetuating use of the term, even in attempts to dismantle it.
     See the following: Christiane Cammerer, Walter Delabar and Helga Meise, eds,
     Fräuleinwunder literarisch: Literatur von Frauen zu Beginn des 21. Jahrhunderts,

of authors came to be associated with the *Fräuleinwunder*, including Tanja Dückers, Karen Duve, Alexa Hennig von Lange, Judith Hermann, Felicitas Hoppe, Zoë Jenny, Tanja Langer and Terézia Mora. While each author had her own relationship to the label, there is no question that the marketing strategy and its surrounding hype drew attention to these authors, many of whom had just published their debuts.

Part of the problem with the *Fräuleinwunder* label was its implication that because these authors did not write about politics, their literature was trivial (in the sense of *Trivialliteratur*), as were the authors themselves. All of the *Fräuleinwunder* authors have continued to publish, and many, including Franck, turned to topics from the German past. The publication of *Lagerfeuer* [Camp Fire] in 2003 marked a turn in Franck's writing away from novels situated in the present day.[9] Set in the West Berlin refugee camp Marienfelde in the late 1970s, *Lagerfeuer* is narrated by four characters whose lives meet in the camp. Significant for Franck's oeuvre, the novel established a pattern for her subsequent books: important moments in German history serve as the backdrop for the characters' exploration of self and search for intimacy and meaning. Although Franck fled East Germany with her mother and sisters and spent time in the camp in 1978, the novel is by no means autobiographical. Instead, it and the subsequent novels use a moment from her family's history as the jumping-off point for the story. The first novel about German-German refugees, *Lagerfeuer* points to a wound from the German past. It also firmly established her as an important, rising author.

In 2007, Franck published *Die Mittagsfrau* (published in English as *The Blind Side of the Heart* in 2009) and just weeks later won the *Deutscher*

Inter-Lit (New York: Peter Lang, 2005); Ilse Nageschmidt, Lea Müller-Dannhausen and Sandy Feldbacher, eds, *Zwischen Inszenierung und Botschaft: Zur Literatur deutschsprachiger Autorinnen ab Ende des zwanzigsten Jahrhunderts* (Berlin: Frank & Timme, 2006); and Heike Bartel and Elizabeth Boa, eds, *Pushing at Boundaries: Approaches to Contemporary German Women Writers from Karen Duve to Jenny Erpenbeck* (New York: Rodopi, 2006).

9   Julia Franck, *Lagerfeuer* (Cologne: DuMont Buchverlag, 2003).

Buchpreis for the novel.[10] The announcement of the prize and the subsequent book and interview tours catapulted Franck into prominence in the German-language literature scene. *Die Mittagsfrau* was translated into thirty-three languages and published in thirty-five different countries, and Franck enjoyed financial stability as a writer for the first time in her life. Represented since 2007 by the famous publishing house S. Fischer (which publishes books by other distinguished contemporary authors, such as Clemens Meyer, Günter de Bruyn, Monika Maron, W. G. Sebald, Ilse Aichinger, Wolfgang Hilbig, Judith Hermann and Marlene Streeruwitz), her status as a prominent German-language author is firmly established.

It is likely both this prominence and her interest in working through German history that made Franck an obvious choice to be keynote speaker at the celebration of the fiftieth anniversary of the publication of Günter Grass's *The Tin Drum*.[11] *Die Mittagsfrau* considers the limited opportunities for women, the chaos of Weimar Berlin and the tragedies of Nazi Germany. Yet unlike novelists of previous generations, such as Grass, Franck makes few explicit connections between German history and the everyday lives of her characters in a moralizing way, instead foregrounding subjectivity and individual experience. Inspired by the story of her paternal grandmother, this novel is more concerned with the protagonist's highly individual experience than with the specifically German history that determines it.

Continuing her exploration of the German past, although in a different vein, Franck edited a collection of pieces reflecting on German division, *Grenzübergänge* [Border Crossings], to commemorate the twentieth anniversary of the fall of the Berlin Wall.[12] In the introduction to the collection,

---

10   Julia Franck, *Die Mittagsfrau* (Frankfurt am Main: S. Fischer Verlag, 2007). English translation: Julia Franck, *The Blind Side of the Heart*, tr. Anthea Bell (London: Harvill Secker, 2009). The same translation was published under a slightly different name in the United States: Julia Franck, *The Blindness of the Heart*, tr. Anthea Bell (New York: Grove Atlantic, 2009).

11   Armgard Seegers, 'Julia Franck: "Dieses Buch prägte Deutschland"' *Hamburger Arbendblatt* (14 September 2009).

12   Julia Franck, *Grenzübergänge: Autoren aus Ost und West erinnern sich* (Frankfurt am Main: S. Fischer Verlag, 2009).

Franck writes: 'es geht mir in dieser Anthologie nicht um das Typische, sondern um das Individuelle, das Subjektive' [in this anthology, I am not concerned with the typical, but instead with the individual, the subjective] (21). Similar themes emerge again in *Rücken an Rücken* [Back to Back], Franck's most recent publication.[13] The family at the centre of this novel is by no means 'normal' for East Germany, and Franck does not use them to explore the typical East German experience. Instead, she begins with details about her maternal grandmother and uncle and creates a literary study of complex family relationships that at once transcend national identification and at the same time are inextricably shaped by the country in which they unfold.

Franck once referred to her 'archetypisches Thema – verlassen und verlassen werden von Orten und auch von Menschen' [archetypal theme – to abandon and to be abandoned by places and also by people].[14] Certainly the motif of abandonment surfaces repeatedly throughout her oeuvre, as I discuss at length in this study: fathers walk out on their daughters, mothers reject their children, lovers give up on each other and friends disregard any sense of allegiance. Critics and scholars have expressed dismay with this unfailingly negative representation of relationships, but Franck refrains from making moral judgements and sweeping statements.[15] Instead she says simply that she prefers characters who 'scheitern', or fail.[16] A number of themes run like red threads throughout Franck's work, but at the core her fiction is about intimacy – coupled with the anxiety of attaining it and the fear of losing it – predominantly in the lives of women.

13   Julia Franck, *Rücken an Rücken* (Frankfurt am Main: S. Fischer Verlag, 2011).
14   Kristina Pezzei and Philipp Sawallisch, '"Die Grenze hat sich verändert"', *taz.de* [online newspaper] (16 March 2009). <http://www.taz.de/regional/berlin/aktuell/artikel/1/die-grenze-hat-sich-veraendert-in-20-jahren/?type=98> accessed 1 April 2009.
15   For a scholarly response to this criticism, see Anke Biendarra, 'Gen(d)eration Next: Prose by Julia Franck and Judith Hermann', *Studies in Twentieth and Twenty-First Century Literature* 28/1 (2004), 211–39.
16   Julia Franck, 'Second Interview' [interview with Alexandra Merley Hill] (Berlin: 20 June 2007).

Feminism

Franck's relationship to feminism has been complicated and only recently has it been explicitly connected with her role as an author. The *Fräuleinwunder* was a key point in Franck's career, in part because of its connection to the success of *Liebediener* and *Bauchlandung*, but more important because it marked the start of her public engagement with issues of feminism. Commissioned by *Die Welt* to write an article on the popularity of women's writing, Franck wrote 'The Wonder (of) Woman' in 2000. Rejected by *Die Welt* for being 'fundamentalfeministisch' [hardline feminist], it was first published in *Women in German Yearbook* in 2008.[17] In the essay, Franck critiques the sexist label as one that belittles women's writing as miraculous, much as others had done before her. Yet, while some struggle to free women writers from gender-specific categories, Franck proposes the concept of 'Female Sobriety' as an alternative. She argues that 'a supposedly unifying approach to the erotic', to borrow the words of Peter Graves, does exist in literature by women:[18]

> I have noticed in the books of my female colleagues that they prefer an unemotional narrative style. Where male colleagues demonstrate uninhibited courage in using pathos, female authors – who are much more easily accused of kitsch because of their gender – walk the line between casualness and sobriety. The fear of the sweet and the nice, of the touching and the maudlin, is great.[19]

---

17 Julia Franck, 'Re: Ihre Frage' [email to Alexandra Merley Hill] (6 December 2006) <amerley@german.umass.edu> accessed December 2006. Also: Julia Franck, 'Das Wunder Frau', *Women in German Yearbook* 24 (2008), 229–35. The original German essay was published simultaneously with an English translation: Julia Franck, 'The Wonder (of) Woman', tr. Alexandra Merley Hill, *Women in German Yearbook* 24 (2008), 235–40. Excerpts from this essay are taken from the published English translation.

18 Graves, '"Ein literarisches Fräuleinwunder"?', 196.

19 Franck, 'The Wonder (of) Woman', 239.

In other words, women writers have adopted a certain writing style because they are socially conditioned to do so and because they seek to avoid the criticism that female authors tend to receive.[20]

Like many of her fellow *Fräuleinwunder* authors, Judith Hermann for example, Franck was uncomfortable with being labelled a feminist in the early 2000s. As late as 2006, she pointed out the following distinction: 'Ja, ich halte mich schon für eine feministisch denkende Frau – ob ich eine feministische Schriftstellerin bin, weiß ich nicht' [Yes, I consider myself a feminist-thinking woman – I don't know whether I am a feminist author].[21] She and her colleagues avoided the term in part because it was associated (especially in the German media) with an out-dated conception of the women's movement with which younger generations did not identify. The expectations associated with the idea of feminism meant, for example, that Franck's critics have frowned upon her unsympathetic representation of women who make mistakes and do ugly things.

Since the publication of *Die Mittagsfrau*, Franck has been a much more active and outspoken member of the feminist community. She has worked publicly with some of the icons of early German feminism, such as Alice Schwarzer and Silvia Bovenschen, and remains actively engaged in discussions surrounding women's roles in contemporary German society. She served on the jury for the *Emma* prize, which is named for the German feminist magazine. She also spoke on a forum with Schwarzer on Simone de Beauvoir. Franck has been situated in the media as a representative of women's issues, and she has written newspaper essays and given talks on motherhood, children and education.[22]

---

20   For a lengthier analysis of Franck's essay, as well as its connection to other feminist investigations of women's writing, see Alexandra Merley Hill, '"Female Sobriety": Feminism, Motherhood, and the Works of Julia Franck', *Women in German Yearbook* 24 (2008), 209–28.

21   Julia Franck, 'Re: MLA Vortrag' [email to Alexandra Merley Hill] (12 March 2007) <amerley@german.umass.edu> accessed March 2007.

22   See for example Julia Franck, 'Lust am Leben', *Kölner Stadt-Anzeiger* (29 April 2006) and Julia Franck, 'Staat und Religion', *Der Spiegel* 4 (2009).

Recent years have seen a renewed interest in feminism in Germany, in part inspired by a critique of second-wave feminism in the 1970s and 1980s. Around 2006, the German media began to spread concern over Europe's low birth rates, in some instances placing the blame on white, educated women who choose to prioritize their careers over having large families. With feminism under attack, young German women have been responding with a surprisingly passionate defence, arguing for the continued relevance of feminist ideals, albeit in an updated and somewhat revised form. Books such as *Die neue F-Klasse* by Thea Dorn, *Das F-Wort: Feminismus ist Sexy* edited by Mirja Stöcker, *Neue deutsche Mädchen* by Jana Hensel and Elisabeth Raether and *Wir Alpha-Mädchen: Warum Feminismus das Leben schöner macht* by Meredith Haaf, Susanne Klingner and Barbara Streidl have flooded the shelves.[23] Scholarship has responded in kind, documenting the rise of 'popfeminism' in contemporary German society and literature.[24]

Featured in a *Spiegel* article on feminism in Germany, Franck was represented as a member of a generation that can bridge the gap between the generation of *Altfeministinnen* [old feminists] on the one hand and the new *Alpha-Mädchen* [alpha-girls] on the other.[25] As an author in the privileged position of having a wide (international) readership, Franck also enjoys the benefits of being widely acknowledged as a prominent author and public intellectual in the German literary tradition. Frequently

---

23   Thea Dorn, *Die neue F-Klasse: Wie die Zukunft von Frauen gemacht wird* (Munich: Piper, 2006); Mirja Stöcker, ed., *Das F-Wort: Feminismus ist sexy* (Königstein: Helmer, 2007); Jana Hensel and Elisabeth Raether, *Neue deutsche Mädchen* (Reinbek: Rowohlt Verlag, 2008); and Meredith Haaf, Susanne Klingner and Barbara Streidl, *Wir Alphamädchen: Warum Feminismus das Leben schöner macht* (Hamburg: Hoffmann und Campe, 2008).

24   Some examples include: Sonja Eismann, ed., *Hot Topic: Popfeminismus heute* (Mainz: Ventil, 2007); Katja Kauer, ed., *Popfeminismus! Fragezeichen! Eine Einführung* (Berlin: Frank & Timme, 2009); and a special issue, Contemporary Women's Writing and the Return of Feminism in Germany, of *Studies in Twentieth and Twenty-First Century Literature* 35/1 (Winter 2011).

25   Anke Dürr, Ulrike Knöfel, and Claudia Voigt, 'Weder Muse noch Madonna', *Der Spiegel* (7 July 2008), 136–9.

asked for her opinions on women's issues, she draws a distinction between interviews and essays on current political topics and her explorations of women's experiences in her novels, which are often set in – and therefore shaped by – a particular time period in German history.[26] Yet the daily lives of women lie at the centre of her literary works.

Book Overview

The fictional works of Julia Franck are primarily concerned with the experiences of women, in all of their various roles: women as lovers, mothers, daughters, sisters and *others*. Like many of her generation, Franck is suspicious of the bourgeois image of domesticity that is based on a nuclear family, and she interrogates these gendered roles as social constructs, recognizing 'mother' as one of the most hotly debated roles in contemporary German culture.[27] This study is centred on motherhood in Franck's literary works: the novels *Der neue Koch, Liebediener, Lagerfeuer, Die Mittagsfrau* and *Rücken an Rücken* and the short stories in the collection *Bauchlandung: Geschichten zum Anfassen*.

Chapter 1 begins with a theorization of women's gendered roles as performative identities. Drawing on Judith Butler's theory of the performativity of gender, I argue that Franck's protagonists perform their identities just as they perform the feminine. Inherent in Franck's works is a tension between an internalized *performative* identity and a consciously manipulated *performance* of identity. Her characters exhibit both, which, although related, are distinct concepts. (Throughout the book, I distinguish

---

26   Julia Franck, 'Re: Kunst und das Leben' [email to Alexandra Merley Hill] (2 August 2007) <amerley@german.umass.edu> accessed August 2007.

27   Britta Heidemann, 'Julia Franck: "Ich muss auf vieles verzichten"', *DerWesten* [website] (10 May 2009). <http://www.derwesten.de/nachrichten/nachrichten/kultur/2009/5/10/news-119251422/detail.html> accessed 11 August 2009.

between the two.) This tension can be productive, especially with respect to the idea of drag. According to Butler, drag is an exaggerated, conscious and theatrical performance that highlights the contingency of that which is being performed. Chapter 4 returns to this topic when I explain my theory of 'maternal drag' – in short, a poor or exaggerated performance of the maternal that destabilizes that very role.[28] In Franck's works not just 'mother' but all identities are mutable, as they are both dependent upon and undermined by the spaces in which they are performed.

Space is the focus of Chapter 2, specifically the prevalence of 'non-places' and the search for 'places' in contemporary society. Marc Augé outlined a theory of places (i.e. spaces in which emotional connections are formed) and non-places (i.e. spaces that do not facilitate connection but through which one simply passes) in his 1995 text *Non-Places: Introduction to an Anthropology of Supermodernity*.[29] The overabundance of non-places in the contemporary world means that people spend more time in locations that do not promote human interaction or interpersonal connection. Focusing on Franck's early works, I consider the places and non-places that her characters inhabit. Common to the majority of the protagonists is a longing for emotional connection and rootedness, a condition (Augé argues) common to supermodernity. Thus while the characters are skeptical of the familial structures that defined their childhoods, they still desire a fantasy of family or domestic life that relies heavily on a romanticized ideal.

This longing for home is strongly connected to the role of the mother, and Chapter 3 examines the attitudes of the daughters in Franck's works towards their mothers. Nearly all the protagonists in Franck's long and short works are daughters, and I consequently draw from many texts in this chapter's analysis. In large part, the daughters are disappointed

---

28　I outline maternal drag in an abbreviated form in the following article: Alexandra Merley Hill, 'Motherhood as Performance: (Re)Negotiations of Motherhood in Contemporary German Literature', *Studies in Twentieth and Twenty-First Century Literature* 35/1 (Winter 2011), 74–94.

29　Marc Augé, *Non-Places: Introduction to an Anthropology of Supermodernity*, tr. John Howe (New York: Verso, 1995).

by their mothers, who frustrate their seemingly endless need for love and attention. Seen through the eyes of the daughters, the mothers are cold, reserved and self-absorbed. To explain this perspective, I refer to psychoanalysis and feminist reinterpretations of psychoanalytic theory. Ultimately I argue that even these modified theories rely on some basic assumptions of motherhood (such as passive sexuality) that Franck's characters do not support. Nevertheless, key ideas from Nancy Chodorow's *The Reproduction of Mothering* resonate with Franck's exploration of the mother–daughter relationship and reinforce the idea of both roles as social constructs.[30]

Of course the other side of the mother–daughter story is that of the mother herself, which is examined in Chapter 4. Franck's novels provide insights into both perspectives, but it is only in *Lagerfeuer* and *Die Mittagsfrau* that the mother speaks for herself. Society criticizes the women in these two books for having non-maternal motivations and desires, but Franck also gently critiques the female characters who live only for their children. She undermines the idea that 'mother' is an identity that is biological, 'natural' and inescapable. Using a technique of estrangement that I call 'maternal drag', Franck questions assumptions made about women's roles in society, and she destabilizes these gendered roles without necessarily proposing an alternative.

Chapter 5 considers the implications of Franck's interrogation of gender and gendered roles. While advocating that 'mother' and 'father' be reconsidered, Franck's texts do not move beyond gender. I show this by briefly considering the fathers and sons in her fictional works, who, though significantly outnumbered by mothers and daughters, are nonetheless conspicuous by their absence. Nor are they treated the same way as their female counterparts. Sons, for example, are more deeply wounded than daughters. I also return to the idea of home, which is closely connected with fantasies of attachment that surface in the previous chapters. The destabilization of motherhood points readers in two directions when considering the future

30   Nancy Chodorow, *The Reproduction of Mothering: Psychoanalysis and the Sociology of Gender* (2nd edn, Berkeley: University of California Press, 1978).

of home in Franck's works. The first suggestion is towards an approach to homemaking that is as far from the bourgeois domestic ideal as can be: gender-neutral parenting and perhaps even co-housing. And the second, which is inspired by the destabilization of traditional parent–child bonds, is that the primary attachment in the lives of Franck's characters is between siblings. These sibling relationships, which are never undermined or weakened in Franck's texts, may well be the answer to the search for intimacy and connection.

Roles: Theorizing Performativity and Performance

After the announcement that Julia Franck had won the 2007 *Deutscher Buchpreis* for her fourth novel, *Die Mittagsfrau*, she began a series of interviews, television appearances and photo shoots that would last well into 2008 and that marked the beginning of a media presence that would continue through to the publication of her most recent book, *Rücken an Rücken*. In the aftermath of the Buchpreis announcement, Franck was interviewed for the German edition of *Vanity Fair*. The article included a large colour image of Franck reclining in an upholstered chair, wearing a fur coat and satin dress and looking at the viewer with one eye hidden behind the chair's wing. One of dozens and dozens of photographs taken of Franck after the prize, this image, much more posed and theatrical than the others, reflects her awareness of playing roles in interviews and media representations. 'Es ist also zwingend notwendig Rollen zu spielen' [It is thus urgently necessary to play roles], Franck has said, not only to safeguard one's privacy, but also to exercise some control over the representations that exist of oneself. Keeping in mind the journalistic tendency to manipulate words or take them out of context, she concludes: 'Je genauer man sich dessen bewusst ist, desto besser – alles andere ist naiv' [The more precisely one is aware of this, the better – everything else is naïve].[1] Flexibility of identity can also be positive. As an identical twin, she is certainly familiar 'with the power and seductive potential of an optical illusion', as well as with both playful and unintentional manipulations of identity.[2] This awareness of identity as performance, from experiences both in her personal life and with the media, finds expression in Franck's works of fiction as well.

1   Franck, 'Re: Kunst und das Leben'.
2   Franck, 'The Wonder (of) Woman', 238.

This chapter lays the theoretical groundwork that explores the tension between performance and performativity in Franck's works. Her first novel *Der neue Koch* nicely illustrates Judith Butler's theory of gender performativity, as outlined in the seminal work *Gender Trouble*.[3] As scholars have done before me, such as Katrin Sieg analysing race in *Ethnic Drag*, I extend Butler's theorization of performativity to encompass other types of identity and roles that people play.[4] Somewhat at odds with performativity is the trope of performance that recurs in Franck's work. *Liebediener* is Franck's second novel and is very much concerned with the ways that identities are adopted and discarded, like and via clothing. This red thread links all of Franck's books, including her most recent, *Rücken an Rücken*. The connection between theatrical performance and performative identity comes to the fore with a discussion of drag. This book does not treat drag simply as cross-dressing (although characters in Franck's works do use clothing to signify the adoption of new identities). Instead, the term is used here in Butler's sense, to mean a parody that illuminates the contingency of the identity that is being performed. This is crucial to the theorization of maternal drag, which is discussed in Chapter 4. It is through performance that one can interrogate and destabilize performative identities.

Gender and Performativity

In 1990 Judith Butler published *Gender Trouble*, which articulated the investigation of gender identities that is at the centre of her work. The book's most important contribution to feminist theory is that of gender

---

3   Julia Franck, *Der neue Koch* (Frankfurt am Main: Fischer Taschenbuch Verlag, 2001). Judith Butler, *Gender Trouble: Feminism and the Subversion of Identity*. Routledge Classics (2nd edn, New York: Routledge, 2006).

4   Katrin Sieg, *Ethnic Drag: Performing Race, Nation, Sexuality in West Germany*, Social History, Popular Culture and Politics in Germany (Ann Arbor: The University of Michigan Press, 2002).

performativity. Beginning with Simone de Beauvoir's famous statement that 'One is not born, but rather becomes a woman',[5] Butler regards identity as a process for which there is no end. She describes gender as 'the repeated stylization of the body, a set of repeated acts within a highly rigid regulatory frame that congeal over time to produce the appearance of substance, of a natural sort of being.'[6] That is, gender is not something inherent, but something performed. It is not a biological fact but a series of 'stylized acts' approved by society and learned by the subject.

But who or what is 'doing' gender? The theatrical quality of Butler's theory would lead one to think of gender as a performance, which it is of sorts, but for Butler there is an important difference between 'performance' and 'performativity': 'performance' requires that there be a subject doing the acting. As she points out, 'A great deal of feminist theory and literature has … assumed that there is a "doer" behind the deed,' a natural conclusion as agency presupposes an agent. Yet Butler speaks not of the 'performance' but of the 'performativity' of gender, because she believes that no subject exists prior to or behind the act: 'There is no gender identity behind the expressions of gender; that identity is performatively constituted by the very "expressions" that are said to be its results.'[7] In other words, there is no 'before', no pre-existing or original gender that a subject tries to imitate. Instead, all gender is a copy of a copy of a copy.

Writing about Butler, Sara Salih sums up: 'all gender is a form of parody, but … some gender performances are more parodic than others';[8] in *Der neue Koch*, nearly all identity performances are parodic. The poet, always called 'der Dichter Anton Jonas', dresses in black, walks alone in the woods, and surrounds himself with an air of pensive melancholy.[9] The chamber-

---

5 Simone de Beauvoir, *The Second Sex*, tr. H. M. Parshley (New York: Vintage Books, 1989), 267.

6 Butler, *Gender Trouble*, 45.

7 Butler, *Gender Trouble*, 34.

8 Sara Salih, *Judith Butler*, Routledge Critical Thinkers (New York: Routledge, 2002), 65.

9 Macnab also points out Anton Jonas's parody of the poet. Lucy Macnab, 'Becoming Bodies: Corporeal Potential in Short Stories by Julia Franck, Karen Duve, and Malin

maid, Berta, is a caricature of domestic servitude: she is at work before the narrator awakens and continues to work after the others have gone to bed; she appears in rooms instantly and silently on her rubber-soled shoes; and she scrubs the china so diligently that she has nearly removed the pictures from the tea cups. The most interesting parodies, however, are those performed by Madame Piper, who is a regular guest at the hotel, and by the nameless narrator. Both illustrate Butler's concept of gender as a masquerade.

Madame, a friend of the narrator's late mother, has been visiting the hotel since before the narrator was born, i.e. for over thirty years. The relationship between Madame and the narrator is characterized by ambivalent intimacy: the narrator cleans and cares for Madame's body, sometimes willingly and sometimes less so, and Madame speaks to the narrator in affectionate terms and gives well-meaning advice, which the narrator receives sometimes gracefully and sometimes less so. Madame's instructions to the narrator – 'ich soll mir auch mal ein Kleidchen anziehen, nie hätte ich ein Kleidchen an, ich wolle wohl nicht gefallen' [I should also put on a little dress for once, I supposedly never have a dress on, I probably do not want to please] – seem old-fashioned and silly, referencing ideas of femininity from an earlier era.[10] For example, to resolve the tension between the narrator and the new cook of the title, as well as to solve the financial problems of the hotel, Madame recommends that they marry (112). But the out-dated quality of Madame's ideas draws attention to changing conceptions of masculine and feminine and, by extension, the changeability of gender identities. Madame's suggestion that the narrator put on a dress seems silly at first. After all, one might argue, wearing a dress will not make the narrator into more of a lady. But Butler would argue otherwise: wearing a dress is one example of 'expressions of gender'.

Schwerdtfeger', in Heike Bartel and Elizabeth Boa, eds, *Pushing at Boundaries: Approaches to Contemporary German Women Writers from Karen Duve to Jenny Erpenbeck*, German Monitor (New York: Rodopi, 2006), 107–18.

10   Franck, *Der neue Koch*, 22.

In fact, the very discussion of the dress draws attention to the narrator's gender, which has not yet been mentioned. Although information on the book's back cover and the synopsis inside the book's front page both indicate that the narrator is a woman, the text itself is not explicit. The reader can use a few details in the text to deduce that the narrator is considered a woman by those around her, such as the dress, the suggestion that she marry the cook, frequent comparisons to her mother and that Madame allows her to see and care for her naked body. (Because the narration is first person from the protagonist's perspective, it is difficult to gain an outside or 'objective' view.) Yet to conclude that the narrator is female based on these details would be to adhere to a strict heterosexual matrix that Franck does not support in the rest of her works.[11] It also becomes clear (although this does not help the reader to identify the narrator's gender) that her performative femininity is neither skilled nor convincing. The narrator puts on the stockings and garter belt solely to seduce the cook, but this seduction fails: the cook does not respond to her advances but leaves the room. In this scene it seems that putting on a feminine costume simply draws attention to the contingency of gender.[12]

In the course of the novel the narrator practices 'doing' femininity and gradually strengthens her female gender identity as a *'stylized repetition of acts'*.[13] That she has learned how to 'do' femininity is proven when the narrator successfully seduces Niclas, a married guest staying at the hotel. In a scene that employs a number of clichés of flirtation, the narrator convinces Niclas to sell her a back-dated insurance policy for the hotel, using the promise of sex to secure the deal. She does not sleep with him, however, declaring: 'schon längst habe ich mich entschieden, ihn nicht zu nehmen, schon längst habe ich entschieden, daß auch er nicht derjenige

---

11   The relationships between sisters in both the short story 'Bäuchlings' and the novel *Die Mittagsfrau* are characterized by sexual attraction. Both relationships are considered in Chapter 5.

12   Macnab, 'Becoming Bodies', 110.

13   Butler, *Gender Trouble*, 191. Original italics.

ist, auf den ich gewartet haben will' [I already decided long ago not to take him, I already decided long ago that he is not the one for whom I had intended to wait] (135). It is important to note that this quotation reveals the narrator's virginity, and the sex act can be seen as an important part of the performance of 'woman' that the narrator has not yet incorporated. In light of her sexual inexperience, it seems reasonable to assume that the narrator has learned the performativity of seduction from others around her, such as the cook, who had seduced the narrator before. Significantly, the narrator has learned that one performs seduction when one wants something; just as she wanted the back-dated insurance policy from Niclas, the cook wanted the narrator's promise to sell him the hotel. The cook has not been the narrator's only model in using sex as a bargaining tool. It is likely that the narrator learned – or learned to avoid – such behaviour from her mother.[14]

The narrator illuminates the contingency of gender identity in both her discomfort in performing and the fake or studied quality of her performance. Madame also demonstrates the performativity of gender identity in that she 'over-does' gender, taking elements of femininity to extremes. The function of Madame's character is discussed in greater detail below, in the section on drag. But in addition to exhibiting an awareness of the performativity of gender identity, Franck's texts thematize identity as performance, as well. The next section of this chapter discusses the novel *Liebediener*, in which the main characters assume and discard a number of different identities. For Butler, all identities are constantly in flux, always in the process of becoming. In Franck's work as well, the fluidity of identity is a common theme.

14   See Chapter 3 for more on this aspect of the mother–daughter relationship.

Role Play and Performance

One aspect of performance theory that builds on the work of American sociologist Erving Goffman considers the extent to which everyday life involves playing roles.[15] Putting on a uniform and using certain language are typical elements of adopting one's professional identity, for example, and socially expected behaviour in various situations, such as at funerals, involves performing according to the corresponding scripts. This concept of performance is strongly associated with the theatre, but it extends the stage onto 'all the world', in the Shakespearean sense. There is an important difference between this more general concept of performance and Butler's theorization of performativity. For Butler, no 'I' exists before the performance of gender; instead, the 'I' is constituted through these acts. In performance 'the role is an act that can be put on and put off at will without ever calling the underlying identity of the performer into question.'[16] Franck, herself conscious of playing roles, creates characters whose identities can be 'put on and put off at will'.

Identity is particularly important in the novel *Liebediener*, as the characters are constantly trying to identify themselves and each other, an obsession fueled by the death of Charlotte in the opening pages. In this book that starts almost as a *Krimi* or crime novel, this death brings together the narrator Beyla with her neighbour Albert, and they begin a messy romantic relationship. Throughout the novel she is trying to identify him (and sometimes trying *not* to identify him) as the man driving the red Ford, the car that startled Charlotte into the path of an on-coming tram. Motivated by this curiosity and fear, as well as an obsessive love for Albert, Beyla wants to know everything about him, yet he remains elusive. She says: 'Albert spürte, daß ich alles von ihm wollte, und dagegen wehrte er sich' [Albert

---

15 Erving Goffman, *The Presentation of Self in Everyday Life* (Garden City, NY: Doubleday, 1959).

16 James Loxley, *Performativity*, The New Critical Idiom (New York: Routledge, 2007), 142.

sensed that I wanted all of him, and he resisted it].[17] Perhaps this is true. Perhaps he wilfully resists her desire to know everything. After all, he hides from her the fact that he is a male prostitute, a fact that, once revealed, undermines the basis of their relationship. Yet even after Beyla learns this, there is no sense that she (or the reader) knows the 'real' Albert.

Beyla is guilty of attempting to fit Albert into certain types: she thinks '[t]ypisch Ostler' [typical East German] when he does not want to discuss his job (89). When he reveals that he is a pianist, she disapproves – not of his career choice, but of his inability to satisfactorily play the role of the pianist (88). At the same time she is cognizant of her efforts to 'do' different identities of her own. While flirting with Albert, she compares her behaviour with the gendered expectations of flirtation, i.e. that women should be mysterious and withholding, in order to satisfy men's preferences (68). (According to her own assessment, she is not successfully meeting these expectations.) On their first date Beyla is frustrated with her table manners and suspects that they belie her poor upbringing (86). She is playing the role of someone who does not have her past, which was one of poverty and neglect, and wondering whether Albert can see through her performance. This conscious and studied distance from the performance marks the important distinction between performed and performative identities and implies that there is a whole and authentic Beyla behind the performance.

Her occupation, however, creates another layer of performed identity and unexpectedly makes her 'real' identity all the more confused. Beyla works as a clown with a small circus in Berlin. Although one would expect clowning to be a clear performance, perhaps the most obvious example of putting on a costume and another persona, Beyla feels paradoxically exposed when she enters the circus ring: 'Ich fühlte mich von einer Vielzahl Augen entdeckt' [I felt myself detected by a multitude of eyes] (74). She cannot hide behind her makeup and costume but feels: 'Das Licht der Scheinwerfer stellte mich bloß' [The light of the spotlights laid me bare] (73). Even more complex is the fact that Beyla does not consider herself a

17   Franck, *Liebediener*, 199.

clown, although she consciously assumes that identity: she calls herself a 'verkannte Artistin', or unrecognized artiste, whose skill is more palatable to an audience when toned down to simple clowning (120). The distinction between clown and 'verkannte Artistin' is never revealed. Is Beyla a choreographer, as indicated by her choreographic project that reenacts Charlotte's death? Does she consider clowning to be a more pedestrian, less skilled version of what she is trained to do? Beyla does not return to this subject, but it suggests that she is withholding facets of her identity even from the reader, just as Albert is from Beyla. Her anxiety about being 'ertappt' [caught out] or 'entdeckt' [detected, literally: dis-covered] implies that an identity is hidden under (and at the same time nearly exposed by) her clown costume.

This identity remains out of reach. One has the feeling that, were one to remove the layers of identity and role-play surrounding Beyla, one would never reach the centre. At first the narration has a conspiratorial quality, such as when she confesses to the reader that she regularly lies: about her job, which is her 'Lieblingslüge' or favourite lie, about her feelings and her experiences (34). The reader imagines herself to have access to privileged information. Yet this changes by the book's end, when Beyla suddenly denies her obsessive love for Albert, which seemed to fuel most of her actions to that point. By the end the reader realizes that the search for truth is a red herring; there is no 'real' Beyla, there is no subject behind all the performances. It is utterly unclear how Beyla 'really' thinks, feels and experiences her reality.

Identity and Costume

It is typical of Franck's style that she never paints a complete picture of a scene. Rather, memory-like, only a few details receive attention, and it is up to the reader to assemble these gathered details into a mental collage. It is thus significant that clothing and attire are mentioned more frequently than other aspects of appearance. The clothing usually functions as costume or an outward marker of an (adopted) identity.

In *Rücken an Rücken* siblings Thomas and Ella dress for their mother's fancy dress party: Thomas dresses as a dog, wearing a mask that he has fashioned out of the pelt of a dead rabbit and the woollen lining of a jacket. Other than these two garments, he is naked. He is not ashamed of this nakedness, until an accident at the party causes his mask to slip and the naked body can be identified as his.[18] Ella wears a Pan costume, consisting of a hat with a parrot feather (the feather found at the zoo), a garland of dried leaves and blossoms, and a flute carved by Thomas. Symbolic of Ella's wild and irrational nature and her desire to drink and dance, this costume reappears later in the novel when Ella wears it to an interview for a position as a costume-maker at the Deutsches Theater in Berlin. Pan is also a god associated with fertility, which foreshadows Ella's unwanted pregnancy – a pregnancy that she reveals to her brother while wearing the costume (184). The siblings are used to performing roles: animals, Hänsel and Gretel, a married couple. It is part of their intimacy, a fantasy world that they share. As they grow older, performance is no longer a game but a requirement. In order to secure a place at the university, Thomas must play the role of a socialist: he must join the youth organization *Freie Deutsche Jugend* [Free German Youth], ideally also the Communist party, and spend at least a year working with his hands (148). His inability to make himself play this role that is not only expected but also required leads to his tragic death.

Different from costumes for play are costumes of seduction. The mother in the short story 'Der Hausfreund' [The Family Friend] wears a red velvet dress, dark red lipstick, and a fur coat when visiting her lover Thorsten (the family friend of the title, who is wearing a fur vest).[19] Implying that they share an animal or sexual relationship, these outward markers of luxury could also be the equivalent of the mother's Sunday best. In the course of the story, which is set in East Berlin, she and Thorsten flee to

18   Franck, *Rücken an Rücken*, 173.
19   Julia Franck, 'Der Hausfreund', *Bauchlandung: Geschichten zum Anfassen* (Cologne: DuMont Buchverlag, 2000), 83–94.

West Germany with her two children. Having planned this, the mother likely wanted to bring her best clothes with her, clothes that might indicate a level of affluence commonly associated with West Germany. This desire to fit in is prefigured by the mother's choice of perfume, called Opium, which was a gift from Uncle Klaus in the West (86). From a different story in the same volume, 'Strandbad' [Bathing Beach], the emotionally distant narrator fantasizes about a one-night stand with a man she sees at the beach.[20] Her claim that she does not seek companionship (discussed in greater depth in Chapter 2) as well as her awkward behaviour in the fantasy make it clear that she is not familiar with the scripts of typical social interactions. That she wears a black suit in her sexual fantasy (as does the man) underscores this. It can also be read as an indication of her uncertainty in performing femininity.

This uncertainty is quite the opposite of Luise in the short story 'Bäuchlings' [On Her Stomach].[21] She is very conscious of the role that she is playing and also her success in playing it. Seducing men and women – including her sister – is testament to this success. When the story opens, Luise is sleeping on a sofa, wearing a see-through garment that allows her sister to see her body beneath it (9). Luise continues to sleep and sends her sister to speak with Olek, one of Luise's boyfriends, when he arrives at their door. The narrator goes to him, and she puts on Luise's clothing: a leather bustier and her shoes, under the narrator's own dress. In this story putting on Luise's clothing enables the narrator to put on Luise's identity as well. She tries to adopt her sister's attitude towards Olek and extends a sexually charged interaction with him into a fantasy of him and Luise having sex. Ultimately the narrator cannot become Luise, but, as argued in Chapter 5, this is not her goal.

In *Liebediener* clothing changes Beyla's identity. Her clown costume signifies one kind of performance, one that, as discussed, leaves her feeling

20 Julia Franck, 'Strandbad', *Bauchlandung: Geschichten zum Anfassen* (Cologne: DuMont Buchverlag, 2000), 37–50.
21 Julia Franck, 'Bäuchlings', *Bauchlandung: Geschichten zum Anfassen* (Cologne: DuMont Buchverlag, 2000), 7–16.

exposed. She also exchanges clothing with Charlotte around the time of her death. When Charlotte is hit by the tram, she is wearing a blue dress and Beyla's shoes. Both are mentioned repeatedly as Beyla struggles to accept the truth of the accident, and she in fact uses the shoes as a way of contesting what she has seen: '[...] ich redete mir ein, es sei eine fremde Frau, ich kannte Charlotte, solche Schuhe mit Absätzen hatte sie nicht' [I convinced myself that the woman was a stranger, I knew Charlotte, she didn't have such shoes with heels].[22] Later she realizes that the shoes were her own and remembers that she had loaned them to Charlotte the day before (18). After Charlotte's death, Beyla moves into her apartment, up several floors from the basement apartment that had been her own. This symbolic beginning of a new life is marked by a change in residence (which I discuss in Chapter 2) but also, again, by clothing. That Charlotte died wearing Beyla's shoes comes to symbolize the death of Beyla's former life. Furthermore, on her first day living in her new apartment, Beyla wears a blue dress (62–3). The dress is not Charlotte's, but Charlotte was wearing a blue dress when she died. Thus, Beyla becomes Charlotte, picking up her life (things, clothing, apartment, lovers, even family) where it was interrupted. This change of identity is indicated by the clothing that the women wear, and which are the only items of clothing that feature prominently in this novel.

To return to Butler, one can see that performance is foregrounded in *Liebediener*. The characters assume a variety of identities in the novel, some of which are performed more frequently than others: a woman who did (not) grow up in poverty, a pianist, a clown, a 'verkannte Artistin', a lover, a person with friends, a daughter, and a woman without family, to name a few. There are also examples of gender performativity in the novel in addition to Beyla's conscious attempt to be feminine during her first date with Albert. One could argue that she has internalized any number of guidelines for how to 'do' femininity, upon which she does not critically reflect. Putting on the blue dress, for example, is not an intentionally assumed marker of femininity, but Beyla has presumably long since learned that women (and not men) wear dresses. Of particular interest is a short scene during which Beyla begins to menstruate as Albert is undressing her with his eyes. Here the masculine gaze makes her the object of his desire and in effect makes her a woman (100). And, in fact, Beyla continues to mention menstruating as long as she and Albert are together (189). This is one small but important instance of performativity in a book that focuses predominantly on performance.

Drag

Performance and performativity, while related, are not the same thing. James Loxley describes the relationship between the two as '*asymptotic*: an ever-closer proximity without a final, resolving convergence.'[23] While they do not ever meet, they are two elements of the most common – and most complex – identities that Franck's characters assume: daughter and mother. The theoretical toolkit used to examine these identities in this book is taken from Judith Butler, namely: drag. And it is precisely within the analysis of drag that Loxley identifies the tension between performativity and performance that exists within Butler's own theory.

In this context the term 'drag' does not refer to cross-dressing in general. Instead, Butler uses the on-stage drag performance as an insight into the constructedness of gender. By intentionally 'mis-performing the acts proper', those same stylized acts that make femininity or masculinity, drag disrupts the illusion of the naturalness of gender.[24] In *Gender Trouble*, Butler briefly discusses the risk that drag runs of reifying gender norms but seeks to reclaim it as a potentially subversive act. She says:

> As much as drag creates a unified picture of 'woman' (what its critics often oppose), it also reveals the distinctness of those aspects of gendered experience which are falsely naturalized as a unity through the regulatory fiction of heterosexual coherence.

23 Loxley, *Performativity*, 140. Original italics.
24 Loxley, *Performativity*, 127.

In imitating gender, drag implicitly reveals the imitative structure of gender itself – as well as its contingency.[25]

A man on stage dressed in drag is making 'two simultaneous but incompatible claims', namely that he is 'really' a man but that he is also a woman.[26] Drag in Butler's sense is an exaggerated performance of gender, one in which the markers of gender are taken to extremes: thickly applied make-up, frilly women's clothing, exaggerated feminine curves, and overt attempts at flirtation or seduction. While this performance is an obvious staging of femininity, it elevates femininity to the point of parody. And in drawing attention to the performative quality of gender, it undermines the 'naturalness' of gender.

Butler's theorization of drag is well illustrated in *Der neue Koch*. The character Madame is not a drag queen per se, but her over-the-top performance of femininity does call drag to mind. Very much concerned with appearances, Madame makes typical aspects of feminine appearance parodic. Far exceeding a womanly softness or roundness, Madame is obese, to the point that she can rarely move without assistance. She is an 'excess of flesh [that] is the image of the female body taken to an extreme'.[27] As part of a daily ritual, she has the narrator prepare her body for the public. While advising the narrator how to dress, Madame applies false eyebrows and eyelashes and paints her lips to twice their size. Madame's fashion advice is made laughable by her own modelling of exaggerated femininity. She is actively (although unknowingly) engaging in a parody of female sexuality, grotesque in its extremes but theoretically no different from those of any 'typical' woman (e.g. plucking eyebrows, using make-up, wearing dresses and having a voluptuous figure).

The extremes of Madame's toilette are comic, because the reader understands what Madame is doing wrong. But in reality Madame's exaggerated femininity simply points out the relativity of all femininity. Butler insists

---

25   Butler, *Gender Trouble*, 187. Original italics.
26   Loxley, *Performativity*, 125.
27   Macnab, 'Becoming Bodies', 109.

that there is no 'inner truth of gender'.[28] If there is no true femininity, how can the reader say that Madame is wrong? In fact, Madame's actions say as much about the reader as they do about Madame. Drag serves to illuminate the assumptions and expectations of the viewer: 'If one thinks that one sees a man dressed as a woman or a woman dressed as a man, then one takes the first term of each of those perceptions as the "reality" of gender: the gender that is introduced through the simile lacks "reality," and is taken to constitute an illusory appearance.'[29] Thus the assessment that Madame's performative femininity is somehow 'off' reveals the innate (if unconscious) gender standards in the reader's own mind. In her more recent publication *Undoing Gender*, Butler clarifies that she is less concerned with the subversive potential of drag than with what drag reveals about the constructed quality of gender:

> When one performance of gender is considered real and another false, or when one presentation of gender is considered authentic and another fake, then we can conclude that a certain ontology of gender is conditioning these judgments, an ontology (an account of what gender is) that is also put into crisis by the performance of gender in such a way that these judgments are undermined or become impossible to make.[30]

As a result of Madame's exaggerated femininity, which serves as a benchmark for the other characters in the novel, it becomes difficult to tell whether the narrator is feminine, with or without the dress. Butler cautions that, 'Parody itself is not subversive', but in this case, Madame's parody of femininity is.[31] It both illuminates the expectations of the reader and destabilizes her conception of what is feminine.

The narrator's attempt to dress like her sister Luise in 'Bäuchlings' is another example of a performance that can be described as drag. In this story the narrator uses clothing and behaviour in a conscious attempt to imitate her sister. The performance of this role is not a convincing one, to either Olek or the narrator. An element of parody is also present, at least

---

28   Butler, *Gender Trouble*, 186.
29   Butler, *Gender Trouble*, xxiii.
30   Judith Butler, *Undoing Gender* (New York: Routledge, 2004), 214.
31   Butler, *Gender Trouble*, 189.

to the reader: the narrator is quite literally trying to fill her sister's shoes, which do not fit. Neither does the bustier, which is too big. Reminiscent of a child playing dress-up, the fact that the clothing does not fit draws attention to the ill fit of the persona. Rather than reveal a sense of 'truth' under the costume, however, the narrator's imitation of Luise draws attention to Luise's own performance of her identity, and to the costumes and behaviour that are part of her act of seduction. Early in the story as the narrator admires Luise's body, Luise watches her, aware of her audience and observing the effect of her performance.[32] Thus, this example of performed identity – of drag – serves to destabilize the viewer's conception of what is 'real' and what is a masquerade.

Here again the reader encounters the tension between performativity and performance. Is there a 'true' Luise acting behind the performance? Butler would say no: there is no 'doer' behind the deed. No inherent identity exists prior to the social discourses that shape it. In drag, however, there is necessarily a 'doer' behind the deed. A cross-dressing performer on stage is self-consciously adopting a parodic role, one that is subversive in that it exposes the constructedness of gender identity. This conscious performance of gender is not the same thing as performative gender. But it is clear that these two currents of analysis work together, and I argue that they are both useful in analysing the gendered roles of 'daughter' and 'mother', which form the focal point of much of Franck's work.

To what extent can one be conscious of the discourses that construct one's gender, and to what extent can one intentionally alter the performance of gender? Or of any gendered role? Franck's oeuvre is an examination of the roles that women play: lovers, daughters, mothers and sisters. Yet she does not take these roles for granted. Applying Butlerian theory to these works shines a light on the ways in which Franck undermines the naturalness of these roles, especially the role of mother. What follows is an investigation of performed and performative identities, including drag, that shape Franck's female characters. In *Ethnic Drag* Sieg says, 'As a technique of estrangement, drag denounces that which dominant ideology presents as natural, normal,

32   Franck, 'Bäuchlings', 11.

and inescapable, without always offering another truth.'[33] It is precisely the dissolution of the 'natural, normal, and inescapable' which interests me in my examination of these roles. The concluding chapter argues that Franck does destabilize these roles without offering a concrete alternative.

Chapter 2 begins with women as lovers. Fuelled in part by the alienation of modern life, by non-places that afford little opportunity for fostering bonds, Franck's characters seek intimacy and connection through romantic relationships. Frustrated by these attempts, unsatisfied by their experiences, they find their thoughts turning towards family and home. This desire for intimacy and the consequent manipulation of behaviour to achieve it presupposes an agent – and one conscious of its gendered actions. The analyses point out the different ways in which the characters' identities are created, adopted and undermined, with an eye to the critique of discursively constructed gender roles.

Lovers: The Search for and Failure of Intimacy in Berlin Literature

In the late 1990s, seeking to identify the malaise of the millennium, the media and literary scholars centred their discussions of contemporary German literature on the alienation of modern life. Although anonymity and isolation within urban centres has long been a topic of concern, it was revived here as indicative of the party generation, the 'scenesters', the young Germans who seemed to have no jobs, no motivation, nothing to do and nothing to care about. Deemed worse than their lack of direction or political engagement was their inability to form meaningful relationships with their peers. Love or romance seemed beyond their limited capacity for emotion. Regardless of whether such people really existed among the twenty- and thirty-somethings of Berlin, they existed in German literature, and it is the characters such as those in Judith Hermann's *Sommerhaus, später,* Tanja Dückers' *Spielzone* or Franck's *Bauchlandung* that were frequently mentioned as examples. Katharina Gerstenberger, in the first chapter of *Writing the New Berlin,* points out that in these works the city is 'a lonely and isolating place' and, despite the frequency of sexual encounters in texts by Franck and Hermann, 'sex never leads to the intimacy that the protagonists desire.'[1] Literary critic Iris Radisch spoke of a millennial 'Liebeskatastrophe' or 'catastrophe of love' in German society, putting the blame on 'das völlige Fehlen von Vorbildern gelingender Liebe in modernen Lebensverhältnissen' [the total absence of models for love that works in modern circumstances] in both real life and the media (which

---

1   Gerstenberger, *Writing the New Berlin,* 29.

she understands to include literature).[2] Part of both the *Fräuleinwunder* phenomenon and Berlin literature trend, this concern with failed intimacy overlaps with the spatial turn in scholarship which is an interrogation of the spaces of the city. As scholars have argued, it is no coincidence that these texts are set in urban environments.

This chapter continues the examination of performative identity, focusing on women as lovers. Particularly (but not exclusively) Franck's earlier works are very much concerned with the search for intimacy, both emotional and physical. The novel *Liebediener* (1999) and the collection of short stories *Bauchlandung: Geschichten zum Anfassen* (2000) are examples of the so-called 'Unmöglichkeit der Nähe' [impossibility of closeness] much discussed in the media.[3] Scholars have drawn on the work of Marc Augé for a way to explain in anthropological terms the alienating effects of the urban landscape. Although Augé's theory does seem to dovetail with some of Franck's short stories, the novel *Liebediener* shows that more factors than space alone determine the (im)possibility of emotional connection. Because, as Gerstenberger puts it, 'Franck's Berlin ... offers her protagonists freedom but no home', home becomes romanticized as a space where intimacy seems to be guaranteed.[4] This chapter concludes with a theorization of home borrowed from feminist geography, and home, this highly gendered place, continues to be of importance for subsequent chapters.

2 Iris Radisch, *Die Schule der Frauen: Wie wir die Familie neu erfinden* (Munich: Deutsche Verlags-Anstalt, 2007), 75.

3 This term is derived from Meike Feßman's article 'Poetik der Nähe', in which she discusses the impossibility of forming intimate relationships in a global age. Meike Feßmann, 'Poetik der Nähe: Zur Topologie des Intimen in der Gegenwartsliteratur', *Sinn und Form* 56/1 (2004), 58–76.

4 Gerstenberger, *Writing the New Berlin*, 29.

Alienation in Urban Life

In a review of *Bauchlandung*, Kristina Stockmann used a phrase that is often repeated in critical commentary of contemporary young authors: 'd[ie] Zeitgeistkrankheit, d[ie] "Unfähigkeit zu lieben"' [the illness of the times, the 'inability to love'].[5] Meike Feßmann was among the first to explore this trope in contemporary literature and to consider its causes, regarding it as a malaise of this age of globalization: 'Es geht dabei um das Spannungsfeld zwischen Globalisierung – also Mobilität, Flexibilität, Vernetzung – und dem, was man Näheverhältnisse nennen kann. Je näher uns die Ferne rückt, desto schwieriger ist es, den eigenen Näheraum zu bestimmen' [It has to do with the area of conflict between globalization – mobility, flexibility, connectedness – and that which one can call intimate relationships. The closer distance becomes to us, the harder it is to define one's own intimate space].[6] In her article Feßmann argues that the disappearance of intimacy is closely linked to the disappearance of private space, and, she claims: 'Was öffentlich dargestellt wird, kann niemals intim sein' [What is publicly represented can never be intimate].[7] Following from this is the seeming paradox that sex becomes more and more a subject in literature and the media. Feßmann argues that people are not afraid to talk about it in public venues or media, precisely because sex has lost its intimacy. At the same time, Feiereisen argues, 'Sex und Erotik sind zu Platzhaltern für Liebe und Nähe geworden' [Sex and eroticism have become placeholders for love and closeness].[8] While some, such as Marc Augé, believe that love has become impossible since post-modernism (if not modernism), Feßmann takes this further and argues that even intimacy is no longer

---

5   Kristina Stockmann, 'Erzählungen zwischen Begehren und Scheitern: Julia Francks neues Buch *Bauchlandung*', *Literaturkritik* [online journal] 9 (September 2000). <http://www.literaturkritik.de/public/rezension.php?rez_id=1530&ausgabe =200009> accessed 1 February 2012.
6   Feßmann, 'Poetik der Nähe', 58.
7   Feßmann, 'Poetik der Nähe', 70.
8   Feiereisen, 'Liebe als Utopie?', 185.

possible today. Instead, physical contact seems the best substitute for emotional connection. Stockman agrees: 'Und doch scheint Erotik als einzig
möglicher Ort von Nähe, wenn auch zweifelhaft in seiner Befriedigung'
[And yet sex seems to be the only possible location of closeness, if also
doubtful in its satisfaction].[9] Some critics put the blame on the immature
and unsatisfying male characters in the texts, who often play the role of the
protagonists' sexual partners. For example, Stockman critiques the narrator's sexual partner in Franck's 'Strandbad', who wraps a used condom in
a chocolate wrapper (from the confectionary firm 'Kinder', whose name
means 'children'), a gesture that Stockmann reads as a 'Symbol für die
Infantilität des Mannes' [symbol of the man's childishness].[10] This failure of
men does not, however, address the failure of the protagonists to maintain
close friendships with women.[11]

It is particularly in reference to Franck's short stories that critics
raised the concern of this 'Zeitgeistkrankheit' in her works. One review
of *Bauchlandung* refers to 'Julia Francks eiskalt[e] Liebesengel' [Julia
Franck's ice-cold love-angels] and decrees: 'Julia Francks Geschichten –
und das macht sie auf den zweiten Blick interessant – sind so lieblos wie
eine Hormonausschüttung' [Julia Franck's stories – and that makes them
interesting on second glance – are as loveless as a release of hormones].[12]
Writing for *Die Zeit*, Katharina Döbler opens her review with this strong
claim: 'Liebe ist es nie bei Julia Franck. Es ist Sex, bestenfalls Begehren
und schlimmstenfalls Zerstreuung. Und zugrunde liegt ein ganzes Bündel
unschöner Impulse: Machtinstinkt, Ressentiment, Rache, Rivalität' [It is

---

9   Stockmann, 'Erzählungen'.
10   Stockmann, 'Erzählungen'.
11   One example would be the short story 'Mir nichts, dir nichts' [Just Like That], for
     which Franck won the 3sat Prize in 2000. In this short story, the narrator is having
     an affair with her friend's boyfriend. Her interest in the male partner is purely sexual,
     and she makes clear that she does not like him at all. With a small exception towards
     the end of the story, her attitude towards her friend is cold. Julia Franck, 'Mir nichts,
     dir nichts' *Bauchlandung: Geschichten zum Anfassen* (Cologne: DuMont Buchverlag,
     2000), 95–111.
12   Thomas Wirtz, 'Schmeckt es euch nicht?', *Frankfurter Allgemeine Zeitung* (12 August
     2000).

never love with Julia Franck. It is sex, in the best case desire, and in the worst case distraction. And underlying it is a whole bundle of unattractive impulses: desire for power, resentment, revenge and rivalry].[13] Many of the reviews adopt a similarly bitter tone, betraying perhaps disappointment in the lack of female solidarity or lack of a ceasefire in the 'battle of the sexes'. Regardless of their attitudes towards feminism, however, the majority of reviewers remain concerned with the focus on the erotic (often mistakenly reading *Bauchlandung* as erotica) and the 'menschliche[e] Nähe, die Utopie bleibt' [human closeness that remains a utopia].[14] In what follows, I discuss three short stories from this collection.

Alienation and Supermodernity

Anthropologist Marc Augé puts forth a theoretical framework that can explain the difficulty of forming connection in modern urban life. Augé is one of many scholars working on space and urban life, but I turn to his theory because it has been used by others working on Franck, such as Helga Meise.[15] To illustrate this theory of 'supermodernity', I use one of Franck's short stories often overlooked by critics and scholars, 'Zugfahrt' [Train Trip].[16] In this story, a young woman embarks on a train trip to Italy, for

---

13   Katharina Döbler, 'Schleimhaut inklusiv: Julia Franck will Hautkontakt', *Die Zeit* (28 December 2000).

14   Thomas Fitzel, 'Nähe als Utopie: Julia Francks erotischer Erzählband "Bauchlandung"', *Die Welt* (22 July 2000).

15   Helga Meise, 'Mythos Berlin: Orte und Nicht-Orte bei Julia Franck, Inka Parei und Judith Hermann', in Christiane Caemmerer, Walter Delabar and Helga Meise, eds, *Fräuleinwunder literarisch: Literatur von Frauen zu Beginn des 21. Jahrhunderts* (New York: Peter Lang, 2005), 125–50. Meike Feßmann includes Gaston Bachelard, Otto Friedrich Bollnow and Peter Sloterdijk in her theorization of urban and private spaces. See: Feßmann, 'Poetik der Nähe'.

16   Julia Franck, 'Zugfahrt', *Bauchlandung: Geschichten zum Anfassen* (Cologne: DuMont Buchverlag, 2000), 17–36.

a friend's wedding. She is less than enthusiastic about her trip: 'Ich mag Hochzeiten nicht. Sie geben mir den Eindruck, ich solle mich übriggeblieben fühlen.' [I don't like weddings. They give me the impression that I should feel left over.] As the girlhood friend of the bride, whose groom is Italian, the narrator feels: 'Diese Hochzeit läßt mich nicht nur übrig, sie macht mich auch älter und deutsch' [This wedding makes me feel not only left over, but it makes me older and German] (17). In other words, her sense of being an outsider arises partly from the goal of her journey and the identity forced upon her by her friend and the friend's fiancé, yet it is primarily the journey itself (the focus of the story) that creates the feeling of alienation in the story.

Augé outlines his theory of 'places' and 'non-places' in his book *Non-Places: Introduction to an Anthropology of Supermodernity* (1995). He uses the term 'supermodernity' to speak of the world that these protagonists currently live in, one characterized by three qualities: 'overabundance of events, spatial overabundance, [and] the individualization of references.'[17] In other words, the speed of history is accelerating (events take place closer together, each unofficial 'era' is shorter and more condensed), remote corners of the world are more accessible (thanks to media, technology and rapid transportation) and individual identity is at once insisted on and subsumed into larger frameworks of identification (e.g. generational identification). The primary result of these characteristics of supermodernity is the creation and abundance of 'non-places'. Augé defines the binary of 'place' versus 'non-place' thus: 'If a place can be defined as relational, historical and concerned with identity, then a space which cannot be defined as relational, or historical, or concerned with identity will be a non-place.'[18] In places connections are formed, identity is created or confirmed and history takes place. By contrast, non-places are often spaces through which people merely pass, such as: 'air, rail, and motorway routes, the mobile cabins called "means of transport" (aircraft, trains and road vehicles), the airports and railway stations, hotel chains, leisure parks,

17   Augé, *Non-Places*, 40–1.
18   Augé, *Non-Places*, 78.

large retail outlets' and the virtual spaces created by the internet, television and other media.[19] The connection to 'Zugfahrt' is thus clear: other than a brief introduction set in the narrator's home (we can assume this, as she packs her bag there, but otherwise no interaction or connection with the space takes place), the story is located exclusively in non-places, train stations and the train itself.[20]

According to Augé's theory, human connections are not formed in non-places, partly because identity is dissolved or suspended there. He explains that a person in a non-place 'becomes no more than what he does or experiences in the role of passenger, customer or driver. ... Subjected to a gentle form of possession, to which he surrenders himself with more or less talent or conviction, he tastes for a while ... the passive joys of identity-loss, and the more active pleasure of role-playing.'[21] This is certainly the case in Franck's story. The narrator speculates as to the lives of her fellow travellers, but she is not able to move beyond the surface of the present. That is, the characters do not become anything more to her than fellow passengers on the train: the man eating liverwurst sandwiches and smelling unpleasantly of eau de toilette, the couple arguing about their failing relationship, the father who looks like he is about to cry and the young son counting cows. Similarly, the reader knows that the narrator is giving away

19 Augé, *Non-Places*, 79. While Augé's book was published after the birth of the Internet, it does not – could not – sufficiently account for the connections formed in cyberspace and via social media. That the abstract concept of the Internet is often explained in spatial terms (e.g. chat rooms, surf the web, in the net, on a webpage, MySpace) can support an argument that the Internet has become a virtual 'place' in the sense that Augé defines, where connections are indeed made.
20 The train has long served as a symbol of modernity in literature. One thinks, for example, of Tolstoy's *Anna Karenina*. In *Die Mittagsfrau*, Helene and Martha travel to Berlin by train in the inter-war years, and their inexperience with train travel reflects their old-fashioned, rural upbringing. Much later in the story, Helene is looking for mushrooms in the woods when she stumbles across an escaped prisoner from a concentration camp, not far from train tracks. The association of trains, particularly livestock cars, with the Holocaust has radically altered the symbolism of trains in German cultural history.
21 Augé, *Non-Places*, 103.

very little of her own identity; she reads a newspaper and carries a backpack – both common details – and otherwise betrays no personal information to her fellow passengers. Thinking back on the discussion of identity in Chapter 1, this anonymity lends itself to the performing of a new identity. The traveller can adopt any identity for the other travellers to see, on the one hand, but the traveller is also subject to having other identities thrust upon her. After all, each passenger witnesses just a few fleeting moments of the others' performances and draws conclusions based on those moments.

Two of the fellow passengers, Kitty and Kurt, speak explicitly to the idea of performance. One cannot help but listen to the two of them argue about their failed relationship and someone named Adam. Addressing the protagonist's visible curiosity, Kitty turns to her: 'Mein Mann und ich sind Schauspieler, wir üben für das nächste Stück. Kennen Sie es?' [My husband and I are actors. We are rehearsing for our next play. Do you know it?] (33). It is unclear what the 'truth' of the situation is, but the reader familiar with performance knows that whether they are actors in the professional sense is irrelevant; Franck points out that one is always performing, consciously or no. While details in the story suggest that the characters have other identities outside of this context – for example, the narrator's repulsive companion has a wife at home – anything that exists beyond this moment can only be speculation.

According to Augé, similar to the shallow – or non-existent – engagement that the traveller has with his fellow passengers, the traveller also interacts with space in a fleeting way. Modern travellers experience foreign locations at an accelerated pace, caused by 'double movement: the traveller's movement, of course, but also a parallel movement of the landscapes which he catches only in partial glimpses, a series of "snapshots" piled hurriedly into his memory.'[22] The narrator's only connection with the space through which her train passes is to catch glimpses of it and list them in an inventory of scenes witnessed:

22   Augé, *Non-Places*, 86.

[N]eben mir die Gleise biegen sich und blinken gelb in der Gewittersonne, die durch die grauen Wolken bricht, mitten aus den Häusern stößt ein kleiner Bahnsteig, ein zweiter und ein dritter, sie werden breiter, der erste ist schon vorbei, der zweite wird noch breiter, eine Bank, breiter, ein Schild breiter, mit Ortsnamen, breit, und Uhr, rund, Menschen mit Gepäck. (19)

[Next to me the tracks bend and flash yellow in the thundery sunshine that breaks through the grey storm clouds. A small train platform pokes up from the midst of the houses, a second and a third, they become wider, the first one is already past, the second becomes still wider, a bench, wider, a sign wider, with place names, wide, and a clock, round, people with luggage.]

Note that the acceleration of the train is indicated by the punctuation and rhythm of the sentence. The child's incessant counting of cows reinforces this sense of an inventory of images: '"Sieben Kuh, acht Kuh, neun Kuh, zwei Pferd, zehn Kuh"' ['Seven cow, eight cow, nine cow, two horse, ten cow'] (34). As a consequence of this disconnect from the space through which one travels, 'movement adds the particular experience of a form of solitude' which Augé calls 'a rare and sometimes melancholy pleasure'.[23] In other words, non-places can create the feeling of being alone, lacking connection and even lacking identity: 'The traveller's space may thus be the archetype of *non-place*.'[24]

It is not only in travel that one can feel this solitude of the non-place. Franck's short story 'Strandbad' captures a similar sense of isolation in the setting of a public beach. This story opens with the declaration: 'Ich mag es nicht, wenn Menschen sich ungefragt in mein Leben drängen. Ich komme gut ohne sie zurecht. Die zwei, drei Freunde, die ich habe, die wissen nicht, daß ich sie Freunde nenne, die reichen mir vollkommen, zu den anderen bin ich einfach höflich.' [I don't like it when people crowd into my life uninvited. I get along fine without them. The two, three friends that I have, they don't know that I call them friends, are completely enough for me. To the others I am simply polite.][25] Often cited as a typical example of the

23 Augé, *Non-Places*, 87.
24 Augé, *Non-Places*, 86.
25 Franck, 'Strandbad', 37.

'Unfähigkeit zu lieben', 'Strandbad' is narrated by the lifeguard of a public beach, who spends her day silently observing others. Her attention focuses on a man named Justus, about whom she has erotic fantasies.

This text is another example of failed or missed inter-personal connections. The narrator knows that she is attractive, and she seeks only periodic sexual contact with no strings attached. Feiereisen is critical of this lack of desire to form an emotional connection: 'Das Eindringen in den Körper beim Sexualakt scheint in der Literatur der so genannten "Fräuleinwunder" leichter zu sein als das Eindringen in den seelischen Näheraum.' [In the literature of the so-called *Fräuleinwunder* the penetration of the body during the sex act seems to be easier than the penetration of psychologically intimate spaces.][26] In addition to the short stories by Karen Duve and Judith Hermann, Feiereisen includes 'Strandbad' as an example of this failed intimacy through sexuality. The culmination of the narrator's fantasy is when Justus ejaculates prematurely on her suit, which leaves her feeling 'begehrt und geehrt wie schon lange nicht mehr' [desired and honoured for the first time in a long while] (45). According to Feiereisen, intimacy – let alone love – has no place in the lives of these characters, and awkward sex is satisfying enough.

What Feiereisen overlooks in this interpretation is that the interaction with Justus in 'Strandbad' occurs only in the narrator's imagination. Although the reader can be reasonably sure that the narrator asked Justus for his phone number, it is clear that she did not give him hers. It is this imagined event that starts the chain of fantasy: 'Ich stelle mir vor, ich gebe sie ihm. Ich denke mir aus, wie er sich mir zum Freund macht' [I imagine that I give it to him. I dream up how he makes himself my boyfriend] (40). Often the shift from fantasy to reality is unclear, as the events leading up to the one-night-stand and the reality of her duties at the pool are narrated in rambling, unbroken paragraphs. At other times the break is jarring: 'Im Fahrstuhl sehen wir uns nicht an, das Licht ist grell. Auf der Wasseroberfläche schwimmt reglos eine Hornisse, das ist eher selten' [We don't look at each other in the elevator. The light is glaring. A hornet swims

26   Feiereisen, 'Liebe als Utopie?', 185.

motionless on the surface of the water. That is rather rare] (44). It is perhaps telling that the narrator's fantasy ends not even with an imagined emotional connection but simply with feeling desired. Even in her fantasies she does not seek love or connection. Contrary to previous interpretations of this short story, this daydream is not an attempt at intimacy that failed; rather, no attempt was made.

This fantasy of sexual intimacy is of central importance, however, as the desire for connection is a significant by-product of the non-places of supermodernity. In Augé's words: 'The space of non-place creates neither singular identity nor relations; only solitude, and similitude.'[27] This causes a longing for place, for identity and for connection. Despite the narrator's insistence at the beginning of the story that she gets along quite well without people, her fantasies betray a desire for connection with others. She also reveals that she does not, in fact, have friends, starting another thought with the phrase, 'Hätte ich Freunde gehabt' [If I had had friends] (38). The narrator explains that she, for the most part, is quite content to live alone, working as a lifeguard during the day and reading physics journals at night. It is only from time to time that she is overcome by the need 'mich menschlich und warm und gesellig zu fühlen' [to feel human and warm and sociable] (38). True to Feiereisen's thesis, the narrator uses sex as a placeholder for intimacy. Her frequent sexual encounters only temporarily satisfy her periodic desire to be close to someone. The narrator has an uncomfortable relationship with this need for closeness, and she attempts to ignore it; when she asks Justus for his phone number, she takes his card but tries to satisfy herself with this small gesture and with fantasy.

Similarly, the narrator of 'Zugfahrt' fantasizes about meeting someone with whom she can connect. Her real reason for travelling to Italy by train is her hope of meeting 'einen ..., den ich lieben kann' [some man ... I can love] (20–1). Although she mentions, fleetingly, a relationship that she has with a married man, it is not fulfilling enough to prevent her from considering her fellow travellers as potential lovers. Despite initial negative observations of the man sitting across from her, the narrator struggles

27   Augé, *Non-Places*, 103.

against her inclination to dislike him, hoping that he might prove more appealing. In the course of the train ride, however, this man (who eats liverwurst sandwiches and smells of eau de toilette and detergent) becomes more repulsive to the narrator. He makes annoying small talk, asks invasive questions (e.g. whether the narrator has an eating disorder), and makes advances to her after openly acknowledging that he is married. Yet the narrator does not reject him entirely until the last page of the story, so pressing is her desire for contact. Her attentions turn briefly to the father of the young child – 'Männer mit Kindern übernehmen Verantwortung, manchmal, und manchmal sind sie sympathisch' [men with children take on responsibility, sometimes, and sometimes they are likeable] – but he shows no interest in the narrator whatsoever (35). At the end, desperate for company, she considers inviting the man's little boy to the dining car for a slice of cake but decides against it. The narrators in both 'Zugfahrt' and 'Strandbad' desire intimacy but take no action to seek or obtain it.

By contrast, some of Franck's other narrators both express a desire for connection and actively pursue it. In 'Für Sie und für Ihn' [For Her and For Him], the narrator regales the bartender of her local bar with stories of her neighbour's erotic adventures.[28] In this story, closeness comes through speaking. The narrator explains: '[W]enn ich mich anders nicht loswerde, mich gerne mitteilen möchte, wie heute, das Auf und Ab in meinen vier Wänden satt habe, gehe ich hinunter und kaufe mir die Aufmerksamkeit des Barmanns' [When I can't otherwise get away from myself, would like to communicate, like today, am sick of the going to and fro within my four walls, I go downstairs and buy myself the attention of the bartender] (53). This intimacy is purchased, is a commodity, but it is sufficient for the lonely narrator. She and the barman do not converse about anything personal or exchange intimate information about themselves. Instead, the narrator seeks the simple acknowledgement and interaction of having someone listen to her stories.

---

28 Julia Franck, 'Für Sie und für Ihn', *Bauchlandung: Geschichten zum Anfassen* (Cologne: DuMont Buchverlag, 2000), 53–65.

Today her story is about her neighbour's sexual exploits. Beret Norman interprets this information as the narrator's 'currency at the bar' with which she can purchase the barkeeper's attention.[29] While buying a drink entitles her to some contact with the bartender, it is her story that sustains his attention and seems to promise more intimacy. At the conclusion of her tale, the barman invites himself over to the narrator's apartment, supposedly to watch her neighbour have sex in front of his open window, but perhaps to have sex with the narrator as well. As in 'Zugfahrt' this narrator notes the faults of her potential partner (in this case a pot belly and a flat butt), but she overlooks them in her desire to prolong their interaction. Their plans are disrupted by the revelation that the neighbour's sexual partner is the barman's ex-girlfriend, and the narrator is left alone when the barman, visibly upset, disappears behind the bar. This failed attempt at connection reflects poorly on the narrator. The barman's response to seeing his ex-girlfriend and knowing of her sexual escapades with another man causes deeper emotions in him than the narrator seems capable of feeling or even understanding. The ability to connect with others, to sustain intimacy in either physical or emotional terms, seems altogether absent in the narrators discussed thus far.

In these three short stories the lives of the female protagonists can be characterized by a lack of meaningful relationships with others. The characters in these stories use sex to satisfy a vague desire for closeness, for a deep emotional connection that is usually defined as intimacy. Their behaviour is influenced by their performative identities: they 'do' femininity (sometimes wrongly, as in the case of the narrator in 'Strandbad') according to their gendered socialization. They also more consciously engage in a performance of identity in order to seduce, to deceive or to gain attention. Yet these interactions leave them unfulfilled, and they continue to long for something more.

29   Beret Norman, 'Social Alienation and Gendered Surveillance: Julia Franck Observes Post-*Wende* Society', in Katharina Gerstenberger and Patricia Herminghouse, eds, *German Literature in a New Century: Trends, Traditions, Transitions, Transformations* (Rochester, NY: Berghahn Books, 2008), 237–52; here, 240.

Intimacy and Identity

While some scholars, such as Helga Meise and Beret Norman, find Beyla's search for truth to be the motivating force in the plot of *Liebediener*, I argue that the plot is largely motivated by the tension between the desire for intimacy and the inability to achieve it.[30] (In fact, I read truth as an obstacle to Beyla's fantasies.) *Liebediener* was named 'womöglich *die* Liebesgeschichte der Neunziger' [possibly *the* love story of the nineties] by the *Süddeutsche Zeitung*.[31] It is telling that this novel would earn such a distinction, for it is characterized by a sense of anonymity, alienation and (in the absence of love) obsession and fantasy. At the centre of the novel is Beyla's friendship with the now-deceased Charlotte and her fledgling relationship with Albert, the handsome downstairs neighbour. Beyond this Beyla has few connections to other people. As the novel progresses, even these connections break, prompting Stuart Taberner to describe this 'depressing' novel as centring on 'a woman's absolute isolation in the city'.[32]

Like the narrator of 'Strandbad', Beyla's life is characterized by solitude. Alone in her new apartment, she considers calling a friend to talk about the move, 'aber mir gefiel die Stille' [but I liked the silence], she says.[33] As she is a self-proclaimed liar, this statement takes on the same ring of untruth as the narrator's claim in 'Strandbad' that her friends (who may or may not exist) 'reichen mir vollkommen'. Many days later, Beyla discovers that Charlotte's answering machine is still taking messages, none of which are for Beyla, further suggesting that Beyla has little contact with the outside world. By contrast, there are several messages for Charlotte, although she has been dead for over a week. One wonders, then, whether

30 See Meise, 'Mythos Berlin', 131 and Norman, 'Social Alienation', 241.
31 Michael Bauer, 'Liebe in den Zeiten von Tralala', *Süddeutsche Zeitung* (10 November 1999). Original italics.
32 Stuart Taberner, '"West German Writing" in the Berlin Republic', in Stuart Taberner, ed., *Contemporary German Fiction: Writing in the Berlin Republic*, Cambridge Studies in German (Cambridge: Cambridge University Press, 2007), 72–91; here, 81.
33 Franck, *Liebediener*, 52.

Beyla actually has any friends to call her, especially as the reader sees her in the company of only one friend in the course of the novel. This character makes three appearances, and it is clear in these scenes that she and Beyla know each other quite well, although their relationship gradually sours and fades.

This nameless friend is known only through a few details: she works for a radio station, she is in a long-term relationship and she has a long history with Beyla. They periodically lose track of each other but are pleased to pick up their friendship again, without making an effort to maintain it. They share a distinct familiarity and closeness: they hug, tease each other and are affectionate. Yet when her friend announces that she is pregnant, Beyla's attitude towards her promptly changes. She is not at all happy about this news. This response could be explained in a variety of ways. Perhaps Beyla, who likes to know everything about the few people in her life, does not like being surprised. It also seems likely that she is jealous, anticipating that her friend will have less time for her as she adopts a new lifestyle and new priorities. It could also be that Beyla is jealous of the intimacy between her friend and the father of the child. She knew that they were happy, but, she says: 'jetzt hatte sie mich übertroffen' [now she had beat me] (43). Beyla craves a similar intimacy with Albert and sees, by contrast, that their relationship is not as far along as that of her friend and her boyfriend.

Not even to this friend, however, does Beyla reveal her desire for intimacy. In fact, Beyla has not introduced her to Albert, and they only meet by accident at the movies. When they discuss the relationship, the friend offers her (unsolicited) opinion of Albert: "'Aber wenn du mich fragst, dein Typ ist nicht so ein Vatertyp'" [But when you ask me, your guy isn't really a father-type], clarifying that she means, "'Na, eben einer, der Verantwortung will. Einer, der sich auf die eine Frau festlegen will und kann'" [Well, a man who wants responsibility. A man who wants to and can commit himself to one woman] (138). It is clear that the friend measures all relationships against her own and uses her life as the standard against which to compare Beyla's. When Beyla defends her relationship with Albert, the friend asks: "'Liebt er dich? Wirst du schwanger?'" ['Does he love you? Are you going to get pregnant?'] Beyla responds:

'"Vielleicht will ich gar nicht gleich schwanger werden, wie wär dann das?"' ['Maybe I don't want to get pregnant right away, how would that be?'] (139). Yet she is annoyed, not because she is being held against her friend's standards, but because her friend has pointed out that Beyla and Albert's relationship is far from the point of starting a family.[34] Beyla's jealousy sours her attitude towards her friend, which becomes increasingly negative: she comments on the friend's stupid maternity clothes (142), her constant eating (137) and her private conversations with her belly, held as if others in the room cannot hear her (143). As Beyla's attempts at intimacy with Albert are frustrated, her resentment towards her friend increases, because she serves to remind Beyla of the intimacy that she seeks but that is beyond her reach.

This craving for intimacy coupled with Beyla's insistent and at times blatant spying begs the question of whether she is starved for company and is suffering from the sense of alienation that so concerned the German media. In contrast to Augé's theory, which does not account for the effects of personal history, Beyla's case is much more complex than simply being trapped in a non-place, where it is impossible to form connections. It could well be that Beyla tends to be more isolated because of modern urban life (see below), but it is difficult if not impossible to identify spatial alienation as the specific and sole cause of Beyla's distress. She seems to have difficulty maintaining friendships as an adult, but these difficulties find their root in much earlier relationships.

In the first chapter of the novel she remembers childhood friends, one in particular who was not at all friendly. In fact, all memories of Beyla's childhood playmates are negative. There was, first of all, no true friendship to speak of. Instead, she seems to have used her playmates to gain temporary entry to their apartments and, by extension, their lives (a behaviour she repeats with Charlotte):

---

34   Several chapters earlier, in which Beyla tells Albert of having had an abortion during a previous relationship, she makes it clear to the reader just how much she does want a child. See Chapter 4.

Ich war ein dreckiges Kind. Gerne ging ich mit den anderen Kindern hinauf in ihre gute Wohnungen, die immer sauber und hell waren, in denen die Muttis gute Kleider trugen und die Vatis gute Arbeit hatten, oder andersherum, und wo die Kinder allein waren, Einzelkinder, die sich tagsüber langweilten und freuten, wenn man ihnen Gesellschaft leistete. ... Bei uns gab es keine Mutti und nichts Ähnliches. Nur Kinder. (51)

[I was a filthy child. I gladly went with the other children up into their good apartments, which were always clean and bright, in which the mommies wore good clothes and the daddies had good jobs, or vice versa, and where the children were alone, only children, who were bored during the day and were glad when someone kept them company. ... At our place there was no mommy and nothing like that. Only children.]

Rather than value these children for their companionship, Beyla was primarily concerned – even as a child – with gaining temporary access to a different world. It is during childhood that Beyla starts to become aware of the associations with domestic spaces. Bright and clean apartments signal that the residents have well-dressed mothers and employed fathers, and certain ways of behaving signify that one was raised in such a space. For example, during Beyla's first date with Albert, she is very conscious of what her behaviour is communicating. When Albert hands her a napkin, she worries whether she has spilled something on herself and, more unsettling, whether Albert can see her lack of proper upbringing in her table manners (85–6). Thus, from these childhood experiences Beyla takes three important things. First, trained at an early age to observe others' lives and to participate vicariously, she continues this as an adult. Second, she finds that, through observation, she can gather information that can serve her own adoption of these identities. Finally, observation can lead to a familiarity with a person's life, if not to intimacy with that person.

Observation and performance remain constants in Beyla's life as an adult. Tragically, although perhaps predictably, they prevent her from experiencing the very intimacy she craves, particularly when it comes to Albert. As much as she might desire it, it soon becomes apparent that Beyla is not capable of sustaining an intimate relationship with Albert. In the beginning, the relationship seems to progress smoothly, and, from the perspective of the reader, it seems that Albert pursues Beyla as much as she pursues him. Yet, as Beyla pushes for great and greater intimacy, imbalance and miscommunication become more pronounced. For example, only four days after they first kiss, Beyla tells Albert about becoming pregnant with a previous boyfriend. Through telling him this story, she is seeking an emotional connection, although she acknowledges freely that Albert cannot understand how significant this experience was for her (113). For his part, Albert does seem to be attempting to connect with Beyla in this conversation, via physical contact and listening sympathetically, but this does not satisfy her. She routinely experiences feelings of distance or moments of misunderstanding, which begin as early as their first dinner together and continue throughout their relationship. Rather than adjust her expectations, Beyla forces herself to justify these moments and ignore her disappointment. In other words, although they may not be genuinely connecting, Beyla insists that they continue playing their roles of happy lovers. Her interior monologue reveals both moments of seeing through their performances and moments of believing in the performance. She ascribes to him a greater understanding of her feelings than she knows is possible, thinking for example that he knows that she reserves the gesture of kissing someone's eyelids only for those whom she loves (132). As her demands for both intimacy and the performance of intimacy increase, Beyla is more and more often disappointed by Albert: 'Es verletzte ein wenig, daß Albert mich nicht verstehen wollte, mehr aber, daß er unbedingt anderer Meinung bleiben wollte. Trotzdem war ich entschlossen, glücklich zu sein ...'. [It hurt a little that Albert did not want to understand me, but more that he absolutely wanted to remain of another opinion. Nevertheless, I was determined to be happy] (168). He insists on keeping parts of his life private, such as his childhood or his occupation, which Beyla attempts to justify. She is bothered by the gaps in her knowledge about Albert and is possessed by the desire to know everything about him, perhaps mistaking knowledge for intimacy.

The more Beyla learns that Albert has a life that does not involve her, the more desperate her desire for connection becomes. As her insecurity grows, she becomes unreasonable, knocking on his door once a day or more: 'Zugegeben, manchmal klopfte ich zweimal. ... Ich gestehe manchmal war es auch dreimal am Tag, daß ich an seiner Tür klopfte. ... (Na, und die Male, die ich geklopft hatte und er nicht öffnete, die zählte ich gar nicht erst, wo hätte das auch hingeführt?)' [Granted, sometimes I knocked twice. ... I'll admit, sometimes it was also three times a day that I knocked on his door. ... (Well, and the times that I had knocked and he didn't open, I didn't count those at all. Where would that have led to?)] (169–70). Her desire to know everything motivates her to consider bugging his apartment, and she comments that she finds it strange that one customarily spies on strangers and not the ones that one loves (172). She does not resort to this measure of surveillance, but she does continue to listen to Albert by standing in the hallway and leaning out her window. (Strangely, Beyla does not ever realize that the sounds of conversation and lovemaking she hears through her bathroom vents come from Albert's apartment as well.) This obsession becomes all consuming, and Beyla stops mentioning aspects of her life (her friend, her job, her family) other than Albert.

To return for a moment to the beginning of the book, it is the accident that causes Charlotte's death that first connects Beyla to Albert. It is also this scene in which the power of surveillance and observation is established as a significant theme. Beyla invests herself with significance by being the one who saw the accident, the only one who knows that happened. She identifies Albert as the man in the red Ford, who presumably startled Charlotte into the path of the tram. As Beyla muses, had she not observed the scene, Albert would not 'exist' in relation to this accident. Thus, the fact that Beyla did see this connection is, according to Beret Norman, 'her key to power': Beyla and Albert are united in their knowledge of that day (although it is unclear whether Albert is cognizant of his role in Charlotte's death), and Beyla has power over Albert as the only witness to the scene.[35]

In her article 'Social Alienation and Gendered Surveillance: Julia Franck Observes Post-*Wende* Society', Norman considers the way in which surveillance functions within Franck's works. For Beyla, the knowledge that she gains through observing Albert serves as 'social currency', a term Norman uses to mean 'networks, reciprocal connections, and trust.'[36] This

---

35 Norman, 'Social Alienation', 242–3.
36 Norman, 'Social Alienation', 237.

social currency could be used to gain attention from others, such as the policemen who want to interrogate her or the woman who sells newspapers at the kiosk down the street. Yet when they ask Beyla for information about the accident, rather than seek their attention, Beyla insists that she saw nothing (12, 13). She only wants to use the currency she gained from observing the accident in order to get closer to Albert.

Her knowledge of the accident, her social currency, does provide an initial connection with Albert, but it does not remain the basis of their relationship for long. Instead, the accident is both the context of their meeting and a threat to their intimacy. At times Beyla is able to deny Albert's guilt. At other times, she is afraid to identify him as the driver of the red car. For example, when Beyla and Albert go away for a couple days, he rents a red Ford, and Beyla refuses to let him drive, refuses to see him – both in life and in her memory – in the driver's seat of the car (174–6). Eventually Beyla resigns herself to acknowledging Albert's guilt, and she only wonders whether he feels remorse for what he has done and whether these thoughts torture him (193). But even here the accident functions as a connection between them. Without the accident as her explanation for Albert's silence, she would have to acknowledge that they do not understand each other completely, that Albert has a life and thoughts that are independent of his relationship with her and that she does not know everything about him. For Beyla, knowing everything about Albert is synonymous with the intimacy that she craves.

Paradoxically, Beyla's relationship with Albert comes to an end when she discovers the long-desired truth about his profession: he is a prostitute. She unearths Albert's business card with his photograph, phone number and rates on it, as well as proof of his previous relationship with Charlotte: a stack of bills for time that they spent together. Others' interpretations of the novel's conclusion are based on a cold and emotionally detached Beyla. Martin Hielscher, for example, claims that the revelation of Albert's profession makes Beyla's love 'unmöglich' or impossible.[37] He believes that

37   Martin Hielscher, 'Generation und Mentalität', *Neue deutsche Literatur* 4 (2000), 174–82; here, 181.

the sheer banality of this revelation pops Beyla's inflated image of who Albert is. Consistent with the idea of 'social currency', Norman interprets the ending along socio-economic lines: 'With this information, Beyla gains more of the knowledge she desires; but because [Albert's] profession both repudiates her position in his life and limits his social capital, she fails in her attempt for power.' Norman concludes that Beyla's 'social detachment ... returns.'[38]

The ending can be read very differently. That Albert routinely performs the role of lover for other women poses a challenge to Beyla's possessiveness and is at the same time insulting for her, as she never felt that he performed his role convincingly for her. She confronts him and he tells her everything, but adds that he loves her. She responds by asking why he doesn't love one of his customers instead, and he responds '"Liebe ist nicht zum Erklären"' [Love can't be explained], countering Beyla's desire to catalogue and understand Albert and his emotions (216). Finally Beyla asks who has been paying Albert to spend time with her. He insists that no one has and wonders aloud who would do that for her (218). Just before this discussion, Albert had described some instances in which husbands paid him to flirt with or pretend to start affairs with their wives, in the hopes of making them feel desired and attractive. This rhetorical question to Beyla, wondering who in her life would go to such trouble and financial cost for her pleasure, (although meant to be reassuring about their relationship) is a sad one, as the answer seems to be: no one.

Yet there is one person who seems affectionate towards Beyla, and who has more money than she alone can possibly spend: Mrs Wolf, Charlotte's aunt. It is, after all, Mrs Wolf who urges Beyla to take Charlotte's apartment. During their first encounter, Mrs Wolf muses that it is a shame that all her relatives have died before being able to enjoy her money. Perhaps this is a clue, a hint that she would like to spend some on Beyla, who (at least in Mrs Wolf's mind) was such a good friend of her favourite niece. Another clue is the reference to the fairy tale 'Little Red Riding Hood'. After their first night together, Beyla asks Albert why he is sleeping. Albert's response

38   Norman, 'Social Alienation', 243.

echoes the wolf's: "'Um dich besser zu lieben'" [The better to love you] (106). Later Beyla makes a reference to the tale when she brings food to Albert's apartment: 'nicht immer in einem kleinen Körbchen und fast nie mit einem roten Tuch um den Kopf' [not always in a little basket and almost never with a red scarf around my head] (170). Commonly understood as a sexually charged fairy tale, some versions of 'Little Red Riding Hood' interpret the story as a parable of sexual awakening.[39] The name of Charlotte's aunt, Mrs Wolf, plays with this reference but posits the aunt as the key figure in Beyla's sexual experience.

Mrs Wolf's significance in the story is underscored by her final appearance in the novel, after Beyla and Albert have ended their stormy relationship. She stops by the apartment to pick up any last personal items of Charlotte's that Beyla might have found. She asks Beyla how she is, comments that she looks unwell and asks, patting her on the cheek, "'Ist der junge Mann, Albert, ist der nett zu Ihnen?'" ['Is the young man, Albert, is he nice to you?'] (236). Perhaps this is an innocent question, since it was already revealed at the funeral that Mrs Wolf and Albert knew each other. But perhaps this is another hint that Mrs Wolf has funded their entire relationship. It could be that she paid for Charlotte's hours with Albert and continues to pay for Beyla. In an unspoken acknowledgement of Mrs Wolf's involvement, Beyla gives her Charlotte's box of photos, which contain those of Albert and others whose services Charlotte enjoyed.

Mrs Wolf is very important in the novel, despite her few appearances. In addition to her possible orchestration of the relationship between Beyla and Albert, her protective and supportive role (and its implication of intimacy) is what lures Beyla into the apartment in the first place. Beyla did not want to move into Charlotte's apartment, but her decision to do so, as with many of her decisions throughout the novel, is prompted by her

---

39   For example, Angela Carter's interpretation, 'In the Company of Wolves', proposes an alternate ending in which Red willingly gets into bed with the wolf and stays there, embracing the animal within (i.e. her sexuality) and her transition to womanhood. Angela Carter, 'In the Company of Wolves', *Burning Your Boats: The Collected Short Stories* (New York: H. Holt and Company, 1996), 212–20.

desire for closeness. When she sees Mrs Wolf at Charlotte's funeral, the elderly woman reacts with pleasure. She greets her 'so herzlich, daß ich den Schlüssel in meiner Tasche losließ' [so cordially that I let go of the key in my pocket], the key to Charlotte's apartment, which Beyla had decided not to take (30). Later Mrs Wolf asks Beyla to sit next to her and introduces her to a woman from the property management agency, who would like to settle the affair with the apartment. Although repulsed by the woman's questions and by her interest in Beyla's occupation and financial situation, Beyla agrees to take the apartment, encouraged by Mrs Wolf's warmth. She seems proud of Beyla and shows off both her financial independence and her job as a clown, as if she were her own niece. Beyla is drawn in by this attention, and she is flattered (if puzzled) by how much Charlotte spoke of her to her aunt.

Moving into Charlotte's apartment promises further contact with Mrs Wolf while cleaning out the apartment. Beyla invites her to call at any time, and Mrs Wolf promises another visit to pick up Charlotte's personal things. Even as her attention is focused on Albert, Beyla reveals that Mrs Wolf is still in her thoughts. She claims to be worried that Mrs Wolf will call and ask why she hasn't visited Charlotte's grave, but her disappointment when she does not call suggests that she had hoped for the opposite (160). When Mrs Wolf does visit at the end of the novel, their conversation seems to pull Beyla back from the brink of insanity. After spending days in a delirious state following her break-up with Albert, Beyla seems able to function like a human being again. Her sentences resume a normal length, and her narration here is more grounded in reality, rather than being hysterical and, at times, incomprehensible. Although her intimacy with Mrs Wolf comes at the cost of a genuine relationship with Albert, it is nonetheless reassuring for Beyla. She is so comforted by Mrs Wolf's presence at the end of the novel that she ceases to obsess over Albert.

(Non-)Places

Returning to Augé's interpretation of supermodernity, it is worth considering the spaces in which *Liebediener* unfolds and where (if at all) emotional connections are formed. Augé emphasizes that inter-personal connections are formed in places, while non-places are understood as locations in which such connections are frustrated or impossible. According to Augé, non-places are typically highly trafficked areas, places through which people customarily pass. There are a few non-places in *Liebediener*: Potsdamer Platz, some streets in Berlin and the circus tent, in which Beyla daily endures the feeling of being exposed under the spotlights. The vast majority of the novel unfolds within places, reflective of Beyla's desire to form connections: her former basement apartment, Charlotte's apartment and Albert's apartment. Based on Augé's division of place and non-place, one would expect that connections would be formed in the places, i.e. the domestic areas within the apartment buildings. Yet this expectation is regularly frustrated in the novel.

The stairwell of the apartment building, for example, is one area through which people customarily pass, i.e. it is a non-place. Yet the stairwell in *Liebediener* comes to function as a central meeting point for all the characters, i.e. in this situation, it is a place. Augé speaks of the importance of a town centre 'where individual itineraries can intersect and mingle, where a few words are exchanged and solitudes momentarily forgotten.'[40] For Beyla, the stairwell becomes this social centre, one to which she gains more regular access when she moves out of the basement apartment. It seems that few people visited Beyla's old apartment, and, indeed, the reader's only knowledge of it is that, from the apartment window, Beyla observed others coming and going. When she used to pick up her mail – the only time she had reason to be in the stairwell, as the basement apartment has a separate entrance onto the street – Beyla would run into Charlotte, and

40   Augé, *Non-Places*, 66–7.

it was during these conversations that they became acquainted. By moving into Charlotte's apartment, Beyla more regularly frequents this social place.

Charlotte's apartment also holds the promise of being a place, one where friends can gather. On her moving day Beyla hosts both her pregnant friend and the young girl from the upstairs apartment, although by the end of the visit Beyla's desire to be alone resurfaces, and she wishes that they would leave (47). Others enter her apartment, Ted, Albert and Mrs Wolf, but these three visitors are still connected to the apartment – and thus to Beyla – through Charlotte. It seems that, on some level, Beyla is aware of this, and at times she appreciates the promise of company that the apartment holds. When considering quitting her job, the ability to afford her new apartment is an important factor in making this decision. By the novel's end, however, she contemplates leaving, largely to distance herself from Charlotte: 'Ich konnte die Wohnung aufgeben, ich mußte nicht diese Räume um mich haben, Charlotte's Räume [...]' [I was able to give up the apartment, I didn't have to have these rooms around me, Charlotte's rooms] (235). In addition, the stairwell that began as a place of connection, a place to meet others living in the building and to spend time with them, deteriorates into a non-place, in which Beyla listens at Albert's door, desperate and unable to connect with him.

Domestic Spaces

Despite this disappointment, Beyla does not give up on the apartment and the promise that it contains for her. Previously she had always lived in basement apartments, and she describes the sounds (of water in the pipes) and smells (of mildew) as being homely. Gradually she reveals important parts of her family history, all of which unfolded in those basement apartments: the absence of her mother, the rages and abuse of her alcoholic father and her own feelings of guilt when separated from him. Upstairs apartments were associated with clean, intact and happy families, which

Beyla could only visit. When she moves into Charlotte's apartment, she has the opportunity to step into this 'upstairs' life and make it her own. Estranged from her family, Beyla wants to make a new one, this time as the mother she never knew and with Albert as the father of their child. This fantasy of starting a family (investigated in greater depth in Chapter 4) is synonymous with creating a home. In the novel it remains an unfulfilled fantasy, as Beyla alienates herself from Albert.

Far from being specific to Beyla, this longing for home is exhibited by many of the characters in the novel. The book opens on the day of Charlotte's death, when Beyla is leaving her apartment to meet her brothers and their families for an Easter picnic. She describes, briefly, the idyllic sense of family associated with this event. As mentioned earlier, Beyla's nameless pregnant friend is giving up her single life and starting a family with her boyfriend. Eventually, the reader learns that even Charlotte, known to Beyla for staying out late with friends and having many lovers, desired a family. Mrs Wolf comments that Charlotte used to collect silverware and dishes from flea markets, for the household she hoped to have someday. More than simply a place to feel comfortable, the idea – or ideal – of home in this novel contains the promise of connection and intimacy that the characters do not find in their frequent sexual encounters.

Clearly, the home remains a topic of concern to Franck and her contemporaries, despite an increased focus on transnationalism, globalization and migration in German literature. In other words, Franck's exploration of domestic spaces is part of a larger trend, although this trend has not been explored in scholarship to the same extent as the theme of urban alienation. The idea of home functions in a variety of ways in contemporary literature, but it is often the location of memory and connection – connection via family and family history. In Tanja Dückers' *Spielzone* or Judith Hermann's *Sommerhaus, später*, traditional notions of home are something to rebel against, for they are symbols of bourgeois values and traditional gender roles. Dückers' later novel, *Himmelskörper* [Heavenly Bodies], represents the home as the archive of history. As the protagonist interacts with her mother's and grandmother's collections of things, she encounters evidence of her family's National Socialist past.[41] Political events reverberate in domestic spaces in Katharina Hacker's *Die Habenichtse* [The Have-Nots], when the World Trade Center bombings and the Iraq War impact the personal lives of Germans living in London.[42] Jenny Erpenbeck's *Heimsuchung* [Visitation] takes the most radical stance towards domestic spaces, making a plot of land and the homes on it the real protagonists of the novel.[43] Erpenbeck traces the division and development of the land throughout the twentieth century as German history scars the landscape and domestic sphere. Domestic spaces figure prominently in Franck's works, as the analysis of *Liebediener* has shown, and they will be investigated further throughout this book. A decided lack of connection to place – one might even say a sense of homelessness – plagues the characters in Franck's early works. It is important that home, a strongly gendered sphere, is the locus of fantasies of social connection. This longing for connection can be explained via a theorization of space borrowed from feminist geography, specifically feminist investigations of the home.

Theorizing the Home

A variety of definitions of 'home' exist in both culture and scholarship, which reflects the myriad subjective experiences of domestic space. Cultural geographers Alison Blunt and Robyn Dowling define home as 'both a place/physical location *and* a set of feelings [...]', allowing for the fantasy of home, the messy reality and everything in between.[44] Ideally, 'home symbolizes: community or familial solidarity, fixity, stability, and refuge',

---

41   Tanja Dückers, *Himmelskörper* (Berlin: Aufbau Taschenbuch Verlag, 2003).
42   Katharina Hacker, *Die Habenichtse* (Frankfurt am Main: Suhrkamp, 2006).
43   Jenny Erpenbeck, *Heimsuchung* (Munich: btb Verlag, 2007).
44   Alison Blunt and Robyn Dowling, *Home*, Key Ideas in Geography (New York: Routledge, 2006), 22.

although scholars point out the frequent conflict between this ideal and lived experience.[45] The home is a space – to use Augé's terminology, hopefully a *place* – that 'is invested with meanings, emotions, experiences and relationships that lie at the heart of human life'.[46] As Duncan and Lambert point out, home can have a political meaning as well, when one considers one's country as 'home' or 'homeland', often reinforcing a sense of 'us' versus 'them' or safety versus threat.[47] This book is primarily concerned with the conflict between the characters' fantasies of home and their experience of it. From this conflict arises a productive tension – productive in the sense that it encourages the reader to question her own assumptions or fantasies about home.

The conflict between fantasy and experience can apply to the physical spaces of home as well. As Blunt and Dowling point out, most people carry an image of an 'ideal' home in their minds, but these ideals are culturally determined and shaped by individual experience.[48] In the United States an ideal home may be a suburban, single-family detached home, often with a garage and yard. In Germany, where the majority of families live in apartments, the image may be a radically different one.[49] Regardless of individual and cultural preferences, Blunt and Dowling argue, it is possible to consider some locations 'homely' if they 'correspond to normative notions of home'.[50] There is no strong correlation between the physical description of a place and its homeliness, however. Blunt and Dowling use the example of a woman who is abused in her home to undermine the relationship between outward appearances and feelings of security and connection. Conversely,

---

45   Patricia Price-Chalita, 'Spatial Metaphor and the Politics of Empowerment: Mapping a Place for Feminism and Postmodernism in Geography?', *Antipode* 26/3 (1994), 236–54; here, 239.

46   Alison Blunt and Ann Varley, 'Geographies of Home: An Introduction', *Cultural Geographies* 11 (2004), 3–6; here, 3.

47   James Ducan and David Lambert, 'Landscapes of Home', in James Duncan, N. C. Johnson and R. H. Schein, eds, *A Companion to Cultural Geography* (Oxford: Blackwell, 2003), 382–403; here, 395.

48   Blunt and Dowling, *Home*, 101.

49   Blunt and Dowling, *Home*, 109, 114.

50   Blunt and Dowling, *Home*, 26.

a place not typically considered homely may nonetheless be experienced as home by an individual: 'Home, in other words, can be created, and takes different forms, in unlikely dwellings: student accommodation ...; travelling caravans and mobile homes ..., residential homes for the elderly ..., and squatter settlements.'[51]

Franck's novels are set in locations both homely (apartments and houses) and unhomely (a hotel and a refugee camp). Not only are the hotel and refugee camp among spaces considered unhomely by Blunt and Dowling, but Augé identifies them as non-places as well.[52] Both temporarily house people, and both are characterized by their transitional nature. In *Der neue Koch* and *Lagerfeuer*, the novels set in these locations, connections are indeed made in these places. Contradicting expectations, the traditionally domestic settings are fraught with conflict and characterized by coldness. Beyla, as we have seen, cannot sustain connections to others, regardless of where she lives. Helene, the protagonist of *Die Mittagsfrau*, grows up in a house with her family but experiences physical abuse and emotional neglect as long as she is there. These physical spaces, while promising fulfillment of the ideals of home, are not experienced as homely. From this brief overview, it is clear that home is an important but problematic site for Franck's characters.

Conclusion

What one can take from Augé's theory and apply to Franck's works is the idea that 'in the world of supermodernity people are always, and never, at home.'[53] As a result, they are often seeking connection and rootedness, which is centred on the ideal of home. The following chapters continue

---

51   Blunt and Dowling, *Home*, 121.
52   Augé, *Non-Places*, 97.
53   Augé, *Non-Places*, 109.

to explore domestic spaces in Franck's novels, with a special focus on how these spaces are gendered. Returning to the ideas of performance and performativity, the gendering of the home shapes the role of 'mother' and the ideal of intimacy that she represents. Home becomes a symbol of the emotional state of being 'im Schoß der Familie', or 'in the bosom of the family', as the German expression goes. For the most part, it is the mother's bosom that is conjured in this image, and thus the significance of domestic space in Franck's oeuvre is tied to the significance of the mother. The investigation of the motherhood, therefore, remains closely connected to an investigation of domestic spaces.

Daughters: Psychoanalytic Theory, Domestic Space, and Maternal Desire

For Franck's characters, the difference between a house and a home is the connectedness that they feel to other people within that space. These people can be friends, relations or lovers, but fantasies of connection usually involve an idealized vision of a family, despite – and also because of – the fractured home lives from which the protagonists emerge. In *Liebediener* Beyla wishes to have a child with Albert, and she fantasizes about a life quite different from her own childhood with her abusive father. The narrator of *Der neue Koch* is obsessed with the ways that her mother failed her, and she remains devoted to and resentful of her shell of a home. Helene, the protagonist of *Die Mittagsfrau*, tries to distance herself from her abusive and neglectful parents by moving to Berlin, where she carves out her own life with her lover. And Ella, one of the sibling protagonists in *Rücken an Rücken*, struggles with her disappointed expectations of and growing anger towards her mother Käthe. Almost all female, Franck's protagonists are shaped and weighed down by their fraught relationships with their mothers.

This chapter focuses on the mother–daughter relationship from the daughters' perspective, as they articulate and attempt to process these charged relationships. The majority of scholarly investigations in this vein operate within the matrix of psychoanalysis, be they more conservative investigations that adhere to Freudian theory or feminist reinterpretations such as those by Nancy Chodorow or Jessica Benjamin. In what follows, several of Franck's texts are analysed using psychoanalysis, but this serves the purpose of proving that Franck's mothers and daughters defy and dismantle this psychoanalytic framework. Although the themes of space and performativity are only touched on briefly in this chapter, space, performative identity and the exploded psychoanalytic mother–daughter matrix together form the basis of Chapter 4 and the theorization of maternal drag.

Much of the scholarly literature on mother–daughter relationships that emerged in the 1970s and 1980s considers how the daughter is to respond to the 'self-sacrifice', or loss of self that the mother endured in order to care for her child.[1] Many of the groundbreaking works on daughterhood struggle with the conflicted feelings that women experience towards their mothers. On the one hand, daughters owe their mothers a terrific debt for all that their mothers have sacrificed for them. For the generation of women participating in the women's movement, awareness of their mothers' limited opportunities in the face of increasing freedom for women was doubtless a source of guilt. On the other hand, these daughters feel at the same time that their mothers have held them back in expecting them to emulate the ideals of (passive) femininity that the mothers embody. This feeling is so common that Lynn Sukenick called it 'matrophobia', which Adrienne Rich defines as both the fear of '*becoming one's mother*' and 'the desire to purge once and for all our mother's bondage, to become individual and free'.[2]

It is worth asking, however, whether matrophobia is generation-specific, rather than the universal experience that 1970s feminists claimed it to be. In *My Mother, My Self* Nancy Friday and women of her generation attempt to come to terms with their relationships to their mothers, who seemed, for the most part, to embody the ideal of the 1950s housewife.[3] Julia Franck and women of her generation had very different mothers. Their mothers, who largely belonged to the generation of 1968, did *not* uphold the earlier ideals of passive femininity and selfless mothering. Instead, members of the 1968 generation were often working mothers, sexually

---

1   Petra M. Bagley, *Somebody's Daughter: The Portrayal of Daughter-Parent Relationships by Contemporary Writers from German-Speaking Countries*, Stuttgarter Arbeiten zur Germanistik (Stuttgart: Verlag Hans-Dieter Heinz, Akademischer Verlag Stuttgart, 1996).

2   Adrienne Rich, *Of Woman Born: Motherhood as Experience and Institution* (New York: W. W. Norton, 1976), 236, 35. Original italics.

3   Nancy Friday, *My Mother, My Self* (New York: Delta Publishing, 1977).

active, single parents and/or increasingly independent from the norm of the nuclear family. The legacy they left their daughters is quite different from the legacy of *their* mothers. As a result, many of the characteristics of the mother–daughter relationship that were thought to be universal (at least in the Western world) according to 1970s theory are not relevant to Franck's generation.[4]

Nonetheless, the vast majority of scholarship on the subject continues to assume that all women experience matrophobia and desire to distance themselves from their mothers. Although I would argue that the mother–daughter relationships represented in Franck's works are no less ambivalent than those in, say, Friday's book, Franck's characters are not motivated by a desire to break with their mothers. Common to all of the works by Franck, the mother remains emotionally inaccessible to and distant from her child(ren). Without exception, the protagonists desire greater intimacy with their mothers. Insistence on the continued relevance of matrophobia is likely related to the Freudian model of mother–daughter attachment, in which the daughter must – and desires to – break from the mother to become an independent self. But what happens if this is not the case? What happens if the mother has made minimal effort to connect with her child and the child desires not to detach from the mother but to experience greater intimacy and bonding with her? This is the alternative mother–daughter model that Franck's works contemplate.

4   Other books written by Franck's contemporaries point to the emotional legacy of the 1968 generation. To name just two: *Das Blütenstaubzimmer* [The Pollen Room] by Zoë Jenny tells the story of a nineteen-year-old woman who goes to Italy in search of her mother, who left her to her father's care when she was just a baby. This novel, one of the most popular of the *Fräuleinwunder* texts, has been widely cited as an indictment of the generation of 1968 and the pursuit of personal pleasure over familial responsibility. Tanja Dückers' *Himmelskörper* is narrated by a young, pregnant woman who is investigating her family's Nazi past. Although the narrator's mother is very different from the free-spirited mother in *Das Blütenstaubzimmer*, the daughter's struggle to get to know her mother is a driving force in the book, too. Zoë Jenny, *Das Blütenstaubzimmer* (Frankfurt: BTB Verlag, 1998).

Freud on the Mother–Daughter Relationship

'Der Hausfreund' establishes not only the craving for intimacy but also the fear of loss as connected themes in these texts. Set in East Berlin in the 1970s, the story is told by a nameless narrator, a young girl who is perhaps eight years old. It is the First of May, and, as the narrator waits to attend the day's festivities, her mother is planning their flight, with a younger sister Hanna and the mother's lover, to the West. The children's father – their mother's husband – will be abandoned in the East. The reader learns of this plan obliquely, through details observed by the child narrator, who is neither aware of the flight nor informed of it. Instead, the narrator's primary concern is coming between her mother and the mother's lover, Thorsten, who threatens stability on three levels: first, he repeatedly steals the mother's time and attention, second (although the narrator knows this only subconsciously) his presence threatens to break up the family, and third (an element known only to the reader) he will be the accomplice – and possibly the cause – for their relocation to West Berlin.

The relationship between Thorsten and the narrator is explained by the narrator's commentary, which betrays her young age in its crankiness and naïve honesty: she says that he comes too often, 'und überhaupt kommt er immer dann, wenn wir mit unserer Mutter etwas unternehmen wollen' [and he always comes when we want to do something with our mother].[5] It is clear that the narrator and Thorsten are established as (unequal) rivals for the mother, as both crave her attention, physical contact and an emotional connection. Frustrating attempts to gain closeness to the mother, Thorsten creates mental and at times even physical barriers between her and her daughters. For example, he and she spend the day in his bedroom, with the children on the other side of the locked door. Together, the two adults speak Russian, to keep the girls out of their conversations. They plan the flight to the West without informing either of the children: even after they have arrived in West Berlin, the girls do not know what is happening.

5   Franck, 'Der Hausfreund', 85.

But perhaps worst of all for the narrator is that she is not allowed into the bathroom with her mother at Thorsten's apartment, although it is customary at home (90). This space of physical and emotional intimacy is established at the beginning of the story. The narrator and her mother are in the bathroom together, the narrator watching as her mother brushes her hair, bathes and dresses. This is the only time they are alone without the company of Hanna, their father or Thorsten, and the narrator becomes possessive of this time and, by association, of her mother's body. In fact, she almost takes the tone of a jealous lover when Thorsten is present. Observing her mother flirting with Thorsten, pressing her face against his and leaning over his shoulder, the narrator grudgingly (and precociously) admits: 'Daß Thorsten uns oft besucht, kann ich gut verstehen' [I can well understand why Thorsten visits us a lot] (87).

The story ends ambiguously. The narrator awakens in Thorsten's car. It is 4:30 in the morning, and the reader can identify from the street signs that they have already arrived in West Berlin. The narrator feels nauseated and vomits. Her mother, after trying to catch the vomit in her hands, suggests that the narrator use her scarf to wipe her face. She responds: '"Spinnst du" sage ich zu meiner Mutter, das ist doch mein Pioniertuch, aber meiner Mutter sind Pioniertücher offenbar egal, so egal wie der Erste Mai und die Tatsache, daß mein Vater sich schon Sorgen machen wird, wo wir bleiben' ['Are you crazy?' I say to my mother. That is my Pioneer scarf, but the Pioneer scarf apparently doesn't mean anything to her, like May First and the fact that my father will be worried about where we are] (94).[6] The narrator, of course, has many reasons to be unhappy: she is tired and sick to her stomach, she has missed the May First parade and she has been forced to spend the entire day competing for her mother's attention. Furthermore, it seems that her mother suddenly does not understand her. She speaks out of frustration and a sense of alienation. The narrator's desire for her

6   The Pioneer scarf is a reference to the *Jungpioniere* [Young Pioneers], otherwise known as the *Pionierorganisation Ernst Thälmann* [Pioneer Organization Ernst Thälmann], which was the junior group affiliated with the *Freie Deutsche Jugend* [Free German Youth], a socialist youth organization in East Germany.

mother is heightened nearly to the point of hysteria by the sense that the mother's attention is always just beyond her grasp. As the mother retreats, the narrator pursues her. The story begins with the daughter searching for her mother: "'Wo ist Mama?'" ['Where is Mama?'] are the first words she speaks (83). Franck thus establishes in the narrator a sense of nervousness that she might lose her mother, a sense that she must always be aware of the mother's whereabouts. Although the narrator's mother has taken her daughters with her to the West, Thorsten is along for the ride, suggesting that the competition for closeness will continue.

It is immediately noticeable that the narrator sees Thorsten as a threat. She resents him not just because his presence denies her some of the intimacy to which she is accustomed (such as going to the bathroom with her mother), but also because he reminds her of an intimacy that she cannot have with her. Just as Biendarra noted with respect to the narrator in 'Bäuchlings', here, too, the narrator's gaze is one 'of longing'.[7] She compares her mother to Morgan in the mists of Avalon, while her mother is bathing. She admires her mother's hair, her appearance and her body. Particularly striking is the way in which the narrator aligns herself with her father as her mother's suitor: 'Sie hat einen dunkelroten Lippenstift, den mein Vater sehr gerne hat, und ich auch. Meine Mutter ist die Schönste' [She has a dark red lipstick that my father likes very much, and I do, too. My mother is the prettiest] (87). The daughter's desire for the mother and also her struggle to keep the mother for herself seem to lend themselves to a Freudian analysis, namely that of the mother–daughter attachment in the pre-Oedipal phase.

In his essay 'Female Sexuality' (1931), Freud analyses the 'phase of exclusive attachment to [the] mother' which precedes the Oedipal phase of development and which both male and female children experience.[8] Freud contends that the pre-Oedipal phase, which can last until the child

---

7   Biendarra, 'Gen(d)eration Next', 215.
8   Sigmund Freud, 'Female Sexuality', *The Standard Edition of the Complete Psychological Works of Sigmund Freud*, ed. James Strachey, xxi (London: The Hogarth Press, 1961), 225–43; here, 225.

is five years old, is much more important for the psychosexual development of females than of males, and one of his primary concerns in this essay is to make clear that attachment to the mother serves a very different function for girls than for boys. In the pre-Oedipal phase, both the male and female children take their mother as their primary love-object. The boy comes to see his father as a rival for his mother and develops a desire to kill him. But when the boy witnesses that his sister (or another woman) does not have a penis, he assumes that she has been castrated by the father, and thus he learns to fear that the father will castrate him as well. The boy sublimates his love for his mother, in order that he no longer be his father's rival.[9] As an adult, the boy will eventually replace the mother with a woman who reminds him of his mother, although this does little to change the status of the mother as love-object.[10]

After developing his theory of the Oedipal complex for the sexual development of boys, Freud initially posited a parallel version for the female child, commonly referred to as the 'Electra complex'.[11] In this phase of a girl's development, she desires her father because he possesses the phallus. Her feelings towards her mother are unequivocally negative, because she faults the mother for not providing her with a phallus, and also because she sees the mother as a rival for the father's affection. Eventually, under the pressure of the incest taboo, she turns her desire for her father into desire for other men. This desire for men is motivated by her desire for the phallus (i.e. penis envy), and her wish for a baby is a really a wish for a phallus-substitute. (The male baby is the best phallus-substitute, because she can

9   Freud refers to the Oedipus complex in many of his works. For the purpose of this brief summary, I used: Sigmund Freud, 'The Dissolution of the Oedipus Complex', *The Standard Edition of the Complete Psychological Works of Sigmund Freud*, ed. James Strachey, xix (London: The Hogarth Press, 1961), 173–9.

10   Freud, 'Female Sexuality', 225.

11   For more information on the Electra complex, although Freud does not refer to it in these terms in this essay, see Sigmund Freud, 'Some Psychical Consequences of the Anatomical Distinction between the Sexes', *The Standard Edition of the Complete Psychological Works of Sigmund Freud*, ed. James Strachey, xix (London: The Hogarth Press, 1961), 248–58.

live vicariously through him.) Freud was forced to revise this interpretation when the psychoanalyst Jeanne Lampl-de Groot found evidence of what she called a 'negative Oedipus complex' in female children.[12] Chodorow explains that, in this 'negative' version, the girls competed with their fathers for the mother.[13] As a result of Lampl-de Groot's findings and the discoveries of other psychoanalysts around the same time, Freud was forced to reconsider the mother–daughter bond.

In his revised theorization of this 'pre-Oedipal phase', Freud makes clear that, contrary to his previous understanding, the paths that male and female children take to establishing heterosexual desire are in fact very different. In other words, there is no corresponding female equivalent of the Oedipal complex. Freud maintains in 'Female Sexuality' that the mother is the first love-object for both boys and girls. For male children, this means that the constellation of relationships is already set up for easy progression to the Oedipus complex, as outlined above. Assuming that heterosexuality is the end goal of normal sexual development – an assumption Freud makes – the female child, however, has an additional task: she must somehow replace her mother with a male love-object. In other words, 'a girl's major task is to become oriented to men. In the traditional paradigm, a girl must change her love object from mother to father, her libidinal mode from active to passive, and finally her libidinal organ and eroticism from clitoris to vagina. A boy has to make no such parallel changes.'[14] While the first change (of her love-object) may be more obvious, the other two changes need some explanation, which follows.

Freud posits two characteristics of female sexuality during the pre-Oedipal phase: it is active and focused on the clitoris. Both active sexuality and clitoral fixation are deemed to be masculine, and, in order to make the transition to femininity, girls must adopt passive sexuality and shift their

---

12   Jeanne Lampl-de-Groot, 'The Evolution of the Oedipus Complex in Women' in Robert Fliess, ed., *The Psychoanalytic Reader: An Anthology of Essential Papers with Critical Introductions* (New York: International Universities Press, 1948), 180–94.

13   Nancy Chodorow, *The Reproduction of Mothering: Psychoanalysis and the Sociology of Gender* (2nd edn, Berkeley: University of California Press, 1978), 95.

14   Chodorow, *The Reproduction of Mothering*, 111.

focus to the vagina.[15] Freud suspects the transition from mother to father as love-object and the transition from clitoris to vagina as primary genital area are related, but, by his own admission, he is not sure how.[16] He knows that the female child is initially interested in the physical sensations that she can experience with her clitoris, and he doubts whether the child is able to experience any vaginal sensation until puberty.[17] Furthermore, the daughter experiences many of these sensations for the first time in connection with the mother, because the mother comes into contact with the clitoris while cleaning and caring for the body of the child. If the mother thus triggers the clitoral (or phallic) phase of sexuality in her daughter, Freud argues, it follows that breaking with the mother would be somehow connected to breaking with the phallic phase.[18] According to Freud's theory, when the little girl has moved on to the vaginal phase, in which the vagina is her primary genital area, she is well on the path to establishing her femininity.

Passivity is an equally important aspect of Freud's theorization of femininity. At first, the mother–child relationship – regardless of the child's gender – is necessarily characterized by the baby's passivity. The mother feeds, cleans, and dresses the child, who eventually assumes greater activity, for example by repeating or mimicking the mother's actions. Again, this is a natural progression, and it can often be observed in child's play: when little girls play with dolls, for example, they act out similar patterns of behaviour that they experienced with their mothers, yet with the roles reversed. In other words, the child assumes the active role of the mother and cares for her baby (doll). Yet Freud concentrates on the fact that the female child directs her active sexuality towards her mother. This active sexuality, when repressed, can find expression in a fear of being killed or devoured by her.[19] Regardless, to attain femininity, these active sexual impulses must somehow be turned into passive experiences of sexuality.

15   Freud, 'Female Sexuality', 228.
16   Freud, 'Female Sexuality', 225.
17   Freud, 'Female Sexuality', 228.
18   Freud, 'Female Sexuality', 238.
19   Freud, 'Female Sexuality', 237.

Again, although Freud is not clear on the way in which this is so, the transition is connected to the break from the mother.

Now, how is this break achieved? Freud suggests a number of reasons why the female child turns from her mother. One possible reason is that, when the girl is forced to acknowledge her 'castration' and thereby her inferiority – as well as her mother's inferiority – she blames her mother for this lack and turns to a man (the father) who has a penis. Another is the resentment experienced when the mother prevents her female daughter from masturbating. A third is the general feeling that the mother has not suckled the child long enough (see below). Finally, Freud concludes, somewhat at a loss: 'Perhaps the real fact is that the attachment to the mother is bound to perish, precisely because it was the first and was so intense.'[20] Regardless, this break can have one of three results: the female child rejects sexuality completely, unsatisfied with her clitoris when compared to the penis; the child hopes to eventually gain or develop a penis of her own and clings therefore to her masculinity (which can result in becoming a lesbian); or the child eventually takes the father as object and develops 'normally'. This last path, which Freud calls 'circuitous', involves the rejection of the mother and eventual turning to the father, as the possessor of the phallus.[21]

The reader may already see the relevance of pre-Oedipal bonding to the intense attachment that the narrator of 'Der Hausfreund' feels for her mother. As discussed, the narrator's primary love-object is her mother. She certainly demonstrates no antipathy towards her father, but her mother is the focus of her desire. It seems that the narrator's sister, Hanna, has successfully broken with her mother, as she is somewhat indifferent to her and seeks instead the attention of her father and Thorsten. For example, while their father tickles the narrator, Hanna tries to put herself between them. Decidedly warmer towards Thorsten than the narrator is, Hanna lets him feed her like a baby and lets him bring her things to drink and to

20   Freud, 'Female Sexuality', 234. This logic seems faulty, as Freud does not posit a similar break between a mother and her male child, although he, too, takes the mother as his primary love-object.
21   Freud, 'Female Sexuality', 230.

play with. She attempts to preserve her alliance with her sister by feigning frustration with Thorsten, but the narrator sees through this (91). Within the framework of Freudian psychoanalysis, Hanna has successfully made the adjustment to the Oedipal phase, which suggests that she will continue to be drawn to men in the future and that she is firmly on the path of developing supposedly normal femininity. The narrator, on the other hand, is still in the pre-Oedipal phase of strong attachment to her mother.

Yet what seemed to be a clear connection between Freud's theory and this story soon proves untenable. Take, for example, the motif of jealousy, which runs throughout the novel as a source of tension and an emotional constant for the narrator. Freud cites jealousy as another reason for the child to break with the mother, calling the child's love 'boundless' and saying 'it is not content with less than all.' According to Freud, this desire for love is impossible to satisfy and therefore must be disappointed.[22] He also believes this unsatisfied love, which gives rise to a constant state of jealousy, to be a motivating factor for breaking with the mother. For the majority of the story, however, jealousy serves the opposite function: it drives the narrator to pursue her mother relentlessly, never satisfied with the limited attention and intimacy that she receives from her. By the story's end, there is some suggestion that the mother–daughter relationship may be approaching a turning point, which would mean that the narrator seems to be following the shift from the pre-Oedipal to the Oedipal phase. By this point, the narrator's frustration is palpable, and her tone is changing from annoyance and irritation to resentment and hostility. This is, after all, the first time that the narrator has voiced her anger towards her mother directly ("'Spinnst du?'" ['Are you crazy?']) instead of indirect whining and complaints ("'O nee, ich dachte, wir gehen zum Ersten Mai'" ['Oh no, I thought we were going to May First'] (91). Earlier in the story, the narrator had been possessive of her mother, hesitant to criticize her, and had directed her hostility towards Thorsten instead. It seems that the narrator is shifting her anger from Thorsten to her mother (i.e. breaking with her as a love-object), but, as opposed to Freud's timeline, she does *not* move on

22   Freud, 'Female Sexuality', 231.

to form another connection with a male love-object in her mother's place (i.e. moving successfully into the Oedipal phase). This raises the questions of whether the narrator *is* breaking with her mother, and whether Freud's attachment model is relevant after all.

Central to Freud's theory of the pre-Oedipal phase is that it is a *phase through which children must pass* on their paths to positive psychosexual development. In other words, if daughters do not break with their mothers, they are considered developmentally regressive. There are several ways in which daughters can fail to move on to the positive Oedipal phase: they can remain entrenched in the pre-Oedipal phase, never breaking with the mother; they can reject their sexuality completely; or they can refuse to accept their lack of phallus, clinging to their 'masculinity complex', and, often, choose to take a homosexual love-object. In other words, there are many pitfalls along this 'circuitous' path that the daughter must take away from her mother. To repeat, if the daughter does not break with her mother – and, by association, if she does not make the transition (back) to passivity and to vaginal fixation – she will face psychosexual consequences throughout her adult life. In sum, both the attachment to the mother and the break from her will influence a woman's emotional development as an adult (often negatively). We have already seen one instance of a character who does not make this transition successfully: the young narrator of 'Der Hausfreund'. Freud would read this as evidence of failure in her development. The fault lies not with the protagonist, I argue, but with the theory.

Feminist Revisions of Psychoanalytic Theory

Many other psychoanalysts contributed to a first wave of revising Freud's work on pre-Oedipal attachment, including Anna Freud, Alice and Michael Balint, John Bowlby, Helene Deutsch, Karen Horney, Melanie Klein and

D. W. Winnicott, to name a few.[23] Yet it was during the women's movement of the 1970s that Freud's findings were rigorously questioned, particularly because they are so male-dominant and heteronormative. Feminist scholars refuted Freud's claims that being a woman is always to assume a position of inferiority, and that the end goal of 'normal' psychosexual development is heterosexuality. Chodorow sums up the flaws of Freud's research as follows: '[Freud's claims] grow from unexamined patriarchal cultural assumptions, from Freud's own blindnesses, contempt of women, and misogyny, from claims about biology which Freud was in no position to demonstrate from his own research, from a patriarchal value system and an evolutionary theory to rationalize these values.'[24] Thus began a second round of attempts to revise Freud's paradigms in order to include the development of female subjectivity.

In 1978 Nancy Chodorow published her groundbreaking work of feminist psychoanalysis, *The Reproduction of Mothering*, which uses object-relations theory to expand upon Freud's theories of mother–daughter attachment. According to Chodorow's interpretation of the female Oedipal phase, it is not characterized by a *break* from the mother, but rather an *adding* of the father.[25] As de Marneffe explains, 'human psychological experience does not follow a linear progression from fusion to autonomy; rather, feelings of oneness and separateness oscillate throughout life.'[26] Furthermore, although Chodorow acknowledges and accepts the pre-Oedipal and Oedipal phases, she does not grant them the full significance that Freud does. She argues instead that the Oedipus complex creates models for interpersonal relationships that will be important in later stages of life: 'Post-oedipal (and, in the girl, postpubertal) personality is the relatively stable foundation upon which other forms of relational development will

---

23 For the major feminist developments in psychoanalysis between Freud and the 1970s, see Chodorow, *The Reproduction of Mothering*.
24 Chodorow, *The Reproduction of Mothering*, 142.
25 Chodorow, *The Reproduction of Mothering*, 93.
26 Daphne de Marneffe, *Maternal Desire: On Children, Love, and the Inner Life* (New York: Little, Brown and Company, 2004), 67.

build.'[27] The significance of the mother–daughter relationship, in other words, does not cease once the daughter enters the Oedipal phase. Instead, it remains a complex and shifting relationship throughout a girl's life and is of particular importance when the daughter becomes a mother herself. The significance of *The Reproduction of Mothering* for feminist psychoanalytic scholarship cannot be underestimated, as it created a framework within which the mother–daughter relationship was accorded much greater importance as the model of intimacy and mothering in adulthood. In effect, Chodorow reads the mother–daughter relationship as both a product of the patriarchal society in which it was created and an attachment pattern that reifies this social structure: patriarchy manipulates the concept of motherhood to suit its needs. Women internalize this concept as they become mothers, and then they pass it on to their daughters. The daughters learn how to mother both from their mothers and from patriarchal society, perpetuating the cycle. Contradicting her own belief in the inevitability of the Oedipal complex, Chodorow asks whether the Oedipus complex could in fact be broken or changed if *fathers* were the primary caretakers. This argument provided a path to equal parenting, which was an important step for the women's movement.

Today many scholars point to the fact that the particular political climate in which Chodorow wrote her book likely motivated her to prove that motherhood is a social construct and not a natural state.[28] Appreciative of the significance of the deconstruction of motherhood, I nonetheless find Chodorow's conclusion to be an unstable one. She critically investigates

27 Chodorow, *The Reproduction of Mothering*, 166.
28 Marneffe, for example, points out that the political necessity of proving the social constructedness of motherhood overshadowed considerations of, for example, women who choose and desire to mother. Marneffe, *Maternal Desire*, 63. Chodorow herself, in the 'Preface to the Second Edition', points out her tendency to generalize beyond white, Western culture 'in a period when many feminists wanted to document the universality of gender and male dominance as important objects of study (and politics)'. She also points out that the book does not account for more recent concerns in feminist scholarship, specifically the deconstruction of sexuality, gender and bodies. Chodorow, *The Reproduction of Mothering*, xi and xv.

the social construction of the role of 'mother', insisting that, while women can give birth, there is no reason to assume that women can or should – for any biological or 'natural' reason – adopt this role. Chodorow's insight, however, is strangely limited. She does not extend her investigation into the social construction of the family, of gender roles and sexual identities. Chodorow is willing to destabilize the supposedly natural connection between a woman's biology and her destiny. Yet she paradoxically insists on applying a – granted, feminist – version of Freud's psychoanalytic theories to her examination of the mother–daughter relationship, without treating Freud's theories as social constructs and culturally specific as well. Feminist scholars have since expanded upon Chodorow's work on the mother–daughter relationship, yet they, too, use Freud's patterns of attachments as the basic framework for their own investigations.

Jessica Benjamin is one such scholar, whose book *The Bonds of Love* is among the foremost works of psychoanalysis to investigate 'the problem of domination', particularly its construction as 'a drama of female vulnerability victimized by male aggression'.[29] Tracing domination back to the child's earliest experiences, Benjamin reconceptualizes the mother–daughter relationship according to her theory of 'mutual recognition', which is relevant to the discussion of motherhood in Chapter 4. Yet she continues in the vein of other Freudian psychoanalysts (like Chodorow) to uphold the need for a break with the mother and, although she questions it, even the need for the mother to be primary caregiver. At the end of her book, Benjamin also advocates shared parenting. Here, in her own words: '[T]he issue is not *switching*, it is *adding* partners (a limited number of course).'[30] In effect, Benjamin upholds the basic tenets of Freudian theory and only undermines his assumption that mothers must be the *exclusive* caretakers.

29 Jessica Benjamin, *The Bonds of Love: Psychoanalysis, Feminism, and the Problem of Domination* (New York: Pantheon Books, 1988), 9.
30 Benjamin, *The Bonds of Love*, 209. One cannot help but notice the striking similarity to Chodorow's thesis, which is that the child does not break from the mother but instead becomes attached to the father as well.

Although this text illuminates the psychoanalytic roots of dominance, it, like Chodorow's, remains confined by the discourse of psychoanalysis.[31]

Thus, feminist contributions to psychoanalysis, although they have shaped and honed Freud's theorizations of the human psyche, although they have increased the importance and influence of the mother in the psychoanalytic paradigm, have not fundamentally questioned some of its basic principles. The basic tenets of psychoanalytic theorization of the mother–daughter relationship are as follows: by the time she has given birth to her daughter, the mother has become an embodiment of femininity, in that she has successfully made the adjustment to passive, vaginal sexuality and has taken a heterosexual love-object. Note that, with heterosexuality as the goal of 'normal' development, one can only interpret lesbian relationships, such as those between the sisters in 'Bäuchlings', as regressive. This premise is also based on a clearly defined division between masculine and feminine. As discussed in Chapter 1, Judith Butler has argued gender to be socially constructed, or performative. Taking Butler as a starting point for our investigations, both gender roles and the traditional (i.e. Freudian) psychoanalytic framework for understanding the mother–daughter relationship are undermined.

Feminist reinterpretations of psychoanalysis still seem to work, even taking the destabilization of gender roles as a starting point. One can assume, perhaps, that the mother need not adhere to traditional femininity in order for her daughter to desire her during the pre-Oedipal phase. According to Freud, a break is then necessary for the daughter to turn from her mother and take a male love-object, most likely her father. She will then naturally replicate her mother's own identity and behaviour and eventually make the transition to passive, vaginal sexuality, a claim not sufficiently resolved even by feminist psychoanalysis. The key point in Chodorow's text is that the

---

31   Other works that attempt to open up the feminist possibilities of psychoanalysis include: Juliet Mitchell, *Psychoanalysis and Feminism* (New York: Vintage Books, 1975); Nancy J. Chodorow, *Feminism and Psychoanalytic Theory* (New Haven: Yale University Press, 1989); and Marianne Hirsch, *The Mother-Daughter Plot: Narrative, Psychoanalysis, Feminism* (Bloomington: Indiana University Press, 1989).

daughter will repeat her mother's behaviour by modelling herself on her mother. Thus, the 'reproduction of motherhood', as Chodorow termed it, is a self-perpetuating cycle. Some crucial steps of this cycle are missing in the mother–daughter relationships in Franck's works.

Loving and Loathing the Mother

As Ella, one of the sibling protagonists in *Rücken an Rücken*, grows from a child to an adult, she does try to break with her mother. The novel opens with Ella and her brother Thomas cleaning the house for their mother's return from a work-related trip. Bursting with excitement as she enters the house, they are soon disappointed by her gruff manner and lack of interest in them and their activities. Eschewing any physical affection, Käthe often remonstrates with her children 'Klammert nicht so' [Don't hang on me like that], and the children have learned not to touch her. In rare moments when Thomas does insist on hugging her, she remains 'ein Kanten Holz' [a chunk of wood].[32] So they are pleasantly surprised when she holds her hand out from the table where she is sitting and says, 'komm her' [come here] (18). It turns out that she is calling for her dog. Her shocking coldness causes the reader to wonder whether Käthe is even a relation of Ella and Thomas; it is only later in the book that one can confirm that she is their mother. Hurt and disappointed, the children plan to run away, and they spend the night paddling a rowboat on the nearby lake, in the hopes that Käthe might miss them or at least notice that they are gone (26).

Both children feel a recurring desire for love and affection from their mother, and they are consoled in childhood only by each other and stories they tell of their father, whom they never knew.[33] As they grow up, Käthe begins to favour Thomas with more attention and encouragement, although

32 Franck, *Rücken an Rücken*, 108.
33 See Chapter 5 for more on their father.

she fails completely to understand his wishes and desires. For example, rather than support his interests in journalism or botany, she secures a position for him to study medicine at the university. Starved as they are for her love, both children recognize that that even this self-absorbed gesture is more like love than anything Käthe does for Ella. Towards Ella, her behaviour becomes cruel and aggressive, rather than simply neglectful. She mocks her appearance and calls her a thief in front of house guests (236, 318). For her sixteenth birthday, she gives her daughter ten pounds of sugar and says she must eat it all before she can eat anything else, an attempt to break her of her habit of 'stealing' food and stamps from her (64). Käthe ignores it when her second husband sexually molests Ella and, later, when her tenant rapes her. Only as Ella retreats into insanity does Käthe show some affection, stroking her hair and holding her hand. But when Ella tries to return it, calling her 'Mami' [mommy], Käthe's coldness returns, and she says sharply, 'Hör auf, mich Mami zu nennen. Ich bin Käthe. Und du bist kein Baby. Reiß dich zusammen' [Stop calling me mommy. I am Käthe. And you are no baby. Pull yourself together] (135). The children's desire for their mother does not abate, although they learn to live with her behaviour. Thomas drinks up the affection of his friend's mother, affection expressed through food (192). Ella swims in the lake, where she feels like she is an embryo in the body of a mother (215). As the years pass, Thomas continues to love his mother, despite everything, and Ella feels hate, if she allows herself to feel at all.

Because the entire novel is narrated by Ella and Thomas, it is difficult to ascertain their mother's motivations. From the perspective of her children, however, Käthe seems to be interested only in two inseparable things: her art and socialism. She raises her children as independent people and asks rhetorically 'Bin ich Mutter von Beruf?' [Is being a mother my job?] when she feels that they demand too much of her (230). She expects them to work around the house while she works on her art, and, as she explains to her colleagues, 'Wer die Gesellschaft ändern will, der fange bei seinen eigenen Kindern an' [He who wants to change society starts with his own children] (120). Consequently, she looks to Thomas to pursue studies and a job that that is helpful to socialist society. Although he avoids joining the *Freie deutsche Jugend*, she insists that he complete a year of manual labour before beginning his studies. That the relationship that Käthe has with Thomas is markedly different from her relationship with her daughter is possibly because she does not see any willingness in Ella to assist in the building of a socialist state.

Ella consciously turns her back on politics and is interested primarily in securing her own apartment and livelihood. Her free time is filled with drinking, dancing and sexual encounters with any of the young men that pursue her. Yet her youth, which was influenced most strongly by her mother's cruelty and her experiences of sexual abuse, leave her numb to physical or emotional encounters of any other kind. By the end of the novel, her emotional distance and unpredictable behaviour, which strongly mirror Käthe's, has resulted in the alienation of Ella from all her former acquaintances. In an early chapter, Ella tells her brother, 'Es gibt nur einen Mann, mit dem ich glücklich sein kann' [There is only one man with whom I can be happy] – Thomas – and when he dies, it seems that Ella will never experience an emotional connection with another person again (76).

This mother–daughter relationship, which is the most openly hostile of those discussed in this book, shares commonalities with many of the others: the daughter desires more attention from the mother than she receives, the mother is perceived as cold and self-involved and the daughter to some extent imitates her mother's behaviour. The analysis of 'Der Hausfreund' questioned whether a break from the mother takes place. While there is evidence of Ella's break from her mother in *Rücken an Rücken* – she certainly rejects her mother and seeks male sexual partners – the mother–daughter relationship in this novel still does not fall into line with Freud's model for two reasons: first, breaking with the mother does not result in 'normal' psycho-sexual development in Ella's case and, second, neither Käthe nor Ella exhibits passive, feminine sexuality. In *Der neue Koch*, the concept of prostitution directly conflicts with this second topic. This is a key way in which Franck's characters destabilize the psychoanalytic paradigm.

The Desire for Maternal Intimacy

Der neue Koch was both Franck's first major publication and the first of her texts that focused on the mother–daughter relationship. In this text the reader meets the protagonist when she is already an adult. That is, the reader has no chance to observe the pre-Oedipal mother–daughter relationship and can only extrapolate this from the adult protagonist's account of her relationship with her mother. *Der neue Koch* is typical in its use of the first-person narration.[34] Yet it is significant in this text (as in others by Franck) in that it obscures the 'truth' of the mother–daughter relationship, if such a thing exists. Just as I discussed with regard to Beyla, the unreliable narrator of *Liebediener*, it is nearly impossible to determine whether – or when – the narrator is lying to the reader, partly because the narrator admits to lying to other people. A lack of factual truth is a recurring theme in Franck's writing. The reader is never able to penetrate each character's perspective to determine what 'actually' happened, just as it is impossible to assemble factual information from the conflicting versions of the stories. This is certainly true of the mother–daughter relationships: as will become clear by the conclusion of Chapter 4, the daughters have a very different impression of the mother–daughter bond than their mothers do. In short, the works narrated by the daughters are strongly critical of their mothers. The daughters cannot conceive of their mothers as having an identity beyond motherhood, and they regard any evidence of such an identity with jealousy and resentment.

Psychoanalysis offers several explanations for this resentment, which may inspire the break with the mother. Common to many of these points is denial: denial of a penis, denial of sexual satisfaction and, significantly,

---

34   *Die Mittagsfrau* was the first of Franck's major publications *not* to use a first-person narration. This was a conscious decision that Franck reached as she began work on the novel and a step she considered necessary in representing and exploring such a controversial story. She used the third-person perspective in *Rücken an Rücken* as well.

denial of continued intimacy with the mother, often represented by insufficient time spent nursing.[35] Freud elaborates on the infant's greed for the mother's milk, citing it as one of the primary accusations voiced by the young women under his care. Freud interprets this desire as a sexual one, commenting, 'Such is the greed of a child's libido!'[36] This desire is not necessarily sexual in nature but indicative of the longing for more intimacy with the mother. Nursing is widely recognized as the most important bonding time between mothers and their infants in the first months of the child's life. As the child develops a sense of separateness from its mother, it also experiences both increased desire for her and anxiety about her departure.

In Franck's texts, this forced break with the mother, supposedly normal in childhood, remains a concern well into adulthood. Chodorow explains this separation anxiety in children: 'This disturbance requires [the child] to face the essential difference between love for the mother and mother-love: Its mother is unique and irreplaceable, whereas it is replaceable – by another infant, by other people, and by other activities.'[37] At the same time, it is this very sense of separation that enables the infant to develop a sense of self. Thus the pre-Oedipal period of intense bonding with the mother is inherently characterized by ambivalence: 'Children wish to remain one with their mother, and expect that she will never have different interests from them; yet they define development in terms of growing away from her.'[38] According to psychoanalysis, this separation, though initially undesirable for the child, is in fact a healthy development. But what happens to the adult daughter, who has not moved past the anxiety of separation or whose anxiety has turned to a sense of abandonment? In psychoanalytic terms, this woman would be considered regressive. Without this break, the daughter would theoretically be unable to develop a sense of self. (Conversely, if the daughter did develop a sense of self, she would break with her mother.) The thirty-year-old narrator of *Der neue Koch* regularly

35   In other words, the feminine is equal to lack. See for example Chodorow, *The Reproduction of Mothering*, 157.
36   Freud, 'Female Sexuality', 234.
37   Chodorow, *The Reproduction of Mothering*, 69.
38   Chodorow, *The Reproduction of Mothering*, 82.

voices her frustration towards her now-deceased mother but seems unable to break with her even as an adult.

Already at the novel's beginning, the narrator recalls feeling betrayed by her mother as a child, a memory that makes plain the degree to which the narrator continues to experience intense filial emotions. This scene, an intensely humiliating memory for the narrator, centres on the first visit of the poet Anton Jonas, who became a regular at the hotel. In awe of the fact that he is a poet, the narrator's mother engages him in conversation about his poetry, over dinner with the other guests. Told from the daughter's point of view, the mother is represented as laughable, even more so than the pretentious and pompous Anton Jonas. She criticizes her mother's interest in poetry, belittling it as the kind of verse printed on decorative calendars.[39] Trying to understand Jonas's cryptic responses to her questions, the narrator's mother gawks with her mouth open, and she seems to be counting on her fingers as she thinks (14). The bitterness of this mean-spirited characterization can be explained by what happens to the narrator next: in an attempt to avoid the mother's persistent questions, Anton Jonas asks the narrator whether she has written a poem she could share with the guests. The narrator, shortly before puberty, is gratified by this attention and also grateful that Anton Jonas correctly guessed that she wrote poetry; her mother claims not to have known anything about it. Yet, when the narrator shares her poem, the poet uses it to turn attention back to himself: he harshly critiques the poem, a cheap attack on a young girl, in order to awe the guests with the authority of his knowledge. As one would expect, the narrator directs a great deal of her resentment towards Anton Jonas, continuing to feel spite for him even as a grown woman. She is also angry with her mother, and here the reader gains insight into the tension between mother and daughter. Instead of praising her daughter's poem, her mother simply says 'Naja' [Well] when she has finished reading, and then turns to Anton Jonas for his opinion. When she does not defend the poem or her daughter, the narrator flees from the table, afraid of the laughing adults, and says, 'ich fürchtete auch meine Mutter, die mir

---

39   Franck, *Der neue Koch*, 13.

fremd erschien' [I was also afraid of my mother, who seemed foreign to me] (16–17). Here the narrator complains of the lack of encouragement she receives from the mother and of the sense that the mother does not acknowledge the existence of a bond between them.[40]

The narrator also vividly recalls her mother's criticisms. Even as a child, the protagonist was criticized for not doing anything when so much needed to be done in the hotel on a regular basis (124). Consequently, the narrator did often run errands for her mother, for example, grocery shopping. Although it seems that the narrator viewed many of these actions as expressions of love for her mother or as attempts to please her, her mother's criticisms became worse as the narrator grew older. As the story progresses, the narrator more openly expresses jealousy and resentment towards her deceased mother, although it is at times masked as frustration and condescension. Her primary complaint, although unarticulated, seems to be that her mother did not love her enough (or perhaps at all). The reader sees no evidence of intimacy between mother and daughter in the protagonist's memories. Instead, the mother functions as an internalized source of censure for the narrator.

Maternal Spaces

For many of Franck's protagonists, identity – including identity as a daughter – is intimately connected to space. Place also affects the mother–daughter relationship, as should be clear in both 'Der Hausfreund' and *Der neue Koch*. In 'Der Hausfreund', the narrator experiences the home as a place of intimacy. There her parents are more likely to pay her attention, and at home the narrator is allowed to be in the bathroom with her mother. In

40 This scene recalls the analyses of Chodorow and Benjamin, who point out that the child is alarmed by any indication that the mother does not exist solely for her daughter.

both a symbolic and a very real way, closed doors in Thorsten's apartment separate the narrator from her mother. In this short story, the narrator experiences the greatest intimacy and bonding with her mother while they are in their apartment or home.

The dilapidated hotel in *Der neue Koch* is a confusing mix of public and private spaces. For example, when the narrator tells the young daughter of a guest that she lives in the hotel, 'Das will sie nicht glauben, das sei hier doch ein Hotel und kein Zuhause' [She doesn't want to believe it. This here is a hotel and not a home] (45). Each guest has a private room, the only space that 'belongs' exclusively to its inhabitant. Madame puts a towel on her bed when she arrives at the hotel, as a way of claiming the space as her own, and she insists on having the same room for each visit. At the same time, this sense of ownership exists only as long as the guest remains in the room. Of course Madame's room and Anton Jonas's room 'belong' to other guests during the periods between their visits. And even while the guests are visiting and paying for the temporary ownership of the room, that sense of ownership and privacy is often undermined. Hotel staff regularly enter the rooms to clean them. In a more extreme example, the narrator moves all of Madame's belongings – including the towel – to another room on the ground floor when she is tired of helping Madame up and down the stairs.

Private and public are categories that do not correlate to places and non-places. For example, the narrator's own room is not a site at which connections are formed, although it could be. She is often there alone and, even when others enter her space (such as Niclas or the cook), the characters talk past each other or leave feeling alienated from one another. The space of the hotel is equally ambiguous, and here it becomes clear that the idea of home is also not synonymous with place (although in fantasy or an ideal form it is). For example, although the property does legally belong to her, the narrator often has a sense that she does not possess or belong in the space. She is constantly forced to welcome strangers and acquaintances into her 'home' as paying guests, as the hotel is her only source of income. At times, the narrator can sequester herself in her bedroom, which is tucked among the other guest rooms, but she is forced to leave her room at mealtimes and to work, if nothing else.[41] Thus, the sense of the hotel as a home is severely undermined, although the narrator may wish for it.

Despite her complaints about the hotel, the narrator is quite possessive of it and is determined to defend her claim to it. She speaks, for example, of another guest being in 'her' chair or at 'her' place at the table, but the others have no awareness of this proprietary attitude. It is, in part, the uncertainty of whether the hotel 'belongs' to her that drives the narrator to become increasingly territorial and escalates her conflict with the cook. He (unnamed, referred to only as 'der Koch') claims to have arrived from Puerto Esperanza, Cuba and brings a sense of exoticism and excitement to the hotel not only through his cooking. In the narrator's mind, he threatens to win the loyalty of the guests and take control of the hotel itself, rendering the narrator completely useless and possibly forcing her to leave her home. The narrator tries to manipulate the cook, first through passive-aggressive gestures and later through seduction, but instead the cook wins over the guests, employees and even the locals with his elaborate meals and charming personality. More than anything else, it is the guests' allegiance to the cook that makes the narrator feel like an outsider in her own home.

The conflict comes to a head when the cook offers to buy the hotel from the narrator. By the narrator's own admission, the hotel is not making money, and the cook thinks that he could bring life back to the establishment. He uses the term 'freikaufen' [to buy out; literally, to buy free] when speaking of buying the hotel, suggesting by the positive word 'frei' [free] in the compound verb that the narrator would then be free to move somewhere else and start her life (over). The narrator's response, by contrast, is quite negative: 'Freikaufen? Was er darunter wohl versteht? Mich auszusetzen, aus meinem Hotel hinaus. Wohin? Raus ins Freie, wie schön. Da war ich noch nie, nie weiter als bis vorne zur Bucht, als bis in den Ort zum Einkaufen, nie weiter als bis zur Haushaltsschule, in die ich nie wollte' [Buy out? What does he mean by that? To put me out, out of my hotel.

---

41 It seems that the interactions of greatest intimacy take place in Madame's room, during which the narrator – often unwillingly – forms a kind of bond with Madame. I return to this shortly.

Where to? Out of doors, how nice. I was never there, never farther than up to the bay, than in the town to go shopping, never farther than to the domestic science college that I never wanted to go to] (118). In other words, despite her periodic 'Wunsch, mich endlich allein im Haus zu fühlen' [wish to finally feel alone in the house], the protagonist does not actually desire to leave the hotel (11). The bay on which the hotel is located represents the constant option of escape, of travel to other and new places – an option that holds no allure for the narrator.

At some level, the hotel seems to be a negative space for her. There she is constantly bombarded by reminders of her mother in the stifling, decaying atmosphere of the run-down building. Symbolically, portraits of each of her parents hang over the reception desk, where the narrator sits for most of the day.[42] She also thinks of her mother as she goes about her daily routines, hearing her mother's voice (often criticism) in her mind. Yet at the same time the space serves as a reminder of her family in a positive sense, and the narrator's identity is strongly connected to the place she inhabits.

When she leaves the hotel, even just to shop for groceries, the narrator experiences a shocking degree of alienation. Although she enjoyed leaving the hotel as a child, particularly to run errands for her mother to make herself useful, as an adult she dreads going into the small town: 'Im Supermarkt treffe ich Leute, die ich nicht treffen mag, sie fragen mich, wie es geht, ich will ihnen nicht antworten, ich habe Angst vor ihnen. Ich habe Angst vor den Verkäufern, die andere sind als früher. ... [S]ie ärgern mich, sie ängstigen mich, ich will schnell in mein Hotel zurück' [In the supermarket, I meet people that I don't like to meet. They ask me how it's going. I don't want to answer them. I am afraid of them. I am afraid of the salespeople, who are different ones to before .... They annoy me, they scare me, I want to return to my hotel quickly] (20–1). Clearly, the town is a non-place for the narrator, a space in which no connections are made and no intimacy is experienced (although this is at times by her own choosing). Only by contrast is it clear that the narrator experiences the hotel as

---

42   The narrator's father deserted them shortly after her birth. The motif of the absent father is discussed in the concluding chapter.

a place. Although she at times resents the intrusive familiarity of guests such as Madame Piper, she is still known by the regulars of the hotel and connects with them, albeit infrequently. Now that the narrator has no living biological family, the hotel and its inhabitants provide her with her only opportunities for intimacy and connection. Thus the reader can conclude that, despite her outward complaining and ungracious reception of the regular guests and hotel staff, the narrator is very much connected to them, as she is to the hotel itself.

There are only two times when the narrator attempts to leave the hotel for an extended period of time. The first time was at age sixteen, when the narrator enroled in a domestic science school at her mother's behest. This attempt failed miserably, whether it was because the school was too boring (the narrator's version) or because the narrator was too stupid (the mother's version). The narrator defends herself that she was at least loyal to her mother, returned to the hotel and tried to help by ironing, shopping and doing the taxes. Thus the narrator's return to her mother's hotel was both a sign of failure and a demonstration of love. She was not smart or accomplished enough to aid in the hotel's success or to start her own hotel, yet she was devoted enough to her mother to return and help with menial tasks. The ambivalence inherent in her connection to the hotel – the failure to move on to something better and the simultaneous demonstration of her devotion – mirrors the ambivalence inherent in her relationship with her mother: the narrator has failed to break with her mother and move on with her life, yet she also still desires the intimacy with her mother that she never had during her mother's lifetime.

At the novel's end, the narrator fantasizes about leaving the hotel, and she even buys a plane ticket to Cuba. The night before her planned departure, she feels a sense of rebirth and speaks of 'die Erinnerung an Geburt, den Verlust meiner Fruchthülle' [the memory of birth, the loss of my placenta] (142). This image crystallizes the associations that the narrator has formed between the hotel and her mother. Yet what promised to be a transformative experience for the narrator, a moment of breaking with her mother as symbolized by the hotel, comes to naught. She does not leave for Cuba; even though the cook and Mr Hirschman (significantly, the men) drive her to the airport, the narrator returns hours later after having bought a newspaper and walked home. She, in effect, is unable to break with her mother and the space that symbolizes her.

Furthermore, she is *unwilling* to break with her mother. In a startling confession, the reader learns that the narrator's mother did not in fact leave the hotel to her daughter in her will, as the narrator had claimed and as the reader had assumed. Instead, her mother willed the hotel to Berta, the housemaid. The narrator, after finding the piece of paper on which this was documented, burned it before others could find it. Thus, the narrator's stubborn insistence to remain with the hotel seems based on the desire to cling to the memory of her mother and the suggestion of intimacy that, although sought, was never found. The hotel is one of the last connections that the narrator has to her mother. After the mother's death, the narrator uses the space of the hotel to feel a mother–daughter bond – in effect, turning the hotel into a place. In this place, the narrator can continue to struggle with her feelings for her mother, at times through proxies like the guest she calls the 'Spätmutter' [Late Mother] or Madame. Thus the hotel becomes a highly significant place for the narrator, one that contains the promise of connections that she was not able to form with her parents.[43]

The Abject and the Maternal Body

The strongest reminder of the narrator's mother is the people affiliated with the hotel. Most of them have been connected to the hotel for decades, such as Berta, the maid, whom the narrator 'inherited' with the property. The regular guests, too, are constant reminders, as many of them began

---

43 It is possible to read the strange congress of guests in the hotel as a kind of family, as Macnab points out. Reinforcing this idea is that the regular guests treat the narrator like a child. For example, they seat her at the children's table during the dinner (88) and they call her 'Kleines' [little one], which provokes typically childish behaviour in the narrator, such as crossing her arms and pouting (128).

staying at the hotel while the narrator's gracious and charming mother was still alive. Madame Piper, for example, 'besucht mein Hotel schon länger, als ich lebe, das sagt sie mir häufig' [has been visiting my hotel longer than I have been alive. She tells me that frequently] (7). At dinner Madame retells stories of going dancing with the narrator's mother and of the men who used to follow her admiringly (31). Other guests remember the narrator's mother and, the narrator assumes, think of her mother much more favourably than they do of her. For example, Anton Jonas compliments Berta for keeping the house so welcoming: 'durch sie hätte das Haus nach dem Tod meiner Mutter eine ganz warme Atmosphäre erhalten' [through her the house kept a very warm atmosphere after the death of my mother] (65). The narrator receives no such compliments.

Although it would seem that the narrator is frozen in time, incapable of moving out of her 'regressive' phase of maternal attachment, the psychoanalytic model does not hold here. The narrator is able to process her relationship with her mother indirectly, thanks to the guests of the hotel. When observing one of the first-time hotel guests, a young woman the narrator refers to as the 'Spätmutter', the narrator reveals her own neuroses by projecting her feelings of victimization onto the woman's young daughter, noting 'besonders das Mädchen macht alles falsch' [especially the girl does everything wrong] (17). The narrator's identification with the young girl leads her to believe that the mother is cold and unfeeling towards her daughter, and she observes with interest when the mother withholds affection (e.g. she does not let the girl hold her hand). The narrator assumes that this behaviour was of intentional cruelty directed at the young girl, and she does not think to wonder about other reasons for this action. Madame Piper later reveals that the woman is living in the hotel while her ex-husband moves out of their home, which explains her preoccupied manner. The narrator's myopic attitude in this respect is very similar to that towards her own mother: she perceives all of her mother's actions to be centred on their relationship instead of understanding them as influenced by other concerns.

Of all of the guests, Madame Piper serves the important function of keeping the memory of the narrator's mother alive. It is through her relationship with Madame that the narrator reveals much of the resentment

that she felt – and still feels – towards her mother. She mentions in passing: 'Madame Piper sagt, sie liebt mich wie meine Mutter. Ich weiß nicht,
wie mich meine Mutter geliebt hat' [Madame Piper says, she loves me like
my mother. I don't know how my mother loved me] (7). Gradually she
reveals the extent to which her feelings for the two women are conflated.
Madame and her mother were close friends, and Madame was staying in
the hotel when the narrator's mother died. Because of this, Madame feels
responsible for the narrator, and tries to 'mother' her by making sure she
is running the hotel correctly and making suggestions for improvements,
such as buying freesias, which was her mother's favourite flower. When the
narrator confesses that she buys lilies instead of freesia when Madame is
staying at the hotel, it is not clear whether it is a passive-aggressive retali-
ation against Madame's incessant commentary, whether the narrator is
avoiding reminders of her mother, or whether she is asserting her own
presence in the hotel.[44] The following statement illuminates tension in
the protagonist's relationship with her mother, which comes to light in
the course of the novel: '[Madame Piper] kannte meine Mutter länger als
ich, und ich behaupte, sie meint damit, sie kannte sie besser. Mir ist das
recht, denn ich wollte meine Mutter nie genauer kennen, als ich ohnehin
mußte' [Madame Piper knew my mother longer than I did, and I maintain
she means to say that she knew her better. That is fine with me, because I
didn't want to know my mother more closely than I already had to] (7).
The irritability in this statement and in her confession that she is glad when
Madame leaves betray the intensity of her feelings towards both Madame
and her mother.[45]

   In fact, her relationship with Madame Piper is the second way in which
the narrator can process her relationship with her mother. While it would
seem that the mother's passing only made permanent the impossibility of
closeness that the narrator always felt, she is able to develop an intimate

44   That the narrator would be asserting herself seems unlikely. Although she often
     reflects upon her ownership of the hotel and fantasizes about exerting her power as
     the owner, she never does.
45   This sentiment is echoed by Beyla in *Liebediener*, as discussed in a later section.

relationship – not a romantic one, as the reader might expect (i.e. with the cook of the title) – but with Madame, the substitute mother. Madame allows the narrator to explore the pros and cons of intimacy, its attraction and revulsion. As she adopts a maternal role in the narrator's life, instructing her on how to dress and how to behave, the narrator in turn criticizes Madame and rebels against her. In quiet moments, she begrudgingly admits her genuine affection for Madame: 'Wie Madame mich sieht, sagt sie zu mir: Da ist ja meine Kleine. Ich, die ich sonst nicht ihre Kleine sein mag, freue mich heute morgen ausnahmsweise über die Vertrautheit, die in ihrer Stimme und dem liegt, was sie sagt' [When Madame sees me, she says to me: there is my little one. I, who otherwise do not like to be her little one, am happy today for once about the familiarity that is in her voice and in what she says] (104).

Like her relationship with her mother, the narrator's relationship with Madame is conflicted. They alternate between using the formal and informal terms of address: although Madame exclusively uses 'du' with the narrator, the narrator insists on using the formal 'Sie', which keeps Madame at a distance.[46] On the one hand, Madame is a paying guest of the hotel, and the narrator is the hotel's proprietor. On the other, Madame's friendship with the narrator's mother and her thirty-year history of wintering at the hotel makes her almost a member of the family. On the one hand, the title 'Madame' keeps the narrator at a distance. (The reader never learns Madame's first name.) On the other, the book opens with a scene of great intimacy: the narrator cleaning Madame's obese body.

Madame presents herself as dependent on the narrator's care: she needs help climbing the stairs to her usual room, she requires assistance to clean herself, and she even has the narrator lift her legs into the bed at night. The veracity of this need is unclear; at one point, the narrator realizes that Madame, rushing to investigate a situation on the second floor, has climbed the stairs without assistance (49). At other times, Madame seems so overcome with the exhaustion of supporting her own body that

---

46   This also mimics the interaction between an adult and a child. In other words, these terms of address prevent the narrator from growing up.

she is incapable of moving her limbs. Certainly the sheer size of her body prevents her from bending and reaching with ease. In one scene the narrator confronts her, rejecting Madame's assumption that the narrator is willing and able to care for her. When the narrator suggests that Madame should consider wearing diapers, as she seems unable to get to the toilet in time by herself, Madame protests that diapers are for infants, 'und ich bezahle hier schließlich' [and after all I am paying here]. The narrator responds: 'Ja ... Sie bezahlen ein Hotelzimmer, aber ich gehöre nicht dazu' [Yes ... you are paying for a hotel room, but I don't come with it]. In response, Madame hands her money, which the narrator refuses to accept, in effect admitting that their relationship is not determined solely by business transactions. This decision also enables the narrator to maintain some independence from Madame's demands. Upon the narrator's protests, Madame responds, 'Weißt du was, mein Kind, du forderst mich heraus. Du kennst mich sehr wohl. Und da ich das Pech habe, in deinen Händen älter als deine Mutter zu werden, muß ich wohl dafür bezahlen, daß du mich menschenwürdig behandelst' [You know what, my child, you are provoking me. You know me very well. And as I have the bad luck to grow older than your mother in your hands, I apparently have to pay so that you treat me humanely] (43). Here, even when Madame's pride is wounded, she maintains the illusion that she cannot live without the narrator's help (even though no carer is mentioned for the months that Madame spends at home). It is more likely that Madame wishes to perpetuate their caring relationship, thereby simulating this mother–daughter relationship with the narrator. It is unclear whether Madame does this for the narrator's good or for her own.

Further proof of their intimacy comes, paradoxically, from the disgust that Madame's body inspires. The physical revulsion with which the narrator regards Madame's body is inextricably connected with her intimate knowledge of it. The function of this is highlighted by the novel's opening passage, which describes Madame's obese, sweating flesh in detail, as the narrator, on her hands and knees on the floor, gathers shards of glass from a dropped glass of water. As Macnab points out, this first page makes a parallel between Madame and the narrator's relationship and that of mother and child: the reader is left with the image of the narrator in short pants (suggestive of youth) and crawling on the floor in front of Madame, the source of revulsion and disgust. Later descriptions highlight aspects of Madame's physicality that are first mentioned here: the massive size of the body; the consequent slowness (of movement, of blood circulation and of thought); the porous, almost fluid quality of her body; and the superficial relationship Madame's appearance has with expectations of femininity.

The sheer size of Madame's body inspires a feeling of disgust. The narrator informs us that Madame's hands are so fat that she cannot make a fist, and that her thighs are so large that she can neither cross her legs nor even close her knees. From this enormous body ooze liquids: sweat, urine, tears and faeces. Madame leaves sweaty marks on the wall as she reaches for the switch to turn on the fan. She spills iced tea on herself while she drinks and is unable to locate the liquid on her body and clothing, suggesting that she is desensitized to wetness. The narrator uses a damp cloth to wipe Madame's bosom, but the cloth already smells like mildew, implying that Madame is never dry (5). The repeated references to fluid leaking from Madame's body or spilling over it suggest that: 'Her body is permeable, she is constantly sweating or excreting across the boundaries that separate the inner from the outer, the self from the other'.[47] Madame also prefers her bedroom to be moist, and she uses her humidifier with a few drops of eucalyptus oil in the water (8). And not only liquid drips from her body. At one point, the narrator comments on the stupidity that 'seeps' from Madame's lips (129).[48]

The revulsion and disgust that Madame's body inspires can be read according to Julia Kristeva's theorization of the abject. In her essay 'Powers of Horror', Kristeva theorizes the process by which the child recognizes the distinction between the self and (m)other and begins the process of breaking from her. Before this point, the infant sees no separation between the mother and the self. With the process of abjection, however, this changes. Noëlle McAfee, writing about Kristeva's theory, explains that, until this

47   Macnab, 'Becoming Bodies', 109.
48   Anxiety surrounding fluid female bodies has a link to the German past as well: Klaus Theweleit describes the representation of women as fluid during the National Socialist regime. Klaus Theweleit, *Männerphantasien*, 2 vols (Frankfurt am Main: Verlag Roter Stern, 1977).

point, 'The child is in a double-bind: a longing for narcissistic union with its first love [i.e. the mother] and a need to renounce this union in order to become a subject. It must renounce a part of itself – insofar as it is still one with the mother – in order to become a self.'[49] This is the point at which the infant rejects – or abjects – the mother's body. Kristeva explains the process thus:

> Food loathing is perhaps the most elementary and most archaic form of abjection. When the eyes see or the lips touch that skin on the surface of milk – harmless, thin as a sheet of cigarette paper, pitiful as a nail paring – I experience a gagging sensation and, still farther down, spasms in the stomach, the belly; and all the organs shrivel up the body, provoke tears and bile, increase heartbeat, cause forehead and hands to perspire. Along with sight-clouding dizziness, *nausea* makes me balk at that milk cream, separates me from the mother and father who proffer it. 'I' want none of that element, sign of their desire; 'I' do not want to listen, 'I' do not assimilate it, 'I' expel it. But since the food is not an 'other' for 'me,' who am only in their desire, I expel *myself*, I spit *myself* out, I abject *myself* with the same motion through which 'I' claim to establish *myself*.[50]

In less opaque terms: when the child rejects the mother's body, it finds that there is no clear distinction between itself and its mother (i.e. self and other). Thus the child remains caught in an unresolvable position: it must reject the mother to become a separate self, but the unclear separation between self and other means that it could, at any time, become the mother again.

This is a particularly complicated situation for daughters. Their biological similarity to their mothers makes the distinction between self and other less clear. In fact, if they become mothers, they will attain greater physical and psychological similarities to their mothers than they have simply as daughters. (Hence the significance and prevalence of Sukenick's 'matrophobia'.) Macnab draws on Kristeva's theory in reflecting on the unease that the changeable female body inspires. Especially the mother's

---

49 Noëlle McAfee, *Julia Kristeva*, Routledge Critical Thinkers (New York: Routledge, 2004), 48.

50 Julia Kristeva, *Powers of Horror: An Essay on Abjection*, tr. Leon S. Roudiez (New York: Columbia University Press, 1982, 2–3.

pregnant body blurs the boundary between self and other.[51] Bringing this discussion back to *Der neue Koch*, part of the narrator's disgust that she experiences with regard to Madame's body comes from this recognition of (undesired) similarity. Macnab connects Madame's corpulent body with a fear of 'physical engulfment'.[52] This fear does not refer to the size of Madame's body (although this is certainly applicable) but rather the fact that the narrator came from a maternal body, one that is not clearly separate from her own, and that could thus reincorporate the narrator's body.

After all, what separates the narrator's body from Madame's? Just as Madame's body is forced to move slowly due to her excess weight, the narrator feels that her body is forced to move slowly when she is around Madame (6). The narrator's body is also described with reference to liquid: she wakes up in a sweat one night, she walks in the rain, she lives on the edge of a bay, and, during the scene in which she seduces Niclas, her hair (wet from a shower) drips all over her back and shoulders. The narrator also reveals that she was overweight and slow moving as a young girl (14). Despite her attempts to disregard her sex – she typically wears gender-neutral clothing and has remained a virgin, eschewing all physical contact – she cannot deny the fact that her female body bears some physical resemblance to Madame's.

Nor can she deny the resemblance that Madame bears to her mother. The first pages of the novel reveal that memories of her mother are conflated with her relationship with Madame. Not only does Madame's very presence remind the narrator of her mother, but she sees the two as very intimately connected: 'Ich kenne den Geruch ihres Schweißes wie den meiner Mutter' [I know the smell of her sweat like that of my mother] (8). Perhaps because many characteristics of Madame's body are 'maternal' in nature (e.g. her corpulence, her large breasts, the permeability of her body), the narrator treats Madame almost as an extension of her mother, or at least as a proxy. Thus she is able to continue a mother–daughter relationship, although her biological mother is deceased.

---

51   Macnab, 'Becoming Bodies', 111.
52   Macnab, 'Becoming Bodies', 109.

In time, it is reasonable to expect that the narrator's body could resemble Madame's, as it has in the past (with the narrator's pre-pubescent baby fat). Yet their bodies are currently – and crucially – different: while Madame's body is corpulent, excessive, suggesting overindulgence in a decadent lifestyle, the narrator's remains minimal, chaste, impermeable in body and emotion. The narrator sees herself becoming 'alt und häßlich' [old and ugly], with a heart that is shrivelling up and a body brittle from disuse (67). In the course of the novel, no mention is made of the narrator's own bodily fluids (other than sweat), such as urine, faeces, blood or tears. Indeed, although she twice acknowledges that she is near tears, she does not – or cannot – cry. Towards the end of the novel, the narrator talks about those who are starving, and she refers to herself, in juxtaposition with Madame, for example, who is a glutton for love, contact and human companionship. This implicitly values Madame's maternal body and love of excess over the narrator's chastity and rigidity. Therein lies the tragedy of the novel: the longer the narrator remains shut off from those around her, to those both within and outside of the hotel, the more her identity becomes fixed and rigid.

Motherhood and Prostitution

As Lucy Macnab points out in her article 'Becoming Bodies', the hotel in *Der neue Koch* is 'essentially a parody of the domestic space of home', a space in which the feeling of being at home is bought and sold.[53] In the previous section, I argued that the hotel is indeed a place for the narrator, a space in which she can feel connection with other people. At the same time, one can agree with Macnab that it is not a home in the sense of a private space in which a nuclear – or even single-parent – family resides. This is further complicated by the fact that the narrator's mother supported her business

53   Macnab, 'Becoming Bodies', 109.

by trading sexual favours for help with the hotel. This is a crucial piece of the mother–daughter puzzle in the works by Julia Franck, and this trope of mothers as prostitutes emerges in five texts: *Der neue Koch*, *Liebediener*, 'Der Hausfreund', *Lagerfeuer* and *Rücken an Rücken*.

There are so many feminist interpretations of prostitution that it is not possible to provide an overview here. There are as many attitudes towards prostitution as there are feminisms. Marxist feminism, for example, considers the prostitute as a victim of patriarchal capitalism. So-called postmodern feminism regards 'prostitutes as sexual pioneers and prostitution as a form of political resistance'.[54] A central issue informing all of these various interpretations is that of victimization: is the prostitute a victim (of men, of patriarchy, of capitalism, of violence) or an empowered agent acting of her own accord? The issue is a complex one, and it is difficult to say that the prostitute is one or the other. For example, even if a woman is able to earn a living and support herself and a family through prostitution, a seemingly empowering act, radical feminists would argue that patriarchal society created this situation in which prostitution is this woman's best (perhaps only) means of survival.[55] For the purposes of my investigation, I take a position between these two poles: prostitution is represented in Franck's texts as an economic necessity, often because absent fathers have forced mothers to be sole wage earners. At the same time, Franck represents these women positively, as empowered, taking charge of their financial solvency and providing for their children.

A second point is that prostitution is all but absent from the field of psychoanalysis, feminist or otherwise. In *Reading, Writing, and Rewriting the Prostitute Body*, Shannon Bell discusses the intersection of prostitution and

54 Alison M. Jaggar, 'Contemporary Western Feminist Perspectives on Prostitution', *Asian Journal of Women's Studies* 3/2 (1997), 8. Jaggar's article provides a concise overview of major points to consider.
55 In this discussion, prostitutes who have to answer to pimps, who are beaten or raped or who are victims of international sex trafficking are intentionally overlooked. I am consciously narrowing my scope of investigation to correspond to the situations in Franck's novels, in which the women unofficially and independently turn to prostitution for economic survival.

psychoanalytic scholarship under the aptly titled section 'The Sexualized
Prostitute Body: Pathology and Perversity'.[56] In this section, Bell outlines the instances in which Freud (briefly) engages with the question of
prostitution. In effect, Freud is not concerned with the prostitute beyond
her significance for the male child and as fetishistic object of male desire.
While there is some discussion of the mother as prostitute (i.e. the non-
sexed woman and the sexed woman existing as one and the same), there is
no mention of prostitutes as mothers. These two ideas remain antithetical;
even in feminist scholarship, motherhood and prostitution are examined
nearly exclusively for the purpose of considering patterns of sexual abuse,
neglect and drug use among the children of sex workers. In other words,
the focus is on the effects of the mother's lifestyle on the child and less so
on the perspective and/or experience of the mother. Thus this considera-
tion of mothers as prostitutes and prostitutes as mothers in Franck's work
remains somewhat limited by the dearth of theoretical investigations of
this subject.

    In all of Franck's texts, prostitution is unofficial and referred to only
obliquely. There is not always an exchange of money, yet there is a clear
sense that the female characters in question profit (financially, in terms of a
better living situation, or in other tangible ways) from their sexual relations
with men. In 'Der Hausfreund' prostitution is not explicitly thematized,
quite naturally as the story is narrated through the perspective of a young
child. Yet the connection between sex (the mother's affair with Thorsten)
and the flight to the West is close enough to suggest some ambiguity with
respect to the mother's intentions. It is not clear whether the mother loves
Thorsten and has chosen to flee with him, or whether she is pretending
to have an affair to ingratiate herself with him and ensure her passage
and the passage of her two daughters to the West. Beyla, the narrator of
Liebediener, speaks briefly – but quite clearly – about her mother's profession. The reader finds out very little information about Beyla's mother, but

56   Shannon Bell, *Reading, Writing, and Rewriting the Prostitute Body* (Bloomington:
      Indiana University Press, 1994), 64.

one thing is certain: although she was offered a way out of prostitution (i.e. in becoming Beyla's mother and her father's wife), she chose not to take it. She presumably prefers life without a family.[57]

At times Franck makes the connection between sex and an improved situation for the mother and her child(ren) quite explicit. In *Rücken an Rücken* Käthe willingly makes herself an instrument of the party. She rents a room in her house to a member of the Stasi [*Staatssicherheit*, or East German police], knowing full well that this cooperation will make it easier for her to work.[58] She benefits in many ways from her relationship with East German officials: by living in a large house with a studio, by receiving numerous commissions for sculptures and by acquiring a car easily and without much wait. The connection between her intimacy with the party and the advantages she receives from it is made most clear when Ella walks in on Käthe having sex with a man who may be their Stasi tenant. Moments later Käthe tells her children that she has just received news that Thomas will be allowed to study medicine. As Ella notes, Käthe could only have heard this from the man she had been having sex with, and it is thus implied that this transaction secured Thomas's future.[59]

While the use of sex as currency serves as a harsh critique of the former East Germany and even of capitalism in Franck's works, this chapter is primarily concerned with the psychological effects of maternal prostitution on the mother–daughter relationship. Chodorow asserts that 'A girl's oedipal identification with her mother, for instance, is continuous with her earliest primary identification (and also in the context of her early dependence and attachment)', and it is this primary identification that informs

57 More on Beyla's prostitute mother follows.
58 Franck, *Rücken an Rücken*, 189.
59 The connection between sexual favors and government-granted benefits is also explicit when Ella is raped by the Stasi tenant, who has asked her to become an informant. He threatens to bar Käthe from working and Thomas from studying if Ella refuses to comply with his wishes (185). Thomas is also sexually harassed by the group leader of the mine in Gommern. He offers Thomas an easier time of it, if he will accept the terms of his help (203).

the daughter's sense of self.[60] My interest is in considering the effects of the mother's prostitution on the daughters. For example, in 'Der Hausfreund' both daughters, but especially Hannah, begin to emulate the mother's flirtatious behaviour. Whoring oneself in exchange for favours is a pattern already established by Ella's mother in *Rücken an Rücken*, and, despite her subsequent sexual promiscuity, Ella is left physically and emotionally scarred by her experiences with the Stasi tenant. In *Der neue Koch*, when the hotel suffers financially under the narrator's direction, she twice attempts to use sex to secure the financial stability of the hotel. In other words, as is the case with nearly all mother–daughter pairs in Franck's works, the daughters imitate the patterns of human interaction that they learn from the mother.

Even Beyla, who had little interaction with her mother, has internalized models of behaviour that are connected to her. In *Liebediener* the reader learns little about her family and next to nothing about her mother. This is partly because Beyla herself knows very little about her mother. This lack of information, however, is not indicative of her mother's (ir)relevance; Beyla's mother has influenced her quite seriously. She shares information only when Albert asks questions, such as where Beyla got her name. She explains that she was named for an 'Arbeitskollegin', or work colleague, of her mother's. Albert insists that, as the name is Icelandic, the friend must have been from Iceland, and Beyla answers:

> Zumindest war sie eine Nutte, die Kollegin meiner Mutter. Meine Mutter war Nutte, ich könnte auch sagen: Prostituierte, aber das klingt sehr theoretisch. ... Und außerdem hat sich meine Mutter selbst als Hure bezeichnet oder als Professionelle, aber das Wort Prostituierte hat sie laut meinem Vater albern gefunden.[61]

> [She was a hooker at least, the colleague of my mother. My mother was a hooker, I could also say 'prostitute', but that sounds very theoretical. ... And anyway, my mother identified herself as a whore or as a professional, but according to my father she found the word prostitute silly.]

60   Chodorow, *The Reproduction of Mothering*, 174.
61   Franck, *Liebediener*, 86.

This discussion of names and titles highlights the lack of connection that Beyla had to her mother, i.e. little knowledge beyond these scant details. Beyla is having dinner with Albert in this scene, and, at his prompting, she continues to describe how her parents decided to have a baby (Beyla). (She later admits to the reader that she is not sure how much of this is true.)

> Es ist nicht so, daß ich ein Arbeitsunfall war, nein, das nicht. Mein Vater hat mir immer versichert, meine Mutter sei neugierig auf eine Schwangerschaft gewesen, und sie hätten alles von vornherein abgesprochen, daß er mich dann nimmt, außerdem hat sie sich wohl ein wenig Pause gönnen wollen. (86)[62]

> [It's not that I was a work accident, no, not that. My father always assured me that my mother was curious about pregnancy, and they had discussed everything at the outset, that he would take me then. Besides, she probably wanted to grant herself a little break.]

Albert's unexpected response to the story is that he thinks prostitutes are 'klasse', great. Beyla is annoyed by this response (although the reader eventually understands it) and makes clear to Albert that she neither knows her mother, nor wants to. She muses:

> Ich suchte meine Mutter nicht, ich wußte nicht, warum ich es tun sollte. Es kann sein, daß ich ihr schon auf der Straße begegnet bin, ich hätte sie nicht erkannt, sie mich bestimmt auch nicht, ich weiß nicht mal, ob sie noch in Berlin lebt oder ob sie überhaupt noch lebt. (86–7)

> [I didn't look for my mother. I didn't know why I should. It could be that I have already run into her on the street. I wouldn't have recognized her, she certainly wouldn't have recognized me either. I don't even know if she still lives in Berlin or is still living at all.]

It is likely, however, that, just like the narrator of *Der neue Koch*, Beyla is posturing here. Instead of admitting to feeling hurt or sorry that her mother

---

62   It is not specified whether Beyla's father paid her mother to be pregnant with Beyla and take a 'break' from her job. If so, this would set up a problematic model of acquiring intimacy with money, which would set a precedent for Beyla's relationship with Albert.

showed no interest in her, Beyla tries to mirror her mother's presumed attitude towards her. If her mother does not care about her, then she will not care about her mother. This emotional detachment also reflects her mother's attitude towards both Beyla's father and her clients: this was a business transaction, nothing more. Indeed, after she finds that Albert was perhaps paid to make her think that he was in love with her, Beyla has less of a reason to believe that either Albert or her mother was capable of emotional intimacy. Her ultimate rejection of Albert at the end of the novel is an echo of her emotional rejection of her mother.[63]

As aware as she is of playing roles, however, Beyla should recognize that 'the prostitute' is just another role for someone (in this case, her mother) to play. Beyla is, after all, a clown by profession, and the performance of identity is a constant theme throughout the book. Beyla even makes this connection – briefly – with prostitution. On a walk with Albert, they see prostitutes standing around the phallic *Siegessäule*, and Beyla thinks: 'Die Nutten dort hatten alle lange Haare und Lackstiefel bis in den Schritt, aber sie konnten sie ausziehen, die Stiefel und auch die Haare, darunter waren sie dann nicht mehr so gleich, das machte vielleicht den Reiz aus' [The hookers there all had long hair and patent leather boots up to the crotch, but they could take them off, the boots and also the hair. Then underneath they weren't so similar anymore. Maybe that's what made them exciting]' (109). In other words, she notes that the prostitutes all wear a similar costume. The accusation she eventually flings at Albert ('Jede darf mal anfassen, aber nur außen, nur kurz – bloß nicht innen, bloß nicht tief!' [Every woman is allowed to touch you, but only on the outside, only briefly – just not inside, just not deeply!]) could apply equally well to her mother (205). After all, she knows only superficial details of her mother's life but has no idea of who she is or was. The question this raises is how many roles one can play at once. And are the roles of prostitute and mother incompatible?

---

63   That Beyla conflates her relationship with Albert to that with her mother seems to underscore Freud's observation of parity between these two relationships. See Freud, 'Female Sexuality', 231.

From the perspective of the narrator of *Der neue Koch* – from the perspective of all of the daughters in these texts – the two are incompatible. This has less to do with prostitution per se than with the idea of anything coming between a mother and her child, be it a career or a man. Early on, the narrator explains the manner in which her mother maintained the hotel at relatively little expense. Here the narrator speaks specifically of the carpenter, who built her mother a reception desk, in exchange for 'eine Nacht im Hotel', or a night in the hotel. He liked this so much that he offered to replace the window frames, and continued to perform other services for her. The mother also offered a night in the hotel to the florist, in exchange for the freesias. That the 'night at the hotel' is a euphemism for sexual favours is underscored by the continuation of this passage: 'Den Tischler wollte meine Mutter bald darauf an Madame abgeben, aber der wollte sie nicht, er wollte nur meine Mutter, sagte er und ging lieber ganz' [Shortly after that, my mother wanted to pass the carpenter on to Madame, but he didn't want her. He only wanted my mother, he said, and would rather go away completely] (9). This passage reveals the daughter's knowledge and disapproval of her mother's behaviour. (This knowledge is also confirmed in a flashback of being bullied by a local boy who called her mother a prostitute.) It also gives Madame's name a different connotation, aligning her with prostitution as well, and turning the hotel into a brothel. It hardly needs to be said that this undermines the narrator's sense of the hotel as home. It also feeds the jealousy and resentment that the narrator feels towards her mother. Rather than understand the reasons behind her mother's actions, she resents the male company that kept her mother's attention away from her.

The consequences of this for the narrator are twofold. First, the narrator interprets the sexual exchanges and the men involved as more hurdles to obtaining the desired closeness with her mother. The second consequence of the mother's prostitution is that the narrator models her sexuality, in part, on her mother's. Chodorow explains from the perspective of psychoanalysis:

A girl identifies with and is expected to identify with her mother in order to attain
her adult feminine identification and learn her adult gender role. At the same time
she must be sufficiently differentiated to grow up and experience herself as a separate
individual – must overcome primary identification while maintaining and building
a secondary identification.[64]

This leaves the narrator with two models of femininity, both of which are
problematic from the perspective of psychoanalysis. Her mother is the first
example, and she frustrates the typical pre-Oedipal and Oedipal patterns
in her active sexuality. Remember that the starting point and end goal of
feminine sexual development is the mother's passive, vaginal sexuality
(which is the psychoanalytic equivalent to femininity). If the daughter is
supposed to emulate the mother's model, this would result in a clear break
from Freud's cycle of 'normal' feminine development. To rebel against
this example, the daughter would have to assume passive sexuality or deny
her sexuality altogether. Perhaps most significant, if the mother does not
assume passive sexuality, the entire course of feminine sexual development
is derailed. The Oedipal and pre-Oedipal phases cannot even begin if the
starting point – the mother's passive sexuality – is not met. Consequently,
one cannot assume that the development of a stable self, heterosexual part-
nering and the 'reproduction of motherhood' will consequently follow. As
a result, the psychoanalytic framework of the mother–daughter relationship cannot be applied to Franck's characters.

For the narrator, Madame is the second model of femininity with
which she must contend. The character Madame also brings the discussion
back to Judith Butler and performativity, as outlined in Chapter 1. Here
one must ask: what happens when the model of femininity is already a
grotesque parody? If her mother and Madame are the models of femininity
for the narrator, it is no wonder that she seems uncertain as to how to 'do'
her gender. Indeed, the reader can observe that the narrator, throughout
the novel, is constantly trying out and rejecting different aspects of the
femininity modelled for her by her mother and Madame. As discussed in

64   Chodorow, *The Reproduction of Mothering*, 178.

Chapter 1 with regard to playing roles and performing gender identity, the narrator does not wear skirts, dresses, or make-up. According to Madame, this is simply more proof of 'wie wenig Ähnlichkeit ich doch mit meiner Mutter hätte' [how little similarity I had to my mother] (33). It could well be that the narrator rejects these outward markers of her gender identity as a symbolic rejection of the sexuality that her mother modelled for her. Yet she tries on a garter belt and stockings (one of many sets that she has in her closet), which can be read as an attempt to 'do' her mother's femininity at least outwardly. She later tries to follow her mother's example of using sex as a form of currency when she employs her sexuality to gain the cook's interest and secure his favour. Unfortunately for the narrator, the cook is trying the same tactics and confuses her in her attempts at seduction. For example, he kisses her one evening and suggests that they retire to her room upstairs. After the narrator half-heartedly protests his advances, he offers that they simply sleep next to each other instead. She adjourns to her room to wait for him, and, despite her internal struggle, she finds herself looking forward to the cook's return, as it will be the first time, possibly in years, that she will have someone else in her room.[65] Yet hours pass, the narrator falls asleep, and he does not come. Days later the narrator tries again. This time she puts on stockings and a garter belt under her clothes and tries to seduce the cook in her room. He resists, and they continue their struggle for power on sexual terms. She is more successful with the insurance agent Niclas, so much so that she manages to secure an insurance policy for the hotel without actually sleeping with him. Yet this scene does not deliver the promise of intimacy, which the narrator also so desperately seeks.

---

65 It is unclear whether this suggests that the narrator has had sex before. At another point in the novel, she says she is waiting for a special man. This is a good example of the volatility of truth and the unreliability of the narrator in this text.

Conclusion: Performing 'Mother' and 'Daughter'

In the four texts I have discussed in this chapter, 'Der Hausfreund', *Der neue Koch*, *Liebediener* and *Rücken an Rücken*, the protagonists, who range in age from around six years old to thirty, have in common that their mothers are largely absent from their lives. In *Der neue Koch* this absence is due to death, in *Rücken an Rücken* to work, in *Liebediener* to the terms of the business-like transaction of having Beyla, and in 'Der Hausfreund' the absence is emotional rather than physical. Also common to all these women is that they desire greater connection with their mothers, which is the case even with Beyla, who outwardly protests against this. Because the protagonists feel that they were denied intimacy with their mothers, this drives them, particularly in *Der neue Koch* and 'Der Hausfreund', to pursue their mothers, to follow them relentlessly in an attempt to create or force a connection with them. This conflicts with previous psychoanalytic models of the mother–daughter relationship, which depend on the daughter's desire to break with her mother. Also contrary to psychoanalysis is the fact that the mothers in these three texts demonstrate *active* sexuality, which is directly in opposition to the passive sexuality that should be both the example for and end goal of the daughter's sexual development. According to the psychoanalytic model, if the daughters of women with active sexuality were desirous of breaking with their mothers, they would presumably adopt passive sexuality, which none of Franck's protagonists do. Instead, lacking a desire to break with their mothers, the women model their sexuality on their mothers' example and remain sexually assertive.

This chapter has also shown how spaces either reinforce or complicate filial identity. The narrator of *Der neue Koch* chooses to remain in the hotel, in effect remaining a daughter. If she were to leave the place that is so closely affiliated with her mother, she would lose her identity in a way that terrifies her. The protagonist of the short story 'Der Hausfreund', too, feels more closely connected to her mother at home, when doors are not shut between them. That one's identity as a daughter is contingent on the spaces in which one lives or through which one passes fundamentally conflicts with the static quality of such identities within the framework of psychoanalysis. According to this traditional matrix, mothers and daughters are permanent identities, much in the same way that 'masculine' and 'feminine' are distinct categories within psychoanalysis. (Although some women might achieve successful femininity while others are regressive, 'masculine' and 'feminine' are fixed poles in the familial constellation.) As Judith Butler dismantled the gender binary, so too must women undermine the fixity of the identities 'mother' and 'daughter'.

Common to all the stories narrated by the daughters is their inability to consider the perspective and independent identities of their mothers. This is perhaps not the fault of the daughters; after all, only relatively recent developments in feminist psychoanalysis have theorized the existence of the mother's subjectivity or, indeed, identity outside of the function that she plays in the development of her daughter's psyche. The next chapter examines Franck's protagonists who are mothers from their own perspectives, instead of the perspectives of their daughters. What Franck's works show is that the identity 'mother' is not natural, biological or inherent. Instead, it is performative and can be 'done' like any other.

Mothers: Psychoanalytic Models, the Bad Mother, and 'Maternal Drag'

It is striking that all of the maternal figures in Franck's texts are negative representations of mothers, 'bad' mothers, deeply flawed women who have complicated and troubled relationships with their children. Although this seems, on the surface, to be an unfailingly negative interpretation of motherhood, closer investigation shows that, in Franck's texts, 'mother' is an unstable and fleeting identity. Just as gender and other identities in Franck's texts are performative, so, too, is motherhood. Think, for example, of Madame, whose maternal performance is completely disconnected from a biological connection between herself and the narrator of *Der neue Koch*. Implicit in Franck's works is a critique of society's rigid expectations of women who have children. In *Lagerfeuer* Nelly Senff's supposed failure as a mother sheds light on the ways in which her ideas of motherhood conflict with Western expectations of the maternal. Others, such as Selma and Helene Würsich in *Die Mittagsfrau*, pose such fundamental questions of maternal identity that they drive the reader to re-evaluate her own conceptions of motherhood.

This chapter refers to three texts: *Liebediener*, *Lagerfeuer*, and *Die Mittagsfrau*. I return to *Liebediener* briefly, because, although Beyla does not become a mother, she does express a strong desire to have a child. This section considers the question of maternal desire: why do Franck's female characters (want to) mother? In *Lagerfeuer* the reader experiences the mother's perspective for the first time in Franck's oeuvre. Through an analysis of Nelly Senff, I open up the discussion of motherhood to some questions that figure prominently in Franck's works, including the following: must the mother live exclusively for her child? What makes a mother a good mother? If the mother has a life outside of her children, how does this change the way others perceive her? Also, how do expectations of motherhood vary based on place? With *Die Mittagsfrau* Franck pushes these questions further. What if a woman does not want to become a mother? Is motherhood an irreversible condition? Under what conditions can she reject her child? And if a woman ceases to be a mother, who is she then? The conclusion of the chapter returns to the idea of maternal drag to underscore the performative quality of motherhood.

Maternal Desire

If psychoanalysis does not treat the desire to mother beyond the level of an instinct or drive, this is because the mother does not exist as a subject beyond her contribution to the development of the child. The mother's wishes are irrelevant. Even much feminist scholarship on motherhood, such as Chodorow's *The Reproduction of Mothering*, was shaped by strong political motivations for dismantling the institution of motherhood. As a result, this discourse left no place for those who *desired* to be mothers. This is particularly the case with the women's movement in Germany, and it remains the general consensus in the motherhood debates today: 'Das Versagen der Frauenbewegung in diesem Punkt hat dazu beigetragen, dass Frauen in Deutschland Beruf und Familie so schlecht vereinbaren können wie in kaum einem anderen europäischen Land' [The failure of the women's movement in this matter has contributed to the fact that women in Germany have more difficulty in combining career and family than in nearly every other European country].[1] In an age, however, when

1   Anke Dürr, Ulrike Knöfel and Claudia Voigt, 'Weder Muse noch Madonna', *Der Spiegel* (7 July 2008), 136–9; here, 139.

mothering is becoming more a choice than a given, it is important to ask why women want to mother.[2]

For Beyla, the narrator of *Liebediener*, the desire to have a child can be located at the intersection of these two concerns. Through a child of her own, she wishes to experience the maternal and to secure an intimate relationship with someone whom she can love and someone who must love her in return. (Beyla's assumption is that she and her child would love each other; in her mind, this love is a constant, unlike her changeable relationship with Albert. This also does not reflect her troubled – one could go so far as to say loveless – attitude towards her own mother.) Beyla's desire for a child becomes synonymous with her desire for intimacy. When she breaks up with Albert, this desire becomes obsessive. During a scene in which she confronts him, he asks what she wants, and she answers, 'Ein Kind', a child. His reply, 'Dann such dir eins' [Then go look for one], indicates that neither the child nor intimacy can be part of their relationship but must be sought elsewhere.[3] She seems to sense this as well. By the novel's end she has given up on her relationship with Albert, conflated as it is with prostitution.

Equally important to Beyla's desire to have a child is the *absence* of her own mother. Although she speaks very little about her mother, it is clear that Beyla experienced no closeness or connection with her. As soon as she was born she was under her father's (neglectful) care. Although Beyla claims to have no interest in learning more about her mother, let alone in pursuing a relationship with her, she nonetheless idealizes the mother–child bond as one of closeness and intimacy. In the first chapter of the novel she speaks longingly of the homes of the neighbourhood children in the upstairs apartments, in which the mother is the glue holding

2   Contemporary German investigations of the subject include: Eva Herman, *Das Eva-Prinzip: Für eine neue Weiblichkeit* (Munich: Wilhelm Goldmann Verlag, 2007); Iris Radisch, *Die Schule der Frauen: wie wir die Familie neu erfinden* (Munich: Deutsche Verlags-Anstalt, 2007; Jana Hensel and Elisabeth Raether's *Neue deutsche Mädchen*, and Meredith Haaf, Susanne Klinger, and Barbara Streidl's *Wir Alphamädchen*.

3   Franck, *Liebediener*, 204.

everything together. Her move upstairs into Charlotte's apartment signifies her chance at creating such a life of her own, this time with herself in
the maternal role.

In wishing to have a baby, Beyla wants at once to create an intimate
relationship with her own child and to try to recreate the brief intimacy
she imagined she experienced with her mother until her mother disappeared from her life. Julia Kristeva writes: 'Such an excursion to the limits
of primal regression can be phantasmatically experienced as the reunion of
a woman-mother with the body of *her* mother.' In other words, 'By giving
birth, the woman enters into contact with her mother; she becomes, she is
her own mother; they are the same continuity differentiating itself.'[4] Thus
Beyla imagines that motherhood promises her intimacy on two levels:
intimacy with her child and intimacy with her mother.

Although she never experienced this mother–child bond herself, Beyla
sees that it is possible. Indeed, it seems common. In her adult life other
models of families reinforce her idea that intimacy is implicitly related to
having children. The idyllic image of her brother's family hunting for Easter
eggs, from the beginning of the novel, is a classic image of 'das Ganze und
Gemeinsame' [the wholeness and togetherness] that Beyla associates with
her fantasy of family life (13). Her pregnant friend, as an expectant mother,
also serves to constantly reinforce Beyla's desire for children. The friend
extends her own values onto Beyla's life, criticizing her relationship with
Albert by asking whether they will have a child together. Although Beyla
dismisses these questions, she is annoyed, because she, too, finds having
a child to be the ultimate goal and proof of love. She hides her feelings
during the conversation, but she later confesses to the reader, 'Ein Kind.
Natürlich wollte ich ein Kind mit ihm' [A child. Of course I wanted a
child with him] (201).

---

4   Julia Kristeva, 'Motherhood According to Giovanni Bellini', *The Portable Kristeva*,
     Kelly Oliver, ed. (New York: Columbia University Press, 1997), 301–7; here, 303.

At the beginning of the novel, Beyla claims that she is not close enough to anyone to fear that person's death above all others, but the reader has reason to suspect that this is not accurate (19).[5] This statement seems false especially in the context of the grief with which she refers to her unborn child. During a walk through Potsdamer Platz, which at the time of the book's publication was simply a cavernous construction site, she tells Albert about having had an abortion after becoming pregnant with twins. The location serves as a symbol for Beyla's confession: the giant hole in the ground represents both her empty uterus and the hole in her childless life. Her choice of words, for example, betrays a great intensity of emotion, and she does not shy away from taking responsibility for the act. Rather than the more politically correct term 'abgetrieben' [aborted], which Albert suggests, Beyla uses 'getötet' [killed] and 'herauskratzen lassen' [have scraped out] to describe the abortion (113). She also begins to cry, although with her back to Albert, who does not notice. Beyla remembers that her boyfriend of the time was terrified of having children, and he listed numerous reasons not to. She explains her response:

> Ich glaubte ihm nicht, nicht den Erklärungen und Gründen, aber ich glaubte der Abneigung gegen das Wachsen in mir, glaubte der Angst, die ich von ihm spürte, und mit dieser Angst wollte ich kein Kind bekommen, für mich nicht, für die Kinder nicht und für keinen sonst. Ende, aus. Ich war nicht Mutter von Natur, nur Frau. (114)

> [I didn't believe him, not the explanations and reasons, but I believed the antipathy towards the growing [child] in me, believed the fear that I sensed from him, and I didn't want to have a child with this fear, not for me, not for the children, and not for anyone else. The end, finished. I was not a mother by nature, only a woman.]

This last statement, that Beyla is not a mother by nature, is significant for two reasons. First, it functions to serve as her justification for denying her wish for children. If it is not a natural drive, she argues, then she can will

---

5   Beyla raises this point during a discussion of her father and his death. Despite her seeming distance from her father, she nonetheless reveals herself to be deeply affected by their relationship.

away her mothering impulses. Second, it becomes a theme for Franck's work: women are not natural mothers. Rather, mothering is a learned behaviour. This is the first clue that the maternal is not an inherent predisposition but rather a conditioned, performative identity.

Although Beyla does not actually become a mother in the course of the novel, she is the only one of Franck's characters to explicitly investigate the issue of maternal desire. In *Rücken an Rücken* Käthe never gives a reason for having children (four children, by two different fathers). Thomas and Ella also never speculate about her motives, assuming, perhaps, that none of her children were desired or planned. Nelly, one of the narrators of *Lagerfeuer*, also makes no mention of a wish or motivation to have children. Her two children, younger son Aleksej and elder daughter Katja, were born out of wedlock with her partner Wassilij, whose mysterious disappearance (and presumed death) encouraged Nelly to leave Berlin. During interrogations Nelly eventually reveals that the reason for her flight was to escape memories of Wassilij, memories which she believed were firmly attached to the places in which they had lived. Yet her children have become walking reminders of and connections to their father, more tangible and harder to escape. During one conversation with John Bird (American agent and another narrator in the novel), Nelly speaks of the burden of memory and says, 'Erinnerungen wiegen wie ein Kind. Was meinen Sie, wie schwer so ein Kind werden kann, wenn Sie's alleine tragen' [Memories weigh like a child. What do you think, how heavy a child can become, when you carry it alone].[6] In describing memory this way, Nelly also gives a negative impression of (her) children. They are burdens to be carried, draining, unending, and without relief. They are also physical reminders of memories that one cannot escape. Thus, one reason to have children (although the reader cannot say with any certainty that this was Nelly's motivation) is to maintain a connection to the father. An unintended consequence of this is that the connection cannot then be severed, as long as the children are alive.

6   Franck, *Lagerfeuer*, 69.

This connection, however, does not motivate the mothers in *Die Mittagsfrau*. There are two main characters who are mothers in this novel: Selma Würsich and her daughter Helene, the novel's protagonist. It is difficult to speak of maternal desire with regard to these two women. Selma, mother of the protagonist Helene, is a quintessential madwoman in the attic.[7] Already alienated by her community because of her Jewish heritage, Selma is driven to madness by the deaths of four infant sons. She acts out a grotesque version of maternal domesticity, rocking the small body of her son for days after he has died, conserving orange peels and unidentified seeds for forgotten reasons, and carefully storing her collection of delicate hat trimmings in boxes infested by maggots. She feels no connection to her two living daughters, who learn to flee her verbal and physical abuse. As Selma retreats further into insanity and depression, she refuses to leave her second-floor bedroom, leaving Helene to both long for and fear her mother. In the book's first chapter Helene's sister Martha is combing Selma's hair when Selma bursts into a rage:

> Doch während die Mutter über ihre Töchter schimpfte, fluchte, sie habe eine nichtsnutze Brut geboren, wiederholte Helene wie ein Gebet immer denselben Satz: Darf ich dich kämmen? Ihre Stimme zitterte: Darf ich dich kämmen? Als eine Schere durch die Luft flog, hob sie schützend die Arme über ihren Kopf: Darf ich dich kämmen? Und kauerte sich unter den Tisch. Darf ich dich kämmen?

> [But while Mother shouted at her daughters, cursing and complaining that she'd given birth to a couple of useless brats, Helene kept on and on repeating the same thing like a prayer: May I comb your hair? Her voice quivered: May I comb your hair? As a pair of scissors flew through the air she raised her arms to protect her head: May I comb your hair? She huddled under the table: May I comb your hair?][8]

---

7   The term 'madwoman in the attic' is used in Gilbert and Gubar's analysis of *Jane Eyre*. See: Sandra M. Gilbert and Susan Gubar, *The Madwoman in the Attic: The Woman Writer and the Nineteenth-Century Literary Imagination* (2nd edn, New Haven: Yale University Press, 2000).

8   Franck, *Die Mittagsfrau*, 33. English translation: Franck, *The Blind Side of the Heart*, 27.

This overwhelming desire to experience a maternal bond is echoed by Helene's own son, when she becomes a mother. Despite her coldness towards her son Peter, he refuses to accept the distance between them, clinging to his mother determinedly (which causes anger in Helene, just as her need provoked rage in Selma). In the novel's prologue, narrated from her son's point of view, Helene abandons Peter at a train station. She tells him to wait with their suitcase, that she is going to look for tickets and maybe food. Peter wants to go with her: 'er wollte seiner Mutter suchen helfen, überhaupt helfen wollte er ihr, er öffnete den Mund, aber sie duldete keinen Widerspruch, sie drehte sich um und tauchte in der Menschenmenge unter' ['he'd help his mother look ..., he wanted to help her anyway. He opened his mouth, but she was determined to have her own way, she turned and plunged into the crowd'].[9] And then she is gone.

Although it is difficult to move beyond the brutality with which these women treat their children, it is critical to examine the reasons why each woman became a mother: namely, that someone else wanted her to. Selma seems obsessed with the idea of having a son, so much so that she, during fits of hysteria, will call the name of her most recently deceased child, even ten years after his death.[10] Each death makes Selma question her reasons for living, and the death of the last son, Ernst Josef, turns Selma's eccentricities into insanity. While she is still in mourning for him, her husband seeks to comfort her – or perhaps simply to feel close to her, as her mourning is intensely private – by sleeping with her, and it is during this scene that Helene is conceived. Her birth is described thus:

> Das Kind war ein Mädchen, seine Mutter erkannte nichts an ihm. ...
> Die Mutter hatte keine Augen für Helene, sie wollte das Kind nicht auf den Arm nehmen und konnte es nicht an sich drücken. ... Die Mutter lag reglos im Bett, sie wandte ihr Gesicht ab, wenn man ihr das Kind brachte. Wenn sie von dem Kind sprach, nannte sie nicht seinen Namen, auch mein Kind kam ihr nicht über die Lippen. Sie sagte: Das Kind.

9   Franck, *Die Mittagsfrau*, 24. English translation: Franck, *The Blind Side of the Heart*, 21.
10   Franck, *Die Mittagsfrau*, 34.

[The baby was a girl, her mother could not recognize her as her own. ...
Helene's mother paid her no attention, she wouldn't pick up the baby and could
not hold her close. ... Her mother lay motionless in bed, turning away her face when
anyone brought her the baby. When she spoke of the child she did not say her name,
she could not even say *my daughter*. She called her just *the child*.][11]

Notice that Franck chose, in writing this scene, to refer to Selma as 'die
Mutter' [the mother], underscoring both her role and her failure to meet
its requirements. Even on the night that Helene is conceived, it is clear
that her mother does not want any other children. Specifically, she does
not want to run the risk of losing any more sons.[12] Selma's obsession with
having a son can be explained according to psychoanalysis (as a substitute
for a penis according to Freud, or as a chance to live vicariously through
the son according to feminist reinterpretations of penis envy). It can also
be explained by the time and place in which she is living: having sons to
continue the family name and to provide for the family was commonly
desirable in early twentieth-century Europe. One could argue that Selma
had been socially conditioned to desire an heir and furthermore to base
her own self-worth on her ability to produce one. Her dismissive attitude
towards her daughters reflects society's attitude towards women at the
time. Particularly in their rural village, the female characters in the novel are
confined by their limited roles in society: daughter, mother, wife and nurse.

In recognizing that Selma's experiences as a mother are located in a
particular place and time, it is important to remember that she had no
choice but to have children. Helene also would have been unusual if she
had avoided becoming a mother. She eventually becomes pregnant with
her son because her brutal husband repeatedly rapes her. Even when she
becomes pregnant with her lover, before marrying her abusive husband,
Helene chooses to have an abortion. She never wishes to have a child,
although it was a clear expectation of her as a woman in the first half of

11   Franck, *Die Mittagsfrau*, 67. English translation: Franck, *The Blind Side of the Heart*,
      60–1. Original italics. Here Bell chose to translate 'mein Kind' as '*my* daughter'. The
      literal translation is 'my child'.
12   Franck, *Die Mittagsfrau*, 66.

the twentieth century. Thus with respect to *Die Mittagsfrau*, it seems out of place to speak of maternal desire. Selma wishes to have a son, but she did not desire either of the daughters that she has. Helene does not wish to have any children, as she realizes that it would interfere with her career as a nurse and her hopes for pursuing further education.[13]

In Franck's novels having children is something that just happens, often without a conscious desire for children or a plan to have them. This puts the majority of Franck's characters at odds with the contemporary debate surrounding motherhood, much of which is based on the assumption that women do want to have children but refrain from doing so because of personal, financial or professional considerations. Again, the debate is centred on white, upper-middle class German women, who have both the luxury of choosing to pursue a career and the luxury of choosing to have (or not have) children. Of Franck's characters, only Beyla could fall into this demographic. Both Selma and Helene live in times of more conservative expectations for women, and, for all intents and purposes, they do not have the choice to become mothers. Käthe's and Nelly's situations are more ambiguous. Certainly Käthe's attitude towards her children indicates ambivalent feelings towards them, if not downright antipathy. It is important to remember, however, that these interactions are seen only through the eyes of the children and, as in *Der neue Koch*, reveal more about the feelings of the children than the mothers. In *Lagerfeuer* the themes of performative identity and the connection between identity and space meet the question of motherhood.

13   There is a brief period, after Helene becomes pregnant with Peter, that she hopes she will have a daughter: 'Sie sah ein Mädchen mit schwarzen Haaren, es sollte so dunkle Haare und glühende Augen haben wie Martha und ein so schwarzes Lachen wie Leontine' [She imagined a little girl with dark hair, hair as dark and eyes as bright as Martha's, and an inscrutable smile like Leontine's]. This desire is more for a reunion with her sister and friend than a desire for the child itself. Franck, *Die Mittagsfrau*, 362. English translation: Franck, *The Blind Side of the Heart*, 356.

What Makes a Good Mother?

The novel *Lagerfeuer* is narrated by four people, and this shifting of perspectives allows the reader to experience the main characters from a variety of angles. At times this yields contradictory impressions, and, as is the case with *Liebediener* and *Der neue Koch*, this novel too is characterized by a sense of slipperiness. There is no clear truth, no undisputed reality by which the reader can orient herself. The character Nelly provides insight into the mother–child relationship from the mother's perspective, yet the conflicting impressions of Nelly that the reader encounters through the perspectives of the other narrators are just as valuable. Indeed, the tension that arises among the various interpretations of this character is at the heart of Franck's critique of motherhood.

In the chapters that Nelly narrates she is convincingly devoted to her children. She narrates the opening chapter of the novel, in which she and her children are trying to cross the border with the help of a Western acquaintance. The officials take Katja and Aleksej inside a building for interrogation, and Nelly is consumed with anxiety about them, feeling their absence quite literally: as they part from her, she says, 'Meine Hand rutschte ins Leere' [My hand slipped into emptiness].[14] Even during her own interrogation and a humiliating and invasive examination of her body, she thinks of her children. She asks where they are, although the officer will not answer her questions, and thinks repeatedly that her children must be hungry (24, 34). Her reunion with them at the end of the chapter reflects a deep attachment to them and also awareness of the potential dangers inherent in their situation. Her acquaintance, Gerd, teases her for this concern: "'Du bist ja lustig, du glaubst wirklich, die haben nichts Besseres zu tun, als kleine Kinder festzuhalten'" ['You're funny, you really think they have nothing better to do than to detain small children']. Nelly answers, "'Nicht nur kleine Kinder', ich versuchte mit ihm zu lachen, es gelang nicht wirklich, "bei uns weiß man nie"' ['Not only small children',

I tried to laugh with him. It didn't really work, 'here you never know']
(14). When she returns to the car from her interrogation, she turns her
attention to her children, hiding from them the details of her experience
inside the building. While the children, bored and hungry, relate their own
experiences, she again grasps her son's hand, trying to hold on to her children literally but also metaphorically. Once they arrive in the camp Nelly
must participate in many more days of questioning, this time by Western
(German, American and British) officers. During these interrogations, too,
she asks to see her children, to bring them food and be with them during
mealtimes (57). It seems that, particularly in the context of the emotionally draining and overwhelming experience of extended interrogations,
thoughts of her children and a sense of their routine together function
both as a source of perspective and something to give her a connection to
normal life. They also help her to escape her current situation by thinking
about someone other than herself, and she seems genuinely protective of
them and concerned for their well-being.

There is no question that Nelly loves her children, yet the time they
spend in the camp wears on her, and her relationships with Katja and
Aleksej suffer for it. In the course of the novel she experiences caring for
her children to be more and more of a burden, although one could argue
that her love for them does not change. She relishes moments away from
them, either while they are at school or during an occasion when she can
leave them alone. Shortly after moving into the camp, for example, Nelly
asks Krystyna Jablanowska, the Polish narrator living with her father, to
look after Katja and Aleksej for a few hours. She does not explain where
she is going or offer any information to Krystyna about why she cannot
take her children with her (115). The reader, too, waits for some kind of
explanation but never learns where Nelly goes by herself in this scene. There
are many other moments that she is alone, some while her children are at
school but others when she leaves them in the camp unattended.

Nelly's relationship with her children is the focus of the chapter titled
'Nelly Senff hört, was sie nicht hören will' [Nelly Senff hears what she
doesn't want to hear], and the chapter provides the most thorough examination of this relationship (146). At the chapter's beginning she wakes her
children and gets them ready for school. They are tired and don't want to

get up, like most children, but Katja has a bad cold, likely related to the fact that her clothes are not appropriate for the cold and wet weather. Aleksej's glasses are broken and held on to his head with a rubber band. Both the inadequate clothing and the broken glasses seem to be the fault of the camp, in that the second-hand clothing donations are insufficient for the residents' needs and that the optician is in high demand. Nelly is doing her best to correct these situations. She offers to look for more shoes, and she has made an appointment for Aleksej with the optician. Katja is not satisfied with the idea of a different pair of second-hand shoes and asks her mother for new ones, which Nelly says she cannot afford. In the course of this conversation she learns that her children are being picked on at school, and several boys beat up Aleksej later that day during recess. After this incident Katja brings Aleksej back to the camp (although they are not allowed to leave the school grounds), and their mother calls an ambulance to take him to the hospital.

Once at the hospital the single interpretation of events that Nelly has provided to the reader begins to fracture as other perspectives compound and confuse it. The doctor, for example, does not believe that the children left the school because they were unsupervised there. Instead, he suspects Aleksej of having been abused or at least neglected by Nelly. According to him, Aleksej weighs too little for his age, and he has head lice, neither of which Nelly has noticed. She reacts strongly to this, explaining that there are no scales in the camp, and that no one commented on Aleksej being underweight when he was last at the paediatrician. The doctor's claims, incorrect as they may be, make Nelly so uncertain that even she qualifies her response with: 'zumindest hat da niemand von Unterernährung gesprochen' [at least no one there said anything about undernourishment] (166). They also suddenly cast a different light on her mothering. Previously, the reader, who had depended on Nelly's own characterization of her parenting, had found no reason to question her own assessment that she was doing the best for her children within her severely limited means. After the doctor's pronouncement Nelly seems somewhat disconnected from her children – had she really not noticed Aleksej's small size? Had she really not noticed his head lice? – possibly to the extent of being neglectful.

Aleksej's incident results in a new perspective of Nelly's mothering and illuminates the ways in which she is failing to care for her children according to the standards of Western (as in, West German) society. Although it could well be that Aleksej only recently acquired head lice or that he is not undernourished according to East German standards, other examples of Nelly's possible neglect now rise to the surface. The reader recalls, for example, that Nelly does not help her children with their homework or even check on it until shortly before they are leaving for school (148). Her lack of support for buying new shoes is now also coloured by the fact that Aleksej was not able to run fast enough to escape his bullies. Katja says, "'Siehst du, Mama, wenn er wenigstens Turnschuhe hätte'" ['You see, Mama, if he at least had sneakers'], implying that the mere existence of the new shoes could have prevented the whole incident (163). (Aleksej was beaten up for being and looking different, so Katja's childhood logic is perhaps not inaccurate in this case.) The reader may find it understandable that Nelly is unable to buy things for the children, such as new sneakers, with their small amount of *Begrüßungsgeld*.[15] Yet somewhat later in this chapter, the reader discovers that Nelly has been offered – and has declined – a job. She rejects it on the grounds of not being willing to accept a job so far below and irrelevant to her training. Before fleeing to the West she had been a chemist, and she turns down a position in a beverage shop. She insists, 'Wofür sei die ganze westliche Freiheit da, wenn nicht zur Entscheidung' [What is all the western freedom there for, if not for making decisions] (174). Both her professional reasons for this decision and the pride that prevents her from taking the position can, in some situations, be considered admirable. Yet it is difficult to reconcile them with her role as mother, particularly as the money earned in any job could have bought the children new shoes. Even if new sneakers had not kept Aleksej safe from bullies, winter boots could have kept Katja's feet warm and dry and ameliorated her chronic cold.

Yet to believe that money and things could solve anything or could make Nelly a better mother is to fall prey to the Western standards (not

---

15 *Begrüßungsgeld*, literally 'greeting money', is the term used for the money given to each refugee entering West Germany.

only of parenting) that other characters demonstrate in the novel. Figures from the West routinely judge residents of the camp based on their clothing and appearances. Krystyna's friendly co-worker at the fast food restaurant suggests that she wear deodorant, and her less friendly boss comments about Krystyna to a customer, "'So sind die aus dem Osten, alle gleich. Egal woher'" ['That's what the people from the East are like, all the same. No matter where they're from'] (193). (She says this in Krystyna's presence, assuming that she neither speaks nor understands German.) When John sees Nelly walking along the street, he wonders whether she is a 'kindliche Hure' [childlike whore], partly because of the practiced way that she walks along the Kurfürstendam and partly because of the thin and semi-transparent blouse that she wears under her jacket (200–1). In another scene, the job counsellor at the camp suggests that Hans Pischke buy a new pair of jeans, offering by way of explanation that Hans's corduroy pants will not look good in a job interview. The same character is bemused and eventually frustrated by both Nelly and Hans, who turn down jobs that are unrelated to their training. He says to Hans: "'Ich faß es nicht ... da kommt ihr hierher, ja, ohne alles, ja, ohne Winterschuhe und ohne Waschmaschine, ja, nicht mal die Wäsche für 'ne Waschmaschine reicht, ja, ohne Dach überm Kopf und ohne jede Mark, ja, und haltet die Hände auf und nehmt und lehnt ab, stellt Ansprüche, ja'" [I don't get it ... you come here, yeah, without everything, yeah, without winter shoes and without a washing machine, yeah, there's not even enough wash for a washing machine, yeah, without a roof over your head and without a mark, yeah, and you hold your hands out and take and refuse and make demands, yeah'] (132–3). Franck's critique of the superficial dimensions of Western society is clear in the job counsellor's reaction: he does not consider the refugees' identities beyond the list of things that they left behind or do not have.

Similarly, Nelly is judged as a mother based on what she and her children do not have, some of which are clearly more important than others: proper winter clothing, new school supplies, gifts to bring to birthday parties, scales and new glasses. This concern with outward appearances and with things is underscored by the visit of Olivier, one of the children who beat up Aleksej, and his mother. They arrive at the hospital ostensibly to apologize, but neither one addresses what Olivier has done. His mother only excuses the fact that she has arrived in a riding habit, seemingly on her way to or from stables. Instead, they bring Aleksej a present, 'ein in Glanzpapier eingeschlagenes Päckchen mit einer großen, silbrigen Schleife' [a little package wrapped in glossy paper with a big, silvery bow], which contains a cassette tape recording of *Pippi Longstocking* (179). The inappropriateness of the gift (as the children do not have a cassette player in the camp) and the ostentatious packaging are out of place from Nelly's perspective, but for Olivier's mother they are part of the overall concern with appearances. She and Olivier make their perfunctory appearance, bring a gift and thus feel absolved of their part in Aleksej's incident. From Nelly's point of view, this entire performance was all for show, as neither mother nor son apologizes, neither looks at or speaks with Aleksej himself and neither considers or empathizes with her situation. Instead, Nelly remains the bad mother in the story of Aleksej's fight at school, largely because she has failed to provide outward, perhaps superficial markers of maternal care.

Nelly is deeply upset by this entire incident, and she directs her anger at the school, both for allowing the boys to beat up Aleksej and for letting the children leave unattended. She is also angry at the hospital, for the accusations they make about her parenting. More than anything, Nelly seems to be angry at institutions, at the bureaucratic labyrinth in which she is stuck. For example, when they arrive in this hospital, she must sign a release form, absolving the hospital of any side effects of the x-ray and other tests used to examine Aleksej. But she notes that the examinations were all completed by that time, and that signing the release form was simply a formality (163). When Nelly feels trapped, she begins to shut down and withdraw from her children, wishing to be alone and to cry even though she feels that she is no longer able to (170). Nelly's withdrawal from her family and conflicted feelings towards her children seem especially to be directed at Katja. There is a moment of great insight into the mother–daughter relationship, when Katja, sensing her mother's distress, tries to comfort her and puts her arms around her mother. Nelly does not respond to this gesture, sitting 'wie ein toter Berg' [like a dead mountain] next to her daughter. She continues:

Doch dann kribbelte innen etwas, Scham breitete sich aus, Lava kroch ins Gesicht und an den Händen erkaltete sie. Unbeweglich harrte ich in ihrer Umklammerung aus. Mir wollte einfach keine sinnvolle Handlung einfallen. Auch die Worte schienen nicht mehr zu sein als unnütze Geräusche. (171)

[But then something prickled inside. Shame spread, lava crept into my face and cooled on my hands. Unmoving, I held out in her embrace. No meaningful action crossed my mind. Words too seemed to be no more than useless sounds.]

This moment recalls the interactions between the *Spätmutter* and her daughter in *Der neue Koch* or moments between the narrator and her mother in 'Der Hausfreund'. The child, specifically the daughter, wishes to feel close to her mother, and the mother reacts with silence and coldness. As discussed in Chapter 3, it is incomprehensible from the daughter's perspective that the mother's reactions could have any motivation other than to reject the daughter. The reader can well imagine how Katja must feel at her mother's lack of response. Yet in *Lagerfeuer* the reader understands that, although the moment is not wholly independent of the daughter's desire for intimacy, it has more to do with the mother's experience of difficulties that the child simply cannot comprehend. Nelly is worried about her children, wondering whether it is safe to send them back to school, questioning her own ability as a mother, fending off accusations of child abuse, and feeling alone in a new country. There is much more to Nelly's concerns – indeed, there is much more to Nelly – than just her relationship with her daughter.

At times Nelly seems to suffer from the growing distance between herself and her children, although she either faults the children or treats the change in their relationship as inevitable. Reflecting on the argument she is having with Katja about new school supplies, Nelly asks whether their classmates make fun of them. Her children avoid answering the question, and she wonders whether the children are too proud to admit that they are being bullied or whether they simply made up the story to justify the purchasing of new, West German items. This desire for things makes the children seem foreign to Nelly. 'Die Fremdheit zwischen uns haßte ich, doch je mehr ich haßte, um so fremder wurden sie. Ich mochte sie nicht, wenn sie um Schulmappen oder irgendwelche modischen Stofftierchen bettelten. ... Ihr Gier war mir zuwider geworden' [I hated the foreignness between us, but the more I hated, the more foreign they became. I didn't like them when they begged for school bags or some fashionable stuffed animal. ... Their greed had become repugnant to me] (150–1). Nelly senses the loss of intimacy with her children as they gain independence from her and experiences outside of the camp (i.e. at school). At the same time, she does not pursue them. Instead, she accepts or perhaps even reinforces this loss by turning to strangers for company and intimacy, rather than turning to her children.

In a later chapter Nelly is visited by Dr Rothe, a representative of a supposed goodwill organization that provides assistance to refugees. Unwilling to accept help and uncomfortable with his insistent and threatening manner, Nelly looks into his bag when he is in the bathroom and finds a document inside containing personal information about her situation, as well as the words: *'Verdacht auf Doppelspionage'* [suspicion of being a double agent], *'Semitenverein'* [Semitic association], *'falsche Angaben'* [false details], *'Eliminierung'* [elimination], *'Objekt'* [object], the initials of the father of her children and the abbreviation *'IM',* for *Inoffizielle Mitarbeiter,* a civilian informant to the East German Stasi (234).[16] Unnerved, she flees the situation and wanders around the camp, trying to decide what to do while she avoids further contact with Dr Rothe. She wonders why the camp seems to be abandoned, wonders whether it is a holiday, and eventually her thoughts lead her back to her children. When she returns to their room, the children are home from school and busying themselves with caring for a raven with a broken wing. After making sure that they are safe and that Dr Rothe is nowhere to be seen, Nelly leaves, promising that she will be right back.

But she stays away for much longer. First, she looks for Hans, whom she has befriended, and turns to him for company and reassurance. When he asks her about Wassilij, the father of Nelly's children, the mood changes, and all intimacy between them disappears (249). She avoids the question and leaves his room. Nelly goes next to the laundry room, to finish the laundry that she had been waiting for when Dr Rothe arrived. There she overhears

16   Original italics.

two women talking about Hans and that he is a Stasi spy. This turns Nelly's world upside-down, as Hans was the closest thing to a friend that she had in the camp. Her distress at the news sends her wandering around again, stopping to ask for mail and then leaving the camp to go to a store across the street and buy the children Christmas presents. When she sees John in the shop window, she avoids him and goes instead to a pay phone to call Gerd, the acquaintance who helped them into the West. Through this conversation the reader learns that Gerd is still interested in seeing Nelly (although he has no interest in her children) and that she owes him ten thousand marks. After ending the conversation (and avoiding planning a meeting with him), she returns, slowly, to her children in the camp. Just as this scene provides more information about Nelly's complicated situation, it unsettles the reader's opinion of her as a mother. She does check on her children's well-being shortly after she has fled from Dr Rothe, yet she also leaves them alone again for hours while she seeks comfort elsewhere. Is she being neglectful of her children? Or is Nelly simply seeking the companionship that she needs as an adult?

Here we come to a central issue for Franck in her exploration of the motherhood role: to what extent must or should a woman organize her own identity around her child? The reader's judgment of Nelly comes, in part, from the still common idea that mothers exist primarily, if not exclusively, for their children. Nancy Chodorow and Susan Contratto point out in their 1980 essay 'The Fantasy of the Perfect Mother' that even '[f]eminist writing on motherhood assumes an all-powerful mother who, because she is totally responsible for how her children turn out, is blamed for everything from her daughter's limitations to the crisis of human experience.'[17] In other words, the common idea of motherhood is that mothers are 'all-powerful', that they are supposed to care for every detail of their children's

---

17 Nancy Chodorow and Susan Contratto, 'The Fantasy of the Perfect Mother', in Barrie Thorne and Marilyn Yalom, eds, *Rethinking the Family: Some Feminist Questions* (rev. edn, Boston: Northeastern University Press, 1992), 191–214; here, 192.

lives and, consequently, are responsible for every problem or failure that their children experience.[18]

In her book *The Mother/Daughter Plot*, Marianne Hirsch writes of 'the uneasy relation between feminist discourse and maternal discourse' and argues: 'Feminist writing and scholarship, continuing in large part to adopt *daughterly* perspectives, can be said to collude with patriarchy in placing mothers into the position of object – thereby keeping mothering outside of representation and maternal discourse a theoretical impossibility.'[19] This book was written in 1989 and does not account for literary representations of the mother–daughter relationship since the time of publication. At the same time, Hirsch theorizes that 'maternal anger' could be a useful way of uncovering a mother's subjectivity, which connects to Franck's representations of mothers. Hirsch states: 'A mother cannot articulate anger *as a mother*; to do so she must step out of a culturally circumscribed role which commands mothers to be caring and nurturing to others, even at the expense of themselves.'[20] Hirsch postulates that this anger comes from losing subjectivity and a voice as one becomes a mother. I disagree with this, as I believe that anger can come from a variety of sources, but I do agree that anger and the maternal are still assumed to be antithetical. Thus, in order for a mother to express her anger, she must temporarily cease to be a mother.

The reader has already witnessed Nelly's ability to change roles, notably in the chapter with Dr Rothe. It is significant that this is also among the first times that she expresses her anger in the novel. Scared, frustrated

---

18   Chodorow and Contratto examine the idea of the 'all-powerful' mother specifically within the context of scholarship and personal narratives written on the mother–daughter relationship in the 1970s, including in their survey Nancy Friday and Adrienne Rich. Their essay also critiques feminist scholarship of the mother–daughter relationship that is based on a Freudian framework as models that 'seriously constrain feminist accounts of mothering'. This points to scholars that followed, such as Jessica Benjamin. Chodorow and Contratto, 'The Fantasy of the Perfect Mother', 210.

19   Marianne Hirsch, *The Mother/Daughter Plot: Narrative, Psychoanalysis, Feminism* (Bloomington: Indiana University Press, 1989), 164 and 163.

20   Hirsch, *The Mother/Daughter Plot*, 170. Original italics.

and furious that she has fled one regime of spying and interrogation for another, she leaves her room in the camp and makes the various stops listed above. In doing so, she assumes a variety of roles that seem distinct and discontinuous: ungrateful refugee (with Dr Rothe), absent mother (with Katja and Aleksej), friend (with Hans), anonymous woman doing laundry (with strangers in the laundry room) and flirt (with Gerd). For Nelly, motherhood is a role like any other. It is not – and cannot be – her exclusive concern in her situation. She must also find a source of income, seek out companionship and emotional support to sustain her, protect herself and her children from spies and intelligence agents and guard her own memories of Wassilij. Nelly finds herself in what seems to be an impossible situation, one in which she must be everything to her children and everything to herself.

This is where prostitution enters into Nelly's story: at the intersection of economic and emotional need. Prostitution is an explicit theme in the text, but Nelly does not discuss prostitution in the chapters that she narrates. She recounts the details about their roommate, Susanne, that reveal her source of income: she comes home late, just before the children wake for school; she takes a bundle of bills out of her boots; her clothing includes a miniskirt, boots, stockings trimmed with fake fur, and fancy underwear (147). In another chapter Susanne confesses to Nelly that the directors of the camp have finally figured out that she leaves the camp at night but not to work in a bakery, as she is supposed to. They kick her out, and, when Nelly asks where she will stay, Susanne responds, "'Mal ehrlich, Nelly, es gibt bequemere Betten als die hier, was?'" ['Seriously, Nelly, there are more comfortable beds than these here, what?'] (261). Her parting words are "'Und bleibt nicht zu lange'" ['And don't stay too long'] (262). Nelly does not judge Susanne's actions, only hugs her as a gesture of goodwill, so the reader cannot infer what her attitude towards prostitution is.

It is just days after this scene, however, that Hans seeks out Nelly in her room in the middle of the day and finds her naked. When he knocks on the door, he comments on hearing voices and wonders whether Nelly has a radio. (She does not). She opens the door a crack but will not let Hans in, saying "'Ich bin nackt, ich will dir jetzt nicht aufmachen'" ['I am naked. I don't want to open the door for you now'] (279). Many details support the suspicion that she is using sex as a form of currency in the camp.[21] At the novel's beginning, the employment counsellor asks Hans whether he knows anything about women in the camp resorting to prostitution (131). Much later in the novel Hans tells Nelly that the other women in the camp call her a whore behind her back (252). It is not clear when Nelly begins to see prostitution as a way to improve her situation, but it seems connected to the visit from Dr Rothe. During this chapter (which immediately precedes the one in which Hans finds her naked), as she flees from Dr Rothe, she repeats to herself something that he said to her: '*Sie werden Ihre Situation nicht auf diese Weise lösen*' [You will not solve your situation in this way] (241).[22] It is possible that she is scared enough by this incident that she decides to find some way to effect a change.

The reader knows from an earlier chapter, however, that Nelly has sex with John Bird. John encounters her outside the camp, where she is walking along the street with an empty shopping bag, and he invites her to coffee. When John asks her to go with him to a hotel around the corner, she does, saying "'Warum nicht'" ['Why not'] (203). It is not clear whether Nelly is seeking to obtain anything concrete in this encounter, but the power that he has over her and the influence that he could have on her situation must be factors in her decision. Nelly does not forget their respective roles in this scene: when John asks her why she is not living with friends but continuing to live in the camp, she asks calmly, "'Wollen Sie wieder Namen wissen?'" ['Do you want to know names again?'] (207). There is no mention of her children or of other roles that she might play, but Nelly's ability to adopt and discard roles at will is an asset in this complicated situation – and one that enables her to evade interrogation. Whether she is withholding information or there is simply no relevant information to share, Nelly's shifting identities create a sense that any underlying 'truth' is obscured.

---

21   Here I use the term 'currency' to mean 'social currency', as Beret Norman outlines in her article 'Gendered Surveillance', and which is discussed in Chapter 2. For Norman, 'social currency' is a means to attaining a better social position and acquiring the perks that come with it, such as intimacy.

22   Original italics.

John, by contrast, conveys no sense of mystery. Rather, he seems to be *just* an American agent. This is not a theatrical performance, not a conscious role-play that involves putting on a costume. Instead, it is as inescapable as gender. John does not exist without it. When sleeping with Nelly, he wonders about her status and background and assumes that she is a spy. She expresses surprise that he does not stop 'working' even during sex. He responds, "'[M]eine Arbeit gehört zu meiner Identität. In keinem Augenblick meines Lebens könnte ich aufhören, die Verantwortung zu empfinden'" ['My work belongs to my identity. In no moment of my life could I stop feeling the responsibility'] (208). Later in the chapter he goes further, and, his mind on an upcoming interview with the CIA, he says (to himself) that he has internalized the values and goals of the United States. As they steam up the windows of his car, he thinks, '[I]ch verkörpere selbst die Freiheit' [I myself embody freedom] and thinks about the Statue of Liberty while feeling 'ihren Kopf in meinem Schoß und ihren Mund an der Freiheit' [her head in my lap and her mouth on freedom] (214). In Franck's texts gender is not the only performative identity that becomes so all encompassing. In John's case, it is that of the American agent. In Käthe's case (*Rücken an Rücken*), it is that of the socialist artist. In Wilhelm's case (*Die Mittagsfrau*), it is that of the Nazi engineer. Political and career identities are also performative.

Unlike John, whose marriage fails due to his inescapable performative identity, Nelly's chameleon-like ability to adopt different roles with different people gives her some degree of flexibility. Yet her life remains severely restricted by the situation in which she finds herself. The recurring metaphor of thwarted flight underscores the idea that she is trapped in her life. Although Nelly thought she had fled her old life in the East, she, just like the others in the camp, is stuck between past and future. Hans, for example, recounts his failed attempt to leave East Germany. His 'flight' to the GDR is more of a fall. Hans had climbed to the top of a statue of Lenin to paint it red, and, when startled by the police, he fell to the ground and broke both his legs. (He was later sold to the West as part of a package of refugees.) Many of the characters in the novel, such as John Bird's wife Eunice, plan to escape their situations; Eunice repeatedly threatens to fly back to the United States, but the reader never learns whether she has left.

Instead, she draws designs for tattoos, many of them winged creatures that hint at flight but remain nothing more than marks on paper. Back in the camp, an elderly woman can see no way out for herself other than death. She jumps from her window, but, rather than enjoy even a brief moment of flight, she becomes entangled in a tree, where she is likely strangled to death. Finally, Aleksej and Katja, desperate for company, adopt a raven with a broken wing. The ultimate symbol of impossible flight, he is inside their room in the camp one evening, confronting Nelly with the failure of her flight, as well.[23]

Critique of the Selfless Mother

Based on the representation of motherhood in *Lagerfeuer*, it seems that Franck is critical of mothers who care for their children only superficially, such as Olivier's mother, and is unsympathetic towards those who do not sufficiently prioritize their children, such as Nelly. In *Die Mittagsfrau* a new type of mother emerges: one who cares for her children too much. This maternal archetype contrasts sharply with Helene's own experiences of mothering, which culminates in rejecting her son from her life.

The prologue of *Die Mittagsfrau* is narrated from Peter's point of view and follows him on the day that he is abandoned by his mother. This means that the moment during which Helene abandons her son is not the climax of the novel. Rather, it is the premise, and the novel is concerned with uncovering why she did so. It immediately comes into conflict with basic assumptions (presumptions) of mothering: that the mother will

---

23   The word *Rabe* [raven] also suggests the term *Rabenmutter*, a bad or uncaring mother. This term is regularly used in the motherhood debate in Germany. Some have tried to reclaim it, such as Jutta Hoffritz in her book *Aufstand der Rabenmütter: Warum Kinder auch ohne Baby-Yoga und Early-English glücklich werden* (Munich: Knaur Taschenbuch Verlag, 2008).

always care for her child, that she will put its needs above her own, and that the mother prioritizes her child's existence over her own survival. In the prologue there is evidence that Helene must be frugal but not that she is struggling to survive. Indeed, World War II has ended in Europe, and there is a sense, despite the difficulties of the time, that better days are ahead. Although the reader does not yet have an idea of why Helene has rejected her son, the reader struggles to preserve the idea of motherhood: perhaps something terrible has happened to Helene, preventing her from reuniting with Peter; perhaps she has a reason that her young son cannot fathom; or perhaps she is simply a terrible mother, who puts her own desires above the well-being of her child. This final conclusion assumes the worst about Helene, but it leaves the institution and myth of motherhood intact.

Franck is careful not to judge Helene's decision, providing a number of details that support any number of interpretations of her 'ungeheuerlicher Tat' [monstrous deed].[24] For example, Helene packs a suitcase full of provisions for Peter, including a new pair of pyjamas, money and the name and address of an uncle, his only known living relative on his father's side. For a reader searching for a more positive interpretation, this can be understood as Helene's way of securing her son's welfare. Of course, one could also argue against this, as her son's well-being still depends very much on luck, his own wherewithal and the kindness of those whom he would happen to meet. Also of significance for Helene's mothering is her genetic connection to her mother. There is a hint in the text that Selma's mental imbalance could be hereditary. At one point, Helene visits Selma in a sanatorium, where the doctor is investigating the causes of Selma's mental illness and the susceptibility of her daughters to developing similar symptoms (322). Again, one could argue that Helene abandons Peter when she begins to feel similar reactions towards him as her mother did towards her, but Franck leaves this open to interpretation. It is possible, however, to uncover a critique of certain types of mothers, who appear with some frequency in the text: mothers who exist solely for their children.

24 'Das kalte Herz', *Frankfurter Allgemeine Zeitung* (10 Oct. 2007).

Helene encounters two such women only briefly, both of whom are with their children and do not exist as characters beyond the fact that they are mothers. On her wedding day, she and Wilhelm are picnicking near the harbour in Stettin when she sees a young woman pushing a baby carriage. The child is screaming with hunger and pain as the wind blows the baby's blanket behind them (329). The glimpse of this mother is a foreshadowing of Helene shortly after the birth of her child. Because of an infection and rising fever, Helene is unable to feed her son, who is screaming with hunger. At Wilhelm's command, she wraps her son in a blanket and takes him with her to buy milk. For both women in these moments, nothing exists for them outside of their screaming children and the responsibility they feel towards them.

Helene meets another mother and child, shortly before meeting Wilhelm for the first time, when she goes into a church. She is mourning the death of her lover Carl, and, distraught, she wonders how much longer she must live. The mother and child enter the church when Helene is wondering to herself where Carl is now. As if in response, the mother and child enter into a conversation:

> Wo? Hörte sie die hohe Kinderstimme hinter sich.
> Da, sagte die Mutter, da oben.
> Wo, ich sehe ihn nicht. Das Kind wurde ungeduldig, es jammerte, wo denn, ich kann ihn nicht sehen.
> Man kann ihn auch nicht sehen, sagte die Mutter, nicht mit den Augen, du musst mit dem Herzen sehen, mein Kind.
> Das Kind war jetzt stumm. Ob es mit dem Herzen sah?

> [Where? she heard the clear voice of the child behind her.
> There, said the mother, up there.
> Where? I can't see him. The child was getting impatient, wailing. Where is he? I can't see him.
> No one can see him, said the mother, you can't see him with your eyes. You have to see with your heart, child.
> There was no reply – was the child's heart seeing something now?][25]

25 Franck, *Die Mittagsfrau*, 306. English translation: Franck, *The Blind Side of the Heart*, 300–1.

Rather than interpret this as a sign from God, Helene resolves to accept that Carl died for no reason and not as part of a greater plan. This mother-and-child pair does not foreshadow Helene's motherhood. Nor does it serve the purpose of a spiritual awakening, as one might expect. The exchange between the mother and her child does not encourage Helene to think of Carl – or God – as ever-present and alive in her heart. Instead, the scene of maternal intimacy does not speak to her, and she simply leaves the church.

Only after Carl's death does Helene meet his mother for the first time. Carl's mother (to whom Franck refers almost exclusively as 'Carls Mutter' [Carl's mother], instead of 'Frau Professor' [Mrs Professor] or 'Frau Wertheimer' [Mrs Wertheimer] or 'Lilly') receives Helene on her veranda, where they drink tea surrounded by the almost unnaturally large and beautiful flowers in the garden. Just as the surroundings connect Mrs Wertheimer to a sense of nature and fertility, so, too, does the conversation surround her with an air of the maternal. In fact, she is not able to speak of anything else. Her interest in Helene is purely with regard to Helene's connection to her son. She recounts all that she knows of Carl's death, disregarding Helene's questions or contributions, and concludes with the following:

> Sie sind jung, Ihr Leben liegt vor Ihnen. Carls Mutter nickte jetzt, als wollte sie ihren Worten Nachdruck verleihen, dabei war ihr Blick von einer Warmherzigkeit, wie Helene sie noch nie an einer Frau gesehen hatte. Sie werden einen Mann finden, der Sie lieben und heiraten wird. Schön wie Sie sind und klug.
>
> Helene wusste, dass nicht stimmte, was Carls Mutter ihr da prophezeite, was sie sich selbst und Helene zum Trost sagte. Sie sagte es, und darin enthalten lag der Hinweis auf einen feinen Unterschied: Helene konnte sich einen anderen Mann suchen, sie würde ihn finden, nichts leichter als das. Doch niemand konnte sich einen anderen Sohn suchen.

> [You are young, your life is ahead of you. Frau Wertheimer nodded as if to emphasize what she was saying, and there was warmth in her eyes such as Helene had never seen in a woman before. You will find a man who will love you and marry you. Beautiful as you are, and so clever.

Helene knew that what Carl's mother was foretelling, to comfort them both, was wrong. She was saying it, yes, but her words hinted at a subtle distinction: Helene could look for another man, she would find one, nothing easier. But no one can look for another son.][26]

In this short statement Mrs Wertheimer makes clear several things: first, Helene's grief does not match her own, as Helene (who is mourning for Carl-the-lover) has less of a claim to Carl than does his mother (who is mourning for Carl-the-son). Second, Mrs Wertheimer's identity is first and foremost – if not exclusively – that of Carl's mother. The reader has no reason, either from this scene or from other times that Mrs Wertheimer is mentioned, to think that she has any interests or concerns other than her children. This, coupled with the almost unreal 'Warmherzigkeit' [literally: warm-hearted-ness] in the passage above, makes her into what is almost a caricature of a mother. Carl's mother is a flat, dimensionless woman whose identity depends solely on her children.

The final example of a mother who is obsessed with her children is Selma, Helene's own mother. As discussed earlier, Selma is so distraught over the death of her four sons that she considers taking her life. She experiences no motivation for living and feels no connection towards her surviving daughters. Yet she is not as selfless as Carl's mother, in the sense that she is not without self in the same way that Mrs Wertheimer is. There is some indication throughout the novel that Selma takes pleasure in small things and has a kind of inner life that is perhaps beyond the comprehension of those around her. She collects objects and then stores them, for reasons unknown to the rest of her family. These mundane objects, such as buttons, coins, old shoes and fragments of broken china, have a special value to Selma: 'Einmal fand sie unmittelbar vor der Haustür einen Gänseflügel und weinte Tränen der Rührung' [Once, right outside their door, she found a goose's wing that could be used as a feather duster and wept tears

---

26   Franck, *Die Mittagsfrau*, 290. English translation: Franck, *The Blind Side of the Heart*, 285. Note that in Bell's translation, the character is referred to once as Carl's mother and once as Frau Wertheimer. In the original German, she is referred to exclusively as Carl's mother.

of emotion].[27] Mysterious as her inner life is, it nonetheless provides Selma with another dimension to her character, as does her intense spirituality. (In fact, she regards these objects with a spiritual reverence.) Ostracized within the town because she is Jewish, she is nevertheless soothed and guided by her beliefs. Although one would not refer to Selma as a happy woman, she does find comfort and satisfaction in these two aspects of her non-maternal life. Helene, the only other mother in the novel, does not construct her identity around her child either. Indeed, it is her inability and refusal to do so that leads to the story's conclusion.

The Reproduction of Mothering

To understand Helene as a mother, one must first turn to Selma. As mentioned earlier, Selma Würsich is, quite literally, the madwoman in the attic, a nod to Sandra Gilbert and Susan Gubar's theorization of literary figures such as 'Mr Rochester's mad wife Bertha' in Charlotte Brontë's *Jane Eyre*.[28] Driven mad by the limited possibilities for her life as a woman and expressing anger at her situation (in this case, as a mother desiring sons but destined only to have daughters), Selma's eccentricities and rages strongly parallel those of Bertha. She remains locked in an upper floor of her house, cut off from society and comforted only by the presence of her maid: in Selma's case, Mariechen; in Bertha's case, Mrs Poole. It is important to note that Selma remains locked up by choice. She refuses to leave even for her husband's funeral. Yet one could argue that both the townspeople who shunned her as a Jew and Selma's resulting madness are what drove her to

27 Franck, *Die Mittagsfrau*, 37. English translation: Franck, *The Blind Side of the Heart*, 31–2. Note that the English translation attaches a practical value to the goose wing that Selma does not. She collects birds' wings and hangs them over her bed, where they are invested with spiritual meaning.
28 Gilbert and Gubar, *The Madwoman in the Attic*, 339. Charlotte Brontë, *Jane Eyre* (New York: Vintage Classics, 2009).

withdraw to her chambers in the first place. Furthermore, although Selma does not seem desirous of freedom, she reveals an interest in flight. For example, her collection of bird feathers has a special place over her bed, and she calls it 'Ein Vogelschwarm für das Geleit von Seelen' [A flock of birds to escort souls].[29] This cherished collection implies a desire to fly away, a desire to have her soul depart from this earth.[30] Just as Bertha tries to fly from the top tower of Thornfield, so, too, does Selma hope that her soul will fly to another place. For both women, escape comes only in the form of death.

If Selma's situation echoes that of Bertha, is it possible to read Helene as Jane Eyre? In no way do their stories seem similar: the trajectories of the heroines' lives are completely different, there is no parallel to Mr Rochester in *Die Mittagsfrau* and, while Jane's story is one of self-discovery, Helene's is one of self-erasure. There is one important way, however, that the novels are alike. According to Gilbert and Gubar's reading, 'Bertha ... is Jane's truest and darkest double.'[31] Just as Bertha expresses her rage and acts out against the confinement of female identity, Jane feels – but does not express – that same rage and confinement. Similarly, just as Selma is trapped in her upper-story bedroom surrounded by the accoutrements of womanhood, so, too, is Helene trapped in a destiny that is restricted and marked by her female identity. Selma expresses the anger that Helene also feels, and it is no coincidence that Helene's moments of frustration often coincide with Selma's tantrums. For example, after living in Berlin for many years, Helene learns that her mother has been removed from her home and taken to a sanatorium. She travels there with Wilhelm, at the time already her fiancé,

29 Franck, *Die Mittagsfrau*, 38. English translation: Franck, *The Blind Side of the Heart*, 32.

30 Selma does not seek to escape her daughters, nor does she believe that she can. On the contrary, she tells them: 'Wenn ich tot bin, werden wir uns wieder begegnen, wir werden verbunden sein. Es gibt kein Entrinnen' [When I'm dead we'll meet again, we'll be united. There's no escaping it]. This is somewhat similar to how Nelly discusses the weight of her children, although much more negative. Franck, *Die Mittagsfrau*, 38. English translation: Franck, *The Blind Side of the Heart*, 33.

31 Gilbert and Gubar, *The Madwoman in the Attic*, 360.

to free her mother. Yet she finds that she cannot. As a woman, without the permission of the male doctor, she is unable to take Selma home. Her frustration at her powerlessness increases, until Helene and Wilhelm are forced to leave. Behind them, they hear Selma expressing Helene's anger: 'Am Ende des Flurs hörten sie hinter sich ein gellendes Schreien. Es war nicht deutlich, ob es das Schreien eines Tieres oder eines Menschen war. ... [E]s konnte das Schreien ihrer Mutter gewesen sein' [At the end of the corridor she heard a shrill screech behind her. It wasn't clear whether it came from an animal or a human throat. ... It could have been her mother screaming].[32] Just as Selma's screams are indistinguishable from those of an animal, Jane Eyre refers to the 'bad animal' in her own nature, which, according to Gilbert and Gubar, Bertha embodies.[33]

Helene's frustration at her limitations is regularly aroused: as a child, when she exhausts the knowledge of her school teacher; as a teenager, when she feels that she will be trapped inside the house with her mad mother for the rest of her life; as a woman, when she wishes to study at the university but cannot, due to financial limitations; and as an expectant mother, when she desires to work again as a nurse but needs her husband's permission to do so. She is at all points of her life confined to a certain lifestyle by the fact that she is a woman, although her performative femininity is more subtle than that of many around her, such as Mrs Wertheimer and other selfless mothers, and such as her aunt Fanny and the other women in slinky dresses who seduce men. Once they marry, Wilhelm must instruct Helene on how to become a woman: 'Helene sollte nicht arbeiten, Wilhelm gab ihr Geld, sie kaufte ein und legte ihm die Kassenzettel auf den Tisch, sie kochte, sie wusch und bügelte, sie heizte' [And Helene wasn't to work; Wilhelm gave her housekeeping money, she did the shopping and put the bill on the table for him to see; she cooked, she washed and ironed clothes, she lit the stove].[34] Wilhelm likes the idea of having a wife (he begins to refer

---

32 Franck, *Die Mittagsfrau*, 326. English translation: Franck, *The Blind Side of the Heart*, 320.

33 Gilbert and Gubar, *The Madwoman in the Attic*, 359.

34 Franck, *Die Mittagsfrau*, 333. English translation: Franck, *The Blind Side of the Heart*, 327.

to Helene as his 'Heimchen', or 'little house wife') and expects nothing of her beyond that role.[35]

This becomes particularly clear when Wilhelm discovers that Helene is no longer a virgin, one of the most important parts of her role. During their first night as husband and wife, he assumes that he must teach her what to do. He does not know that Helene had slept with Carl many times, and he is shocked and repulsed when her experience becomes clear and she expresses both a will of her own and even some sexual excitement: 'Ein Tier bist du, ein richtiges Tier' [You're an animal, a real little animal]. He tries, by naming her, 'Meine Frau' [My wife], to make it true.[36] But he cannot reconcile her behaviour with his expectations of a virginal wife. When she deviates from his expectations, Wilhelm turns against Helene. Because she falls short of the role of wife, he treats her instead as a whore. For Wilhelm, 'wife' and 'whore' are binaries in the same way that 'masculine' and 'feminine' are.[37] Women must fit into one category or the other, and he expects Helene to play both roles to his standards. Once he regards her as a whore, he provides financial support in exchange for domestic chores and sexual availability. Wilhelm rapes Helene repeatedly throughout the course of their marriage, and, although she seems to become passive in the face of his brutality, her anger continues to grow.[38]

---

35   Franck, *Die Mittagsfrau*, 334. English translation: Franck, *The Blind Side of the Heart*, 328.

36   Franck, *Die Mittagsfrau*, 344. English translation: Franck, *The Blind Side of the Heart*, 338.

37   Some have criticized the character of Wilhelm for its lack of depth and dimension, such as Christoph Schröder, 'Das abgestorbene Innenleben', *Frankfurter Rundschau* (18 September 2007). Instead of seeing Wilhelm as a one-dimensional character, I believe that he is actually living up to his own standards of masculinity in the same way that he expects Helene to meet his standards of femininity. Noteworthy, for example, is the extent to which Wilhelm hides Helene's supposed failings from his colleagues and society in general.

38   Helene periodically expresses her anger, although it is quickly overshadowed by Wilhelm's violence. When he refuses to accept their son as his child, claiming that she must have slept with someone else, he nonetheless agrees to remain married to Helene and, to a limited extent, support her financially. Helene points out that his

This anger finds its expression when she is with Peter. After becoming pregnant against her will,[39] after desiring a daughter and having a son, after being abandoned by Wilhelm, who has begun to take jobs farther and farther away from their home, Helene is left with a young child to support as Germany stands on the brink of war. Her anger, which had mounted over years of trials, loss and frustration, is now directed at her son. She tries at all times to contain it. Rather than yell at him, she prefers to say nothing. When Peter, still very young, throws his food onto the floor, Helene struggles to control herself: 'Helene riss ihm den Löffel aus der Hand und hätte ihn am liebsten auf den Tisch geknallt, sie musste an ihre Mutter denken, das böse Funkeln in den Augen ihrer Mutter, die Unberechenbarkeit, Helene legte den Löffel auf den Tisch' [Helene snatched the spoon away from him and felt like banging it down on the table. She thought of her mother, the angry light in her eyes, her unpredictability. Helene laid the spoon gently on the table].[40] Seeing the connection between her behaviour and her mother's, trying to squash the 'bad animal' within her, Helene struggles for self-control. She is successful when she withdraws from Peter and avoids all emotion in his presence, speaking only when necessary. Her anger is still evident. When they are riding in a crowded train, Peter inadvertently causes his mother to stumble, provoking her fury: 'Niemals hätte sie aufgeschrien, sie knurrte nur widerwillig. ... Ihre Augen funkelten böse, Peter entschuldigte sich, doch die Mutter schien es nicht zu hören, ihr Mund blieb schmal verschlossen, sie drückte seine Hand von sich' [She would never have cried out, she just uttered a sound of annoyance. ... Her

---

gesture is not one of generosity but of fear, as Helene might reveal to party members that he obtained false papers for her. Her decision to stay with him is likely motivated by fear as well, as she is living and working with falsified papers.

39   Even on their wedding night, Helene is primarily concerned with preventing pregnancy. When Wilhelm begins to ask her about her sexual past, she misunderstands and assures him that it is possible to avoid conception. Wilhelm cannot understand why she would want to (344). This is another way in which Helene fails to live up to his expectations of femininity.

40   Franck, *Die Mittagsfrau*, 387. English translation: Franck, *The Blind Side of the Heart*, 381.

eyes were sparkling angrily, Peter said he was sorry, but his mother didn't seem to be listening; her mouth stayed closed, her lips were narrowed, she pushed his hand away].[41] As Peter grows older, it becomes more and more difficult for Helene to keep her feelings contained.

Her distance from her son comes from two connected causes: first, her attempt to control her emotions and, second, her gradual erasure of self. Both result in an increasing silence. Beginning with Carl's death, Helene feels less of a desire to speak. Once missing, their relationship, which had become such an integral part of her emotional and intellectual identity, leaves Helene without a sense of self. The only role that is appealing to her is that of the nurse, which provides her with distraction from her loss, some degree of anonymity (as nurses are all called 'Schwester' [sister] and wear the same uniform) and a sense of purpose or activity. Being allowed to adopt this role is of crucial importance to Helene. There is a sense that she marries Wilhelm only because he promises to secure false papers proving her non-Jewish heritage, which are necessary for her to continue working in the hospital.

Acquiring the papers means adopting a false name and history and experiencing further disconnection from her other selves and lives. Significantly, Wilhelm gives her the history of a childhood acquaintance, a young girl named Alice who had run away from home.[42] Already from the first time they meet, Wilhelm decides that Helene looked more like an 'Alice' than a 'Helene', and he insists on calling her Alice throughout their courtship. When they marry, she takes his last name and, effectively, a completely new identity: that of Frau Alice Sehmisch. Adopting a new identity means forsaking her old one, partly because of the danger inherent in having Jewish 'blood'. Consequently, she effectively loses her sister Martha and friend Leontine, both of whom have to correspond with Helene under pseudonyms, and who can correspond only with increasing difficulty

---

41 Franck, *Die Mittagsfrau*, 26. English translation: Franck, *The Blind Side of the Heart*, 20.

42 This story is pleasing to Helene, and she enjoys the idea of being someone who disappeared (331).

as more communication lines are broken during the war. While living as Frau Alice Sehmisch, Helene also learns that her mother has died, further severing ties between the identities of Helene and Alice. During this time Helene notices that she speaks less and less, communicating only briefly with Wilhelm or with shop clerks in the town (362). Silence increasingly becomes her only option, as she must withhold any incriminating personal information from those around her. As Alice, she forms no connections with other people, avoiding even the company of the other nurses.

When Peter is born, Helene does feel love for him. In the hospital she already experiences her first moment of intimacy with her son (376). Yet, as he grows older and begins to ask questions, she finds that she cannot answer them. When he is only about three years old, he asks his mother where she is all day when he is at day care. She says she is working, but she is not able to explain more. Because she cannot think of an appropriate lie and because she is not able to share with him the unpleasant truth about what she does all day (Helene is haunted by images of her patients and their suffering when she comes home from work), she does not say anything (383–4). In another scene, Helene overhears Peter singing an anti-Semitic rhyme, and she reprimands him for it. Yet she cannot reprimand him too harshly, as it would put them both in danger if Peter spoke out publicly against such rhymes (401). Nor can she explain to him why it is particularly hurtful for her to hear her son singing such a song. He cannot know the truth about her own Jewish background, and that is only a fraction of what he does not know about his mother. For Helene, intimacy is bound with the ability to speak. As she retreats into herself, she becomes less able to talk about herself and therefore to form connections with others, including Peter. So, too, is her emotional rejection of Peter related to the different identities that she must perform – or must not perform. Peter, as with all of the children in Franck's texts, only knows about his mother what he can see. In this case he cannot know about Helene's other identities (sister, daughter, nurse, lover), none of which she performs in his presence and most of which she has given up.

Maternal Drag

According to Marianne Hirsch's theory, put forth in *The Mother/Daughter Plot*, anger is at odds with the maternal. There is a fear of maternal anger, Hirsch contends, and she cites Medea as the most common example of the danger inherent in it.[43] Medea is dangerous precisely because, in her anger, she ceases to be a mother and instead becomes a lover seeking revenge. It is not a coincidence that Helene's anger grows as the novel approaches its end. The closest thing to an outburst of anger from her is the rage that Peter witnesses in her moments before she leaves him at the train station. In other words, as Helene becomes angry, she ceases to be a mother. Just like her other identities, Helene's identity as a mother is performative as well. And, just as she had ceased to perform her other identities, she ceases to perform 'mother', too.

This is precisely what is scandalous and controversial about *Die Mittagsfrau*: that Helene simply ceases to perform (seemingly ceases to be) 'mother'. This conclusion conflicts violently with the popular Western conception of the maternal. Indeed, this idea is so difficult to comprehend that I have seen no publication or media report of the book that considers the possibility. Some dismiss Helene as a bad mother, an unforgivable mother, but always a mother. Others consider her a selfless mother, one who trusts that Peter would have a better life anywhere except at her side.[44] Any solution is sought that leaves the institution of motherhood intact, because it is easier to condemn a mother than to dismantle the institu-

---

43   Hirsch, *The Mother/Daughter Plot*, 170–1.
44   Even Franck, who tries to leave all interpretations open, seems to suggest that this interpretation is likely. She was cited in an article as having said: 'Als die Frau, die nicht mehr lebt, sondern nur noch überlebt, mit ihrem Sohn kein Gespräch mehr führen kann, meint sie zu erkennen, dass das Kind es überall besser habe als bei ihr' [When the woman who is no longer living but only surviving can no longer have a conversation with her son, she thinks that she realizes that her child would be better off everywhere else than with her]. Martin Whittmann, 'Ausgesetzt: Julia Franck liest aus ihrem Buch *Die Mittagsfrau*', *Frankfurter Allgemeine Zeitung* (24 September 2007).

tion of motherhood. In *Die Mittagsfrau* the reader meets many women who represent points along the spectrum from selfless to selfish mothers. While readers with a feminist perspective can criticize mothers like Mrs Wertheimer, who has no stable identity after the death of her son, such women are ultimately more sympathetic than those such as Selma, who abuse and neglect their own children. But even Selma seems 'better' than Helene, because Selma's depression and madness are ostensibly – or at least possibly – caused by the deaths of her four sons. 'Die Mutter sei am Herzen erblindet' [her heart had gone blind] Martha says about Selma, effectively excusing her behaviour.[45] To attempt to claim the same thing about Helene points more to the sanctity of motherhood than the awareness of Helene's suffering. In other words, it continues to find fault with individual women rather than question the institution of motherhood itself.

What Franck demonstrates in her novels is that, just as her characters perform a variety of identities, so too do they perform 'mother.' Butler argues that anyone who identifies or is identified as female is aspiring to perform a femininity for which there is no original. Women who have given birth to children aspire or are pressured to meet expectations of motherhood, which is also a copy of a copy, for which there is no original. That Helene fails as a mother has more to do with the reader's expectations of mother-hood than with Helene's inability to care for her child. Outwardly she does what a mother is supposed to do: feed and clothe her child, tuck him in at night, talk to him and do things with him. Yet the reader, even before Helene abandons Peter, has criticized if not condemned her mothering.

Helene's performance of the maternal is so empty that it becomes parodic. The clothing and outward markers of motherhood do not fit her. For example, when a stranger on a bus compliments Helene on her son, she not only does not experience pleasure, but she avoids the conversation altogether. The woman says that she should be proud, but 'Helene empfand keinen Stolz. Warum sollte sie stolz darauf sein, dass sie ein Kind hatte? Peter gehörte ihr nicht, sie hatte ihn geboren, aber er war nicht ihr Eigentum und nicht ihre Errungenschaft' [Helene did not feel

---

45 Franck, *Die Mittagsfrau*, 119. English translation: Franck, *The Blind Side of the Heart*, 114.

proud. Why should she feel proud of having a child? Peter didn't belong to her, she had given birth to him but he was not her property, not her own great achievement].[46] Helene's response here sharply contradicts popular expectations of motherhood. It is clear that she is not 'doing' motherhood convincingly. To connect Helene's failed performative identity to drag, consider this quotation from Judith Butler: 'If one thinks that one sees a man dressed as a woman or a woman dressed as a man, then one takes the first term of each of those perceptions as the "reality" of gender: the gender that is introduced through the simile lacks "reality," and is taken to constitute an illusory appearance.'[47] In other words, just as men's clothing on a woman is identified as out of place, so maternity seems incorrect on someone who does not fit expectations of the maternal. Furthermore, the disconnect produced in this conflict between the 'reality' and the 'simile' highlights the performative quality of 'reality'.

Drag simultaneously depends on and challenges certain assumptions, namely, what is feminine and what is masculine. Franck constructs motherhood in her works so that it functions in a similar way: at the same time that it relies on general expectations of mothering (e.g. in order to identify Helene as a bad mother), it undermines the very assumptions upon which the judgments of good and bad mothering are based. The question in Julia Franck's works is not what is a good mother or what is a bad mother, which depends on an identity as socially constructed as 'male' or 'female'. Instead, the question is: how is the maternal performed? At the end of Franck's novels the reader must contend with a litany of maternal figures, some of whom, such as Nelly and Helene, fail to meet society's expectations of mothers. Other figures, such as Madame, insist on performing the maternal, although they fail to meet other prerequisites of maternal identity (i.e. a biological or legal connection to the child being mothered). Taken together, these figures question and undermine simple definitions of motherhood. Just as gender identity has been destabilized, so, too, has maternal identity.

---

46   Franck, *Die Mittagsfrau*, 385. English translation: Franck, *The Blind Side of the Heart*, 379.
47   Butler, *Gender Trouble*, xxiii.

Fathers and Sons: Absent Fathers, Sisters and Siblings, and Looking for Home

Franck's works of fiction demonstrate an interest in interrogating gender roles and gendered expectations for women in the workplace, in public and private spaces and in family life. This is not to say that Franck's characters have moved beyond gender, nor that she treats them in a gender-neutral manner. While the mothers in these texts tend to be 'bad' mothers or women who in some way challenge the expectations of motherhood, the fathers are typically absent, weak or ineffectual, creating a strong sense of matriarchy in these family histories.[1] This book has focused on mothers and daughters, but sons are increasingly prominent in Franck's later books. They tend to be more sensitive and greatly affected by negative social and familial developments. Two of these male children are also brothers who function crucially for their sisters' growth. This chapter, while far from a thorough investigation, provides an overview of the fathers, sons and brothers, while pointing towards scholarship on Franck's oeuvre that remains to be done.

1   Valerie Heffernan uses the concept of *historia matria*, or maternal history, to theo-rize the strongly matrilineal narratives in Franck's works that take place against the backdrop of German history. Valerie Heffernan, 'Julia Franck, *Die Mittagsfrau*: *Historia Matria* and Matrilineal Narrative', in Lyn Marven and Stuart Taberner, eds, *Emerging German-Language Novelists of the Twenty-First Century*, Studies in German Literature, Linguistics and Culture (Rochester, NY: Camden House, 2011), 148–61.

Fathers

Fathers figure less prominently than mothers in these texts, partially – and crucially – because they are largely absent. There are several ways in which one can speak of the absence of the fathers, and one paternal character can be absent in more than one way. First, they disappear from the narrative, as in the case of 'Der Hausfreund'. In this short story, the father's cameo is brief, yet he remains a primary object of the narrator's affection. As she leaves the apartment with her mother, she thinks that she would gladly stay at home with her father.[2] She thinks of him again at the story's end, when she is sure that he will be worried about their absence, and the idea of him becomes synonymous with normalcy. A second type of absence is that caused by death, such as in *Lagerfeuer*. Despite the physical absence of Wassilij Batalow, Nelly's former lover and father of her children, he is very much present in the children's thoughts. When Aleksej is in the hospital after his accident, he asks his mother whether he is dead like his father, and he expresses anxiety about the idea that his father has the ability to live on through his children.[3] A third type of absence is that of the ineffectual father: one who (for a time, at least) remains in his daughter's life in a limited or altogether unsuccessful capacity. The father of the narrator in *Der neue Koch* is absent in this way, having left his family when the narrator was only five years old. The narrator claims that she does not know where he is and implies that she does not care. Although she does not mention him again after the opening pages of the novel, she lives with the painting of him hanging above the reception desk, a regular reminder that he has failed her as a father.[4] The fathers with the most profound impact are those who are absent in more than one sense.

This paternal failure features prominently in four works: *Liebediener*, *Die Mittagsfrau*, *Rücken an Rücken* and the short story 'Streuselschnecke'.

---

2   Franck, 'Der Hausfreund', 87.
3   Franck, *Lagerfeuer*, 163–4.
4   Franck, *Der neue Koch*, 9–10.

In all four the protagonists lose the father (each through death) without having ever achieved the closeness that they desired. In *Liebediener* Beyla feigns disregard for her father. She insists that she barely had a father whose absence she can now miss.[5] Because she made similar and false statements about her mother and even Charlotte, one can assume that this is also disingenuous. The reader finds further proof of her father's significance in the course of the novel. Through her relationship with Albert, with whom her father shared some common characteristics (e.g. both were musicians), Beyla finds herself reliving her relationship with her dad. At first small details trigger memories. For example, she hears Albert playing the piano and identifies the piece as one that her father enjoyed. Other memories being to overwhelm her, and the reader learns more about Beyla's complex paternal relationship: he had affairs with numerous women, he at times flew into rages, drank and became violent. The reader learns that Beyla had not seen her father for three years before he died but that she attended his funeral, hoping, for one last time, to feel close to him. Instead, she was struck by the performative quality of her role as daughter at the funeral, and she observed herself adopting the role of the mourning daughter. She found the role difficult to assume: 'an mir konnte ich nichts Töchterliches entdecken' [I couldn't detect anything daughterly about myself], she says, other than her biological connection to the deceased (28). The emotional connection she expects father and daughter to have is lacking between them.

In the course of the novel Beyla reveals more information to the reader about her relationship with her father (although it would be inaccurate to think that the reader approaches the 'truth' about this relationship). This is partially because Albert and her father become increasingly conflated in her mind, and thoughts of one often lead to thoughts of the other. At the novel's end Albert cries when Beyla leaves him, reminding her of her father's tears of regret and apology after his regular outbursts of rage (218). The relationship patterns that she learned with her father also apply to her relationship with Albert. For example, her father would hit her when he

5   Franck, *Liebediener*, 29.

was angry, and Beyla always tried to hide his abuse (125). Eventually her brothers contacted a child services organization, and she and her brothers were taken away from their father, an act that Beyla understands as betrayal. She extends this to her romantic life and believes it is inevitable that Albert will betray her (i.e. by hiding his 'true' identity from her). In Beyla's mind, one must love someone unconditionally, despite abuse, despite secrecy, despite lies. In this sense, deciding to leave Albert is her betrayal of him, as well.

In *Die Mittagsfrau* Helene's father, Ernst Ludwig Würsich, demonstrates another failed paternal performance. He is so preoccupied with love for Selma that he barely notices his daughters. When he is with his wife, even his manner of speaking changes. Instead of limiting his communication to matter-of-fact sentences, as he does with Helene, Ernst uses terms of endearment.[6] He seems almost unaware that he has a paternal role to play. When Helene's teacher speaks with both parents about Helene's remarkable intelligence, Ernst is friendly and polite but defers to his wife. As Selma feels no love towards her daughter, she of course makes no effort to praise or encourage her. Even when Helene begins to help her father with the accounts in his printing shop, he recognizes neither her ability nor her hard work, unwilling or perhaps unable to do so. Instead, she only hears him muttering to himself when she makes a mistake (55).

Both Helene and Martha are unflaggingly loyal to him, however, and they are drawn to him, likely because he is infinitely more gentle and patient than their mother. Helene for example loves it when her father pets her like he pets his dog (139). (The reference to Ernst's dog, Baldo, is not an insult, as he loves his dog more than anyone except Selma.) Helene spends her childhood seeking validation from her father, yet she never receives the love, encouragement or even approval from him that she so desperately seeks. After her father goes off to war (World War I), the distance between them grows. Seriously injured after only a few weeks away from home, Helene's father remains in the hospital, unable to find a way back to Bautzen until two years after the war's end. When he returns, he

6   Franck, *Die Mittagsfrau*, 68.

is too ill to speak often, although Helene continues to talk to him. She begins to address him with the formal 'Sie', unable to dissolve the distance between them (103–4). Ernst becomes a mute and unresponsive shell, a kind of paternal altar at which his daughters demonstrate their devotion. After some time under their diligent care, he dies. The daughters grieve for him properly and respectfully, but neither Martha nor Helene mentions him again in the novel. The primary relationship constellations remain centred on Selma or on Martha. Although Helene was determined to love her father, this failed connection is only one of many blows that she suffers on her path to adulthood.

The biological father of the two child narrators in *Rücken an Rücken* is almost completely unknown to them, having died shortly after they were born, at the end of World War II. Denied love and gentleness by their mother, Ella and Thomas console each other with the image of their painter father. Ella claims to remember him, and she regularly narrates the memory of seeing him, on leave from the army, climbing a hill to where Käthe was living with the children, and then lifting Ella into the air in his happiness to see her again. Telling the story becomes a ritual, and especially Ella is attached to these memories: 'Sie liebte den toten Vater, und der war leicht zu lieben' [She loved her dead father, and he was easy to love].[7] Several years later when sexual abuse has driven Ella to the brink of madness, she tells Thomas that she made all these stories up. Instead she says that she only remembers her parents closing the children out of the house. Ella banged on the door, and both the children screamed, but their parents ignored their cries (131).[8] Regardless of the factual truth of this scene, it expresses well the children's feeling of being shut out and denied parental love.

Of the four stories in which the father–daughter relationship figures prominently, 'Streuselschnecke' is the most optimistic about the

---

7   Franck, *Rücken an Rücken*, 46.
8   This scene is reminiscent of the narrator of 'Der Hausfreund', banging on the bedroom door when Thorsen and her mother close the narrator and her sister out of the room.

possibility of forming an intimate attachment between father and daughter.[9] Intimacy, however, is cut short in this story by the father's early death. In spite of the story's concision, the subtleties of the relationship are no less pronounced. In just two pages, the fourteen-year-old narrator tells of meeting an unidentified man who calls to ask 'ob ich ihn kennenlernen wolle' [if I want to get to know him] and charts the progression of their relationship, which is ambiguous and seems to be sexually charged (51). Franck uses the reader's associations with stories such as *Lolita* to create dramatic tension, and the actual relationship (estranged father and daughter) is not revealed until the last sentence. It is clear that a connection is slowly growing between the two until the father is hospitalized three years later with a terminal illness. He confesses his fear of dying and asks his daughter for assistance in acquiring morphine, with the intent of quickening or easing his death. This gesture of intimacy is overwhelming to the narrator, who fears getting caught, worries about procuring the drug and likely does not want to hasten her father's demise. Thus, despite the depth of emotion that motivated her father's question, the narrator avoids it; she does not answer when he questions her about the morphine but asks instead whether he would like anything to eat (52). Her father requests *Streuselschnecken*, seeming to tacitly acknowledge her mixed emotions.[10] In a quixotic gesture of love and apology, she bakes two cookies sheets full of *Streuselschnecken* and brings them to the hospital still warm. In response, her father tells her that he would have enjoyed living with her, that he would have liked to try it, but time runs out (52). While it seems likely that the father and daughter of this story would have continued to develop a relationship (perhaps not without its problems), the narrator is deprived of this opportunity. Again, this absence is on more than one level: first, the father never assumed a parental role in the life of the narrator and, second, death prevents him

---

9   Julia Franck, 'Streuselschnecke', *Bauchlandung: Geschichten zum Anfassen* (Cologne: DuMont Buchverlag, 2000), 51–2.

10 *Streuselschnecken* are rolls of pastry dough cut into disks and covered in streusel topping, similar to an American danish pastry.

from doing so in the future. As we have seen with all the examples thus far, the father is a father in name only. He is the biological progenitor of the protagonist(s), but he falls short of fulfilling any of the expectations that society has of fathers.

From even this brief survey of the father figures in Franck's works, it should be clear that they fail to meet expectations of the paternal, just as the mothers fail to meet expectations of the maternal. In this failure, they highlight the performativity of the paternal role. Beyla, reflecting on her role as a daughter, points to the discrepancy between what one thinks of as a father and how her father behaved. These fathers, however, do not simply fail to live up to expectations; they fail so spectacularly that their characters are parodic. It is quite possible to speak of paternal drag with respect to Franck's works.

This is different from maternal drag. Mothers parody motherhood, and fathers parody fatherhood. The fathers are caricatures or types of fathers: the abusive alcoholic, the one who ran out on his wife and child, and the husband who takes no interest in his children. Similarly, the mothers fall into their own types: the madwoman in the attic, the single mother trying to care for her children, the sexualized (and thus less maternal) mother and the mother who abandons her child(ren). These identities, however, are neither interchangeable nor gender-neutral. There are no abusive alcoholic mothers or madmen in the attic. Some actions, such as abandoning children, seem applicable to both parents at first glance. For example, Helene abandons Peter in *Die Mittagsfrau*, and Hans, the only father to narrate in Franck's works, has abandoned his pregnant girlfriend in the East. A crucial difference, however, is the greater censure that falls on the mothers than on the fathers, either from characters within the texts or from the texts' readers. A father who abandons his child may be pardonable: Hans did not know that his girlfriend was expecting their baby. But a mother who abandons her child is considered monstrous.

Sons

One might also ask whether 'daughter' and 'son' are performative identities similar to 'mother' and 'father', or whether children are treated in a gender-neutral manner in Franck's works. Up to the publication of *Rücken an Rücken*, the answer to this question was complicated by the fact that daughters feature much more prominently in these texts than do sons. In general, it does seem that sons have different experiences than daughters. For example, Beyla's brothers are married and have children, while she remains single. Nelly's relationship to Aleksej in *Lagerfeuer* is much less antagonistic than her relationship to her daughter Katja. None of these male characters narrates his own story, however, which limits the representation of the mother–son relationship to being told from the mother's perspective. Before Thomas's chapters in *Rücken an Rücken*, only the prologue and epilogue of *Die Mittagsfrau* and Hans' chapters in *Lagerfeuer* were narrated by a son. Both of these sons were abandoned by their mothers, and, hurt and unable to understand this, both sons reject their mothers out of hand. Even Peter, when Helene tries to meet him nearly ten years later, refuses to see her.

The sons in Franck's texts are usually children, and the most recent is Thomas, the younger sibling of Ella in *Rücken an Rücken*. Both suffer from the emotional neglect of their mother and the absence of their father, but their responses indicate – again – that their experiences are shaped by their gender. Ella seeks refuge in detaching emotions from sexual relationships, as both a result and means of surviving her sexual abuse. She has no friends; her attitude towards male suitors is nearly emotionless; and she oscillates between affection and rage towards Käthe and even Thomas, with whom she is closest. Thomas does not experience love from Käthe, but it is clear to both siblings that he is the favoured child. The time that he spends modelling for her sculptures affords him greater interaction with his mother. While she does not (will not, or maybe even cannot) get to know him, she gives him advice and assistance to help him thrive in the socialist society of fledgling East Germany.

Thomas is unable to resign himself to what he perceives as his limited opportunities there, despite his desire to please his mother and sister. Käthe, who is focused on his career, dismisses his interest in writing as bourgeois and wants him to develop his talent in metallurgy. In her mind, only a future in the service of the state is of any value. Ella is not at all interested in politics and only wants to escape her mother's home and the abuse she suffers there. Because of Ella's intensely negative sexual experiences, Thomas is horrified by his own sexuality. Nearly until his death, he represses it. In both his private and public life he is dominated and inhibited by the strong-willed women in his family. He appeals to his uncle who is living in New York but receives no help from him either. Marie, a nurse at the hospital where Thomas is interning, feels equally trapped in her situation. While divorce would allow her to leave her abusive husband, he would then withhold her child. She says to Thomas: 'Ohne mein Kind kann ich nicht leben. Mit meinem Mann nicht, und ohne dich nicht' [I can't live without my child. Not with my husband, and not without you].[11] Together they plan to escape through death.

In *Rücken an Rücken*, Thomas is a lightning rod that conducts the intensity of the charged political and personal situations. He diverts the danger away from his family, Ella and Käthe. Both women are blind, perhaps wilfully so: Ella refuses to acknowledge the political events unfolding around her, and Käthe only sees socialism in its ideal (and unreal) form. Thomas cannot look away, and he cannot perform the socially prescribed roles necessary to successfully weather this storm. At the same time, he cannot (or will not) abandon the roles of 'son' and 'brother'. When Käthe describes his options as staying or leaving, he asks, 'Um euch nur noch alle paar Jahre zu sehen?' [To see you only every couple years?] Defeated, he concludes, 'Das kann ich nicht. Ich will euch nicht verlassen' [I can't do that. I don't want to leave you] (150). Unlike his sister, he does not have the ability to emotionally distance herself from a situation to survive it. And unlike his sister, he is well aware of his attachment to his family.

11   Franck, *Rücken an Rücken*, 345.

Home?

For Thomas, East Germany is not home, but Ella and Käthe are. He feels much more of a connection to the people than to the spaces that they inhabit, but he does assert his presence in their house as well: he knows the plants in the garden and the path from the house to the lake, he spends hours modelling for his mother in the atelier, he has scrubbed the kitchen top to bottom and he reclaims the tenant's room for his own. There he paints the walls black, Ella spills paint on the rug, and Thomas and his friend Michael use a small pistol to shoot holes into the picture of Erich Honecker hanging on the wall. This room is where he spends time with Marie. In the atelier he has the longest conversations with his mother. And he is with Ella all over the house. This building, although at times full of tension and arguments, is a place and a home for Thomas.

Not every typically domestic space in Franck's works becomes a home. Beyla's cellar apartments are filled with memories of her unhappy childhood. Her new apartment (Charlotte's) is a home and the locus of connection with Mrs Wolf at the very least. Helene's childhood home in *Die Mittagsfrau* is a place from which she and her sister long to escape. She does not feel comfortable or welcome in her aunt Fanny's apartment. Instead, she feels most at home in Carl's small apartment that smells like him and is full of books. When she later marries Wilhelm, she makes their residences clean and comfortable, but their physical characteristics cannot compensate for her unhappiness and the abuse that she suffers there. The narrator of *Der neue Koch* feels tension between the hotel as a place of business and the hotel as her home. Ultimately, though perhaps unexpectedly, she does think of it as her home, largely because of the extent to which it is connected with memories of her mother. Blunt and Dowling define home as 'both a place/physical location *and* a set of feelings', which in an ideal form can include comfort (physical and emotional), security, attachment and connectedness. While places are not necessarily homes, the fantasy of home is of home as a place. The most unhappy of Franck's characters are those who do not feel at home and are those without connections to other people.

The bond between siblings serves as an anchor for many of Franck's protagonists; the loneliest characters in her oeuvre are the only children, such as the narrator of *Der neue Koch*, Peter from *Die Mittagsfrau*, Nelly in *Lagerfeuer* and narrators of the short stories in *Bauchlandung*. Beyla is not an only child, but she is not close to her brothers and fantasizes about having had a sister.[12] When she moves into Charlotte's apartment and gradually adopts elements of her life, she thinks about her with growing fondness, to the point that she imagines a sisterly relationship between them. Because she is such an unreliable narrator, it remains challenging to determine how close the two women were before Charlotte's death. Beyla insists that she did not know Charlotte well, but the reader gradually learns that Beyla was familiar with details regarding her clothing, job, family history, friends and behaviour. Mrs Wolf also insists that Charlotte spoke of Beyla frequently (55). The longer that she lives in Charlotte's apartment, the more strongly she feels a connection to her. Using and living among her possessions is part of this, but Beyla also develops feelings of guilt towards Charlotte regarding her relationship with Albert. Her dreams reveal the extent to which these thoughts bother her (71). At the end of the novel, when Albert and Beyla's relationship has fallen apart, she continues to think about Charlotte, choreographing a clowning routine of the accident that caused her death. If Charlotte can be considered the primary object of Beyla's interest and even longing, then Albert is merely an intermediary or a means of getting closer to her lost friend.

The narrator of 'Bäuchlings' similarly desires to be close to her sister Luise, to the point of wanting to meld with her. Anke Biendarra sees this as the narrator wanting to be like her sister. To an extent, she interprets the narrator's desire as the desire to model her behaviour on Luise's 'emotional and sexual independence, a desire that culminates in the fantasy of slipping into her sister's body.'[13] I disagree that the narrator wants to emulate her

---

12   Franck, *Liebediener*, 95.
13   Biendarra, 'Gen(d)eration Next', 216.

sister. Instead, I understand the narrator's efforts as attempts to get as close as she can to Luise, to get inside her skin if possible. She does this by two means: wearing her clothing, as discussed in Chapter 1, and flirting with Luise's boyfriend Olek. The narrator's attempt to perform Luise is to gain insight into her experiences and access to her perspective, which extends to fantasizing about being Luise having sex with Olek. It is not Olek that is the object of the narrator's desire, but Luise. Franck has described him as 'eine Bande (wie im Poolbillard)' [a tie (like in pool)] that connects the separate spheres – in this case, the sisters.[14]

This fantasy is so successful in blurring any distinction between Luise and the narrator that it is unclear at times what is fantasy and what is reality, whether Luise is having sex with Olek or whether the narrator is. Yet the fantasy is curtailed by the corporeal inevitability of the narrator's body: 'Ich stelle mir vor, wie er hinter Luise steht … und wie er ihr Kleid hochschiebt und in sie stößt … und ich sehe ihre Locken in seinen Händen, die Locken, die plötzlich schwarz und meine sind' [I imagine how he stands behind Luise … and how he hitches up her dress and thrusts into her … and I see her curls in his hands, the curls that are suddenly black and mine].[15] Despite the fluidity of the narrator's psychic identity, the physicality of her body, separate and distinct from Luise's, ultimately keeps the two sisters apart, perhaps indicating a limit to performativity in Franck's texts.

Other sibling pairs exist in Franck's works: Katja and Aleksej in *Lagerfeuer*, Helene and Martha in *Die Mittagsfrau* and of course Ella and Thomas in *Rücken an Rücken*. Common to all of them is an extremely strong attachment. Even when the siblings consider themselves on good terms with other family members (such as Katja and Aleksej), it is clear that they understand each other better than others understand them. When Aleksej is beaten up, for example, Katja knows with which stuffed animal to comfort him and sings to him in a maternal way, out-performing their mother Nelly. Ella and Thomas care for each other even as children:

14   Franck, 'Re: Ihre Frage'.
15   Franck, 'Bäuchlings', 14.

Ella goes into the basement for Thomas, knowing that he is afraid of the dark, and when she falls down the stairs he cleans and bandages her scrapes. Helene and Martha are farthest apart in age, and, as a result, Martha's attitude towards Helene is at times as maternal as sisterly. Even after they drift apart during their time in Berlin and lose track of each other during the war, Helene sets out to find her after she has abandoned Peter: clearly Martha is more important to her than anyone.

Although these relationships are not completely harmonious, they are critically important both to the characters and taken as a whole. When fathers are absent and mothers fail to provide the requisite emotional support, siblings provide each other with support and love. Even Käthe's nearly feral twin girls, who were raised by foster parents and whom Thomas and Ella barely know, have each other. It is notable that no siblings in Franck's oeuvre turn against each other, although parents and children, lovers and even friends disappoint and betray each other. Perhaps siblings are the source of unconditional love and security associated with an idealized version of home. Based on Franck's texts, this relationship seems stronger and more important than any other. It also functions differently from 'mother' and 'father' in that it does not seem to be so easily adopted and discarded, and it does not conflict with other performative identities the way that, for example, 'mother' and 'lover' do. This privileged relationship remains to be explored in future scholarship on Franck.

Conclusion

This book has shown that the identities of Franck's characters, shifting as they are and further destabilized by their contingency on place, are performative. This performativity extends to many identities in Franck's oeuvre, including the identities 'daughter' and 'mother'. Just as Judith Butler has shown that one 'does' one's gender identity, just as Katrin Sieg has observed the performance of ethnicity, so, too, have I theorized the performativity of the maternal. This raises the question: what about fathers? If we accept the performativity of motherhood, which is connected with Butler's destabilization of gender, then fatherhood, too, must be performative. While the paternal is also performative, even parodic in the sense of maternal drag, Franck's works do not move beyond gender. She interrogates the gendered roles of 'mother' and 'father' and destabilizes them, but her characters, which exist in a society familiar to our own, are not gender neutral.

Home also remains gendered, and domestic spaces are still more commonly associated with women than with men. This puts the pressure on women to create homely spaces, while men have fewer such expectations placed upon them. Women are still typically thought of as the primary caretakers, and fathering is generally understood to be different from mothering. Scholars have argued for the shift away from mothering and fathering to *parenting*, and, as Franck's texts indicate, this shift is by no means complete. But there is progress. Blunt and Dowling argue: 'Moreover, home is a *process* of creating and understanding forms of dwelling and belonging. ... What home means and how it is materially manifest are continually created and re-created through everyday home-making practices, which are themselves tied to spatial imaginaries of home.'[16] Reminiscent of Judith Butler's theorization of gender as a process, this remarkable conclusion means that home must be imagined – and can be reimagined in new configurations and unlikely settings. In other words, just as 'mother' and 'father' can be resignified, so too can 'home'.

Feminist geography is opening up the theorization of home in ways that echo Nancy Chodorow's call for gender-neutral parenting. Blunt and Dowling point to co-housing as one way to reimagine domestic space, which 'involves unsettling the normative assumption that an "ideal" home is one inhabited by a nuclear family and rather suggests ways in which people can live in more collaborative, collective or cooperative ways.'[17] The feminist appeal of this configuration is shared domestic work (of cleaning, cooking and childcare), and the human appeal is shared experience and emotional

16   Blunt and Dowling, *Home*, 254.
17   Blunt and Dowling, *Home*, 262.

support. One can speak about the domestic arrangements in *Der neue Koch*, *Lagerfeuer* and even *Rücken an Rücken* as a kind of co-housing: the residents elect to share spaces, responsibilities and lives with each other, to some extent independent of familial relationships. In Franck's texts, nuclear families rarely exist, and families in any form do not guarantee the fantasy of bonding and connection that is related to the idea of home. New interpretations of family might be necessary for creating home in the non-places of supermodernity.

Bibliography

Adelson, Leslie A., *Making Bodies, Making History: Feminism and German Identity*, Modern German Culture and Literature (Lincoln: University of Nebraska Press, 1993).

Adorján, Johanna, 'Mädchenhaft brav', *Frankfurter Allgemeine Zeitung* (30 March 2008).

Allen, Virginia M., *The Femme Fatale: Erotic Icon* (Troy, NY: The Whitston Publishing Company, 1983).

Augé, Marc, *Non-Places: Introduction to an Anthropology of Supermodernity*, tr. John Howe (New York: Verso, 1995).

Baer, Hester, 'Frauenliteratur "After Feminism": Rereading Contemporary Women's Writing', in Mark W. Rectanus, ed., *Über Gegenwartsliteratur: Interpretationen – Kritiken – Interventionen: Festschrift für Paul Michael Lützeler zum 65. Geburtstag* (Bielefeld: Aisthesis Verlag, 2008), 69–85.

—— 'Introduction: Resignifications of Feminism in Contemporary Germany', *Studies in Twentieth and Twenty-First Century Literature* 35/1 (Winter 2011), 8–17.

Bagley, Petra M., *Somebody's Daughter: The Portrayal of Daughter-Parent Relationships by Contemporary Women Writers from German-Speaking Countries*, Stuttgarter Arbeiten zur Germanistik (Stuttgart: Verlag Hans-Dieter Heinz, 1996).

Baier, Uta, '"Die Mittagsfrau": Wie die Generation der um 1970 Geborenen nach ihren Wurzeln sucht', *Die Welt* (19 November 2007).

Bailey, Cathryn, 'Unpacking the Mother/Daughter Baggage: Reassessing Second- and Third-Wave Tensions', *Women's Studies Quarterly* 30/3–4 (2002), 138–54.

Bammer, Angelika, 'Feminism, *Frauenliteratur*, and Women's Writing of the 1970s and 1980s' in Jo Catling, ed., *A History of Women's Writing in Germany, Austria and Switzerland* (Cambridge: Cambridge University Press, 2000), 216–32.

Bartel, Heike, and Elizabeth Boa, eds, *Pushing at Boundaries: Approaches to Contemporary German Women Writers from Karen Duve to Jenny Erpenbeck* (New York: Rodopi, 2006).

Bauer, Michael, 'Liebe in den Zeiten von Tralala', *Süddeutsche Zeitung* (10 November 1999).

Beauvoir, Simone de, *The Second Sex*, tr. H. M. Parshley (New York: Vintage Books, 1989).

Beck-Gernsheim, Elisabeth, *Die Kinderfrage heute: Über Frauenleben, Kinderwunsch und Geburtenrückgang* (Munich: Verlag C. H. Beck, 2006).

—— *Reinventing the Family: In Search of New Lifestyles*, tr. Patrick Camiller (Cambridge: Polity, 2002).

Bell, Shannon, *Reading, Writing, and Rewriting the Prostitute Body* (Bloomington: Indiana University Press, 1994).

Ben-Ze'ev, Aaron, *The Subtlety of Emotions* (Cambridge, MA: The MIT Press, 2000).

Benjamin, Jessica, *The Bonds of Love: Psychoanalysis, Feminism, and the Problem of Domination* (New York: Pantheon Books, 1988).

—— *Like Subjects, Love Objects: Essays on Recognition and Sexual Difference* (New Haven, CT: Yale University Press, 1995).

—— *Shadow of the Other: Intersubjectivity and Gender in Psychoanalysis* (New York: Routledge, 1998).

Bennets, Leslie, *The Feminine Mistake* (New York: Hyperion, 2007).

Beutel, Carolin, 'Berlin feiert Beauvoir', *Die Berliner Literaturkritik* (10 March 2008).

Biendarra, Anke S., 'Gen(d)eration Next: Prose by Julia Franck and Judith Hermann', *Studies in Twentieth and Twenty-First Century Literature* 28/1 (2004), 211–39.

Blunt, Alison, and Robyn Dowling, *Home*, Key Ideas in Geography (New York: Routledge, 2006).

Blunt, Alison, and Ann Varley, 'Geographies of Home: An Introduction', *Cultural Geographies* 11 (2004), 3–6.

Bort, Julie, Aviva Pflock and Devra Renner, *Mommy Guilt: Learn to Worry Less, Focus on What Matters Most, and Raise Happier Kids* (New York: American Management Association, 2005).

Bovenschen, Silvia, 'Is There a Feminine Aesthetic?', in Gisela Ecker, ed., *Feminist Aesthetics* (Boston: Beacon Press, 1985), 23–50.

—— *Über-Empfindlichkeit: Spielformen der Idiosynkrasie* (Frankfurt am Main: Suhrkamp, 2000).

Brockmann, Stephen, 'Berlin as the Literary Capital of German Unification', in Stuart Taberner, ed., *Contemporary German Fiction: Writing in the Berlin Republic*, Cambridge Studies in German (Cambridge: Cambridge University Press, 2007), 39–55.

Brunswick, Ruth Mack, 'The Preoedipal Phase of the Libido Development', in Robert Fliess, ed., *The Psychoanalytic Reader: An Anthology of Essential Papers with Critical Introductions* (New York: International Universities Press, 1940), 231–53.

Bude, Heinz, *Generation Berlin* (Berlin: Merve Verlag, 2001).

Bullough, Vern L., and Bonnie Bullough, *Cross Dressing, Sex, and Gender* (Philadelphia: University of Pennsylvania Press, 1993).

Butler, Judith, *Bodies that Matter: On the Discursive Limits of 'Sex'* (New York: Routledge, 1993).

—— *Gender Trouble: Feminism and the Subversion of Identity*, Routledge Classics (2nd edn, New York: Routledge, 2006).

—— *Undoing Gender* (New York: Routledge, 2004).

Caemmerer, Christiane, Walter Delabar and Helga Meise, 'Die perfekte Welle: Das literarische Fräuleinwunder wird besichtigt. Eine Einleitung', in Christiane Caemmerer, Walter Delabar and Helga Meise, eds, *Fräuleinwunder literarisch: Literatur von Frauen zu Beginn des 21. Jahrhunderts*, Inter-Lit (New York: Peter Lang, 2005), 7–12.

——, eds, *Fräuleinwunder literarisch: Literatur von Frauen zu Beginn des 21. Jahrhunderts*, Inter-Lit (New York: Peter Lang, 2005).

Carter, Angela, 'In the Company of Wolves', *Burning Your Boats: The Collected Short Stories* (New York: Henry Holt and Company, 1995), 212–20.

Chodorow, Nancy J., *Feminism and Psychoanalytic Theory* (New Haven, CT: Yale University Press, 1989).

—— *The Reproduction of Mothering: Psychoanalysis and the Sociology of Gender* (2nd edn, Berkeley: University of California Press, 1978).

—— and Susan Contratto, 'The Fantasy of the Perfect Mother', in Barrie Thorne and Marilyn Yalom, eds, *Rethinking the Family: Some Feminist Questions* (Boston: Northeastern University Press, 1992), 191–214.

Cleto, Fabio, ed., *Camp: Queer Aesthetics and the Performing Subject. A Reader* (Ann Arbor: University of Michigan Press, 1999).

Conrad, Bernadette, 'Alle reden, und Helene verstummt', *Die Zeit* (18 Oct. 2007).

Delabar, Walter, 'Reload, remix, repeat – remember: Chronikalische Anmerkungen zum Wunder des Fräuleinwunders', in Christiane Caemmerer, Walter Delabar and Helga Meise, eds, *Fräuleinwunder literarisch; Literatur von Frauen zu Beginn des 21. Jahrhunderts*, Inter-Lit (New York: Peter Lang, 2005), 231–49.

Detering, Heinrich, 'Fäden an den Hufen der Worte', *Frankfurter Allgemeine Zeitung* (27 April 1998).

Dillaway, Heather, and Elizabeth Paré, 'Locating Mothers: How Cultural Debates about Stay-at-Home Versus Working Mothers Define Women and Home', *Journal of Family Issues* 29 (2008), 437–64.

Döbler, Katharina, 'Peterchens Mutter', *Die Zeit* (6 September 2007).

—— 'Schleimhaut inklusiv: Julia Franck will Hautkontakt', *Die Zeit* (28 December 2000).

Domosh, Mona, and Joni Seager, *Putting Women in Place: Feminist Geographers Make Sense of the World* (New York: The Guilford Press, 2001).

Dorn, Thea, *Die neue F-Klasse: Wie die Zukunft von Frauen gemacht wird* (Munich: Piper, 2006).

Downing, Christine, *Psyche's Sisters: ReImagining the Meaning of Sisterhood* (New York: Harper & Row Publishers, 1988).

Druxes, Helga, *Resisting Bodies: The Negotiation of Female Agency in Twentieth-Century Women's Fiction*, Kritik: German Literary Theory and Cultural Studies (Detroit: Wayne State University Press, 1996).

Duncan, James, and David Lambert, 'Landscapes of Home', in James Duncan, N. C. Johnson and R. H. Schein, eds, *A Companion to Cultural Geography* (Oxford: Blackwell, 2003), 382–403.

Dückers, Tanja, *Himmelskörper* (Berlin: Aufbau Taschenbuch Verlag, 2003).

——*Spielzone* (5th edn, Berlin: Aufbau Taschenbuch Verlag, 2007).

Dürr, Anke, 'Julia Franck und das Leben', *Emma* (November/December 2007), 16.

——Ulrike Knöfel and Claudia Voigt, 'Weder Muse noch Madonna', *Der Spiegel* (7 July 2008), 136–9.

Duve, Karen, *Regenroman* (5th edn, Frankfurt am Main: Eichborn Verlag, 1999).

Ecker, Gisela, ed., *Feminist Aesthetics* (Boston: Beacon Press, 1985).

Eigler, Friederike, *Gedächtnis und Geschichte in Generationenromanen seit der Wende*, Philologische Studien und Quellen (Berlin: Erich Schmidt Verlag, 2005).

Eismann, Sonja, ed., *Hot Topic: Popfeminismus heute* (Mainz: Ventil, 2007).

Encke, Julia, 'Kräftiger Hände Arbeit', *Frankfurter Allgemeine Zeitung* (12 October 1999).

Erpenbeck, Jenny, *Heimsuchung* (Munich: btb Verlag, 2010).

'Eva Hermans Buch schon auf der Bestsellerliste', *Die Welt* (13 September 2007).

Feiereisen, Florence, 'Liebe als Utopie? Von der Unmöglichkeit menschlicher Näheräume in den Kurzgeschichten von Tanja Dückers, Julia Franck und Judith Hermann', in Lea Müller-Dannhausen, Ilse Nagelschmidt and Sandy Feldbacher, eds, *Zwischen Inszenierung und Botschaft: Zur Literatur deutschsprachiger Autorinnen ab Ende des 20. Jahrhunderts*, Literaturwissenschaft (Berlin: Frank & Timme, 2006), 179–96.

Felski, Rita, *Literature after Feminism* (Chicago: University of Chicago Press, 2003).

Feßmann, Meike, 'Poetik der Nähe: Zur Topologie des Intimen in der Gegenwarts-literatur', *Sinn und Form* 1 (2004), 58–76.

Fitzel, Thomas, 'Nähe als Utopie: Julia Francks erotischer Erzählband "Bauchlandung"', *Die Welt* (22 July 2000).

Franck, Julia, 'Absätze', in Eckhard Schneider, ed., *Thomas Demand: Phototrophy* (Vienna: Kunsthaus Bregenz, 2004), 112–13.

——'AW: AW: Grüße' [email to Alexandra Merley Hill] (19 September 2011) <hilla@ up.edu> accessed September 2011.

—— *Bauchlandung: Geschichten zum Anfassen* (5th edn, Cologne: DuMont Buchverlag, 2000).

—— 'Bäuchlings', *Bauchlandung: Geschichten zum Anfassen* (Cologne: DuMont Buchverlag, 2000), 7–16.

—— *The Blind Side of the Heart*, tr. Anthea Bell (London: Harvill Secker, 2009).

—— *The Blindness of the Heart*, tr. Anthea Bell (New York: Grove Atlantic, 2009).

—— 'Die Dame mit Biß' *Frankfurter Allgemeine Sonntagszeitung* (16 October 2005).

—— 'Der Hausfreund', *Bauchlandung: Geschichten zum Anfassen* (5th edn, Cologne: DuMont Buchverlag, 2000), 83–94.

—— 'First Interview' [interview with Alexandra Merley Hill] (Berlin: 19 June 2007).

—— 'Ich bin kein Mensch mit zehn Versicherungen', *Das Magazin* (August 2003), 16–20.

—— *Lagerfeuer* (Cologne: DuMont, 2003).

—— *Liebediener* (Cologne: DuMont Buchverlag, 1999).

—— 'Lust am Leben', *Kölner Stadt-Anzeiger* (29 April 2006).

—— 'Mein Portier', in Ulrike Ostermeyer and Sophie Zeitz, eds, *West-östliche Diven* (Munich: Deutscher Taschenbuch Verlag, 2000), 11–17.

—— 'Mir nichts, dir nichts', *Bauchlandung: Geschichten zum Anfassen* (5th edn, Cologne: DuMont Buchverlag, 2000), 95–111.

—— *Die Mittagsfrau* (Frankfurt am Main: S. Fischer Verlag, 2007).

—— *Der neue Koch* (Frankfurt am Main: Fischer Taschenbuch Verlag, 1997).

—— 'Politik und Literatur', in Heinz Lunzer, Klaus Amann and Ursula Seeber, eds, *Ungefragt: Über Literatur und Politik* (Vienna: Czernin Verlag, 2005), 66–71.

—— 'Re: Fragen zum Lagerfeuer' [email to Alexandra Merley Hill] (30 March 2007) <amerley@german.umass.edu> accessed March 2007.

—— 'Re: Frühling' [email to Alexandra Merley Hill] (10 April 2008) <amerley@german.umass.edu> accessed April 2008.

—— 'Re: Ihre Frage' [email to Alexandra Merley Hill] (27 November 2006) <amerley@german.umass.edu> accessed November 2006.

—— 'Re: Ihre Frage' [email to Alexandra Merley Hill] (6 December 2006) <amerley@german.umass.edu> accessed December 2006.

—— 'Re: Kunst und das Leben' [email to Alexandra Merley Hill] (2 August 2007) <amerley@german.umass.edu> accessed August 2007.

—— 'Re: die Mittagsfrau' [email to Alexandra Merley Hill] (25 August 2007) <amerley@german.umass.edu> accessed August 2007.

—— 'Re: MLA Vortrag' [email to Alexandra Merley Hill] (12 March 2007) <amerley@german.umass.edu> accessed March 2007.

—— 'Re: Mutterschaft' [email to Alexandra Merley Hill] (10 November 2007) <amerley@german.umass.edu> accessed April 2008.

—— 'Re: Vanity Fair' [email to Alexandra Merley Hill] (8 December 2007) <amerley @german.umass.edu> accessed April 2008.

—— 'Re: Weiter geht's' [email to Alexandra Merley Hill] (16 February 2008) <amerley @german.umass.edu> accessed April 2008.

—— *Rücken an Rücken* (Frankfurt am Main: S. Fischer Verlag, 2011).

—— 'Second Interview' [interview with Alexandra Merley Hill] (Berlin: 20 June 2007).

—— 'Staat und Religion', *Der Spiegel* 4 (2009).

—— 'Strandbad', *Bauchlandung: Geschichten zum Anfassen* (5th edn, Cologne: DuMont Buchverlag, 2000), 37–49.

—— 'Streuselschnecke', *Bauchlandung: Geschichten zum Anfassen* (5th edn, Cologne: DuMont Buchverlag, 2000), 51–2.

—— 'Was ich heimlich lese', *Cicero* 4 (April 2008).

—— 'The Wonder (of) Woman', tr. Alexandra Merley Hill, *Women in German Yearbook* 24 (2008), 235–40.

—— 'Das Wunder Frau', *Women in German Yearbook* 24 (2008), 229–35.

—— 'Zugfahrt', *Bauchlandung: Geschichten zum Anfassen* (5th edn, Cologne: DuMont Buchverlag, 2000), 7–16.

——, ed., *Grenzübergänge: Autoren aus Ost und West erinnern sich* (Frankfurt am Main: S. Fischer Verlag, 2009).

Freud, Sigmund, 'The Dissolution of the Oedipus Complex', *The Standard Edition of the Complete Psychological Works of Sigmund Freud*, ed. James Strachey, xix (London: The Hogarth Press, 1961), 173–9.

—— 'Female Sexuality', *The Standard Edition of the Complete Psychological Works of Sigmund Freud*, ed. James Strachey, xxi (London: The Hogarth Press, 1961), 225–43.

—— 'Some Psychical Consequences of the Anatomical Distinction between the Sexes', *The Standard Edition of the Complete Psychological Works of Sigmund Freud*, ed. James Strachey, xix (London: The Hogarth Press, 1961), 248–58.

Friday, Nancy, *My Mother, My Self: The Daughter's Search for Identity* (New York: Dell, 1977).

Frisch, Christine, 'Powerfrauen und Frauenpower: Zur deutschsprachigen Frauenliteratur der Neunziger', in Thomas Jung, ed., *Alles nur Pop? Anmerkungen zur populären und Pop-Literatur seit 1990*, Ostoer Beiträge zur Germanistik (New York: Peter Lang, 2002), 103–16.

Fuchs, Anne, *Phantoms of War in Contemporary German Literature, Films and Discourse: The Politics of Memory* (New York: Palgrave Macmillan, 2008).

Fuld, Werner, 'Ideales Versteck für Schriftsteller', *Welt am Sonntag* (14 November 1999).

Ganeva, Mila, 'From West-German *Väterliteratur* to Post-Wall *Enkelliteratur*: The End of the Generation Conflict in Marcel Beyer's *Spione* and Tanja Dückers's *Himmelskörper*', *Seminar* 43/2 (2007), 149–62.

Garber, Marjorie, *Vested Interests: Cross-Dressing and Cultural Anxiety* (New York: Routledge, 1992).

Gerstenberger, Katharina, *Writing the New Berlin: The German Capital in Post-Wall Literature* (Rochester, NY: Camden House, 2008).

——and Patricia Herminghouse, eds, *German Literature in a New Century: Trends, Traditions, Transitions, Transformations* (New York: Berghahn Books, 2008).

Gilbert, Sandra M., and Susan Gubar, *The Madwoman in the Attic: The Woman Writer and the Nineteenth-Century Literary Imagination* (2nd edn, New Haven, CT: Yale University Press, 2000).

Goffman, Erving, *The Presentation of Self in Everday Life* (Garden City, NY: Doubleday, 1959).

Grätz, Katharina, 'Das Andere hinter der Mauer: Retrospektive Grenzkonstruktion und Grenzüberschreitung in Julia Francks *Lagerfeuer* und Wolfgang Hilbigs *Das Provisorium*', in Barbara Besslich, Katharina Grätz and Olaf Hildebrand, eds, *Wende des Erinnerns? Geschichtskonstruktionen in der deutschen Literatur nach 1989* (Berlin: Erich Schmidt, 2006), 243–57.

Graves, Peter J., 'Karen Duve, Kathrin Schmidt, Judith Hermann: "Ein literarisches Fräuleinwunder"?', *German Life and Letters* 55/2 (2002), 196–207.

Großman, Karin, 'Gleiche Löffel für die Bildungstöpfe', *Sächsische Zeitung* (10 March 2008).

Guignard, Florence, 'Maternity and Femininity: Sharing and Splitting in the Mother-Daughter Relationship', in Alcira Mariam Alizade, ed., *Motherhood in the Twenty-First Century*, Psychoanalysis and Women (New York: Karnac, 2006), 97–111.

Haaf, Meredith, Susanne Klingner and Barbara Streidl, *Wir Alphamädchen: Warum Feminismus das Leben schöner macht* (Hamburg: Hoffmann und Campe, 2008).

Hacker, Katharina, *Die Habenichtse* (Frankfurt am Main: Suhrkamp Verlag, 2006).

Hage, Volker, 'Ganz schön abgedreht', *Der Spiegel* 12 (1999), 244–6.

—— 'Die neue Lust am Erzählen: Generation Bestseller', *Deutschland* (February/March 2008), 22–5.

Haines, Brigid, and Margaret Littler, *Contemporary Women's Writing in German: Changing the Subject* (New York: Oxford University Press, 2004).

Halberstam, Judith, *Female Masculinity* (Durham, NC: Duke University Press, 1998).

Harder, Matthias, and Almut Hille, eds, *Weltfabrik Berlin: Eine Metropole als Sujet der Literatur* (Würzburg: Königshausen & Neumann, 2006).

Heffernan, Valerie, 'Julia Franck, *Die Mittagsfrau*: *Historia Matria* and Matrilineal Narrative', in Lyn Marven and Stuart Taberner, eds, *Emerging German-Language*

Novelists of the Twenty-First Century, Studies in German Literature, Linguistics and Culture (Rochester, NY: Camden House, 2011), 148–61.

Heidemann, Britta, 'Julia Franck: "Ich muss auf vieles verzichten"', *DerWesten* [website] (10 May 2009). <http://www.derwesten.de/nachrichten/nachrichten/kultur/2009/5/10/news-119251422/detail.html> accessed 11 August 2009.

Hensel, Jana, and Elisabeth Raether, *Neue deutsche Mädchen* (Reinbek: Rowohlt Verlag, 2008).

Herman, Eva, 'Die Emanzipation – ein Irrtum?', *Cicero* (May 2006), 114–17.

—— *Das Eva-Prinzip: Für eine neue Weiblichkeit* (Munich: Wilhelm Goldmann Verlag, 2007).

Hermann, Judith, *Sommerhaus, später* (Frankfurt am Main: S. Fischer Verlag, 1998).

Hielscher, Martin, 'Generation und Mentalität', *Neue deutsche Literatur* 4 (2000), 174–82.

Hill, Alexandra Merley, '"Female Sobriety": Feminism, Motherhood, and the Works of Julia Franck', *Women in German Yearbook* 24 (2008), 209–28.

—— 'Motherhood as Performance: (Re)Negotiations of Motherhood in Contemporary German Literature', *Studies in Twentieth and Twenty-First Century Literature* 35/1 (Winter 2011), 74–94.

Hirsch, Marianne, 'Mothers and Daughters', in Deborah Pope, Jean F. O'Barr and Mary Wyer, eds, *The Ties that Bind: Essays on Mothering and Patriarchy* (6th edn, Chicago: The University of Chicago Press, 1990), 177–200.

—— *The Mother/Daughter Plot: Narrative, Psychoanalysis, Feminism* (Bloomington: Indiana University Press, 1989).

Hoffritz, Jutta, *Aufstand der Rabenmütter: Warum Kinder auch ohne Baby-Yoga und Early-English glücklich werden* (Munich: Knaur Taschenbuch Verlag, 2008).

Hook, Elizabeth Snyder, *Family Secrets and the Contemporary German Novel: Literary Explorations in the Aftermath of the Third Reich*, Studies in German Literature, Linguistics and Culture (Rochester, NY: Camden House, 2001).

'In größter Nähe doch so fern', *Frankfurter Allgemeine Zeitung* (9 April 2001).

'Ingeborg Hunzinger: Widerstand in Stein', *Tagesspiegel* (22 July 2009).

Irigaray, Luce, *This Sex Which Is Not One*, tr. Catherine Porter and Carolyn Burke (Ithaca, NY: Cornell University Press, 1985).

Jäger, Christian, 'Der literarische Aufgang des Ostens: Berlin-Romanen der Nachwendezeit', in Erhard Schütz and Jörg Döring, eds, *Text der Stadt – Reden von Berlin: Literatur und Metropole seit 1989* (Berlin: Weidler Verlag, 1999), 16–31.

Jaggar, Alison M., 'Contemporary Western Feminist Perspectives on Prostitution', *Asian Journal of Women's Studies* 3/2 (1997), 8.

Jenny, Zoë, *Das Blütenstaubzimmer* (Frankfurt am Main: btb, 1998).

Jung, Thomas, 'Trash, Cash oder Chaos? Populäre deutschsprachige Literatur seit der Wende und die sogenannte Popliteratur', in Thomas Jung, ed., *Alles nur Pop? Anmerkungen zur populären und Pop-Literatur seit 1990* (New York: Peter Lang, 2002), 15–27.

'Das kalte Herz', *Frankfurter Allgemeine Zeitung* (10 Oct. 2007).

Kauer, Katja, ed., *Popfeminismus! Fragezeichen! Eine Einführung* (Berlin: Frank & Timme, 2009).

Kocher, Ursula, 'Die Leere und die Angst – Erzählen "Fräuleinwunder" anders?', in Christiane Caemmerer, Walter Delabar and Helga Meise, eds, *Fräuleinwunder literarisch: Literatur von Frauen zu Beginn des 21. Jahrhunderts*, Inter-Lit (New York: Peter Lang, 2005), 37–52.

Kofman, Eleonore, 'Feminist Political Geographies', in Lise Nelson and Joni Seager, eds, *A Companion to Feminist Geography*, Blackwell Companions to Geography (Malden, MA: Blackwell Publishing, 2005), 519–33.

Köhler, Andrea, '"Is that all there is?": Judith Hermann oder Die Geschichte eines Erfolgs', in Thomas Kraft, ed., *Aufgerissen: Zur Literatur der 90er* (Munich: Piper, 2000), 81–9.

Kolesch, Doris, 'Geschwisterliebe: Inzestuöse Liebe und Sexualität bei Marguerite Duras und Katarina von Bredow', in Gertrud Lehnert, ed., *Inszenierungen von Weiblichkeit: Weibliche Kindheit und Adoleszenz in der Literatur des 20. Jahrhunderts* (Opladen: Westdeutscher Verlag, 1996), 81–100.

Korsmeier, Antje, 'Blindheit des Herzens', *Die Tageszeitung* (29 September 2007).

Kraft, Helga, and Elke Liebs, eds, *Mütter – Töchter – Frauen: Weiblichkeitsbilder in der Literatur* (Stuttgart: Verlag J. B. Metzler, 1993).

Krekeler, Elmar, 'Das erkaltete Herz', *Die Welt* (29 September 2007) 2007.

Kristeva, Julia, 'Motherhood According to Giovanni Bellini', *The Portable Kristeva*, ed. Kelly Oliver (New York: Columbia University Press, 1997), 301–7.

—— *Powers of Horror: An Essay on Abjection*, tr. Leon S. Roudiez (New York: Columbia University Press, 1982.

—— 'Stabat Mater', *The Portable Kristeva*, ed. Kelly Oliver (New York: Columbia University Press, 1997), 308–31.

Kuhn, Anna K., 'Women's Writing in Germany Since 1989: New Concepts of National Identity', in Jo Catling, ed., *A History of Women's Writing in Germany, Austria and Switzerland* (Cambridge: Cambridge University Press, 2000), 233–53.

Lampl-de Groot, Jeanne, 'The Evolution of the Oedipus Complex in Women', in Robert Fliess, ed., *The Psychoanalytic Reader: An Anthology of Essential Papers with Critical Introductions* (New York: International Universities Press, 1948), 180–94.

Lange, Nadine, 'Invasion der Freundinnen', *die tageszeitung* (15 July 2000).

Ledanff, Susanne, *Hauptstadtphantasien: Berliner Stadtlektüren in der Gegenwarts-literatur 1989–2000* (Bielefeld: Aisthesis Verlag, 2009).

Lehnert, Gertrud, 'Identitäts(er)findung: Literarische Entwürfe lesbischer Adoleszenz', in Gertrud Lehnert, ed., *Inszenierungen von Weiblichkeit: Weibliche Kindheit und Adoleszenz in der Literatur des 20. Jahrhunderts* (Opladen: Westdeutscher Verlag, 1996), 101–18.

Lennox, Sara, '"Nun ja! Das nächste Leben geht aber heute an": Prosa von Frauen und Frauenbefreiung in der DDR', in Peter Uwe Hohendahl and Patricia Herminghouse, eds, *Literatur der DDR in den siebziger Jahren* (Frankfurt am Main: Suhrkamp, 1983), 224–58.

—— 'Oppositional Criticism: Marxism and Feminism, 1970–80', in Peter Uwe Hohendahl, ed., *German Studies in the United States: A Historical Handbook* (New York: The Modern Language Association of America, 2003), 231–42.

Lenz, Daniel and Eric Pütz, eds, *LebensBeschreibungen. Zwanzig Gespräche mit Schriftstellern* (Munich: Edition Text + Kritik, 2000).

Lewis, Thomas, Fari Amini and Richard Lannon, *A General Theory of Love* (New York: Vintage Books, 2000).

Littler, Margaret, 'Cultural Memory and Identity Formation in the Berlin Republic', in Stuart Taberner, ed., *Contemporary German Fiction: Writing in the Berlin Republic*, Cambridge Studies in German (Cambridge: Cambridge University Press, 2007), 177–95.

Loxley, James, *Performativity*, The New Critical Idiom (New York: Routledge, 2007).

McAfee, Noëlle, *Julia Kristeva*, Routledge Critical Thinkers (New York: Routledge, 2004).

McCarthy, Margaret, 'Feminism and Generational Conflicts in Alexa Hennig von Lange's *Relax*, Elke Naters's *Lügen*, Charlotte Roche's *Feuchtgebiete*', *Studies in Twentieth and Twenty-First Century Literature* 35/1 (Winter 2011), 56–73.

Macnab, Lucy, 'Becoming Bodies: Corporeal Potential in Short Stories by Julia Franck, Karen Duve, and Malin Schwerdtfeger', in Heike Bartel and Elizabeth Boa, eds, *Pushing at Boundaries: Approaches to Contemporary German Women Writers from Karen Duve to Jenny Erpenbeck*, German Monitor (New York: Rodopi, 2006), 107–18.

Magenau, Jörg, 'Berlin-Prosa', in Erhard Schütz and Jörg Döring, eds, *Text der Stadt – Reden von Berlin: Literatur und Metropole seit 1989* (Berlin: Weidler Buchverlag, 1999), 59–70.

Maidt-Zinke, Kristina, 'Ein Macho wie die Axt im Walde', *Süddeutsche Zeitung* (27 September 2007).

Marneffe, Daphne de, *Maternal Desire: On Children, Love, and the Inner Life* (New York: Little, Brown and Company, 2004).

Marven, Lyn, 'German Literature in the Berlin Republic – Writing by Women', in Stuart Taberner, ed., *Contemporary German Fiction: Writing in the Berlin Republic*, Cambridge Studies in German (Cambridge: Cambridge University Press, 2007), 159–76.

Marven, Lyn, and Stuart Taberner, eds, *Emerging German-Language Novelists of the Twenty-First Century*, Studies in German Literature, Linguistics and Culture (Rochester, NY: Camden House, 2011.

März, Usula, 'Lasst mich in Ruhe!', *Die Zeit* 22 (26 May 2011).

Matt, Beatrice von, 'Die Dämonie von Lust und Unlust: Julia Franck schreibt Körpergeschichten', *Neue Zürcher Zeitung* (7 September 2000).

Matthias, Bettina, *The Hotel as Setting in Early Twentieth-Century German and Austrian Literature: Checking in to Tell a Story* (Rochester, NY: Camden House, 2006).

Meise, Helga, '"Ist die Liebe etwa ein Gefühl?": Judith Hermanns *Sommerhaus, später* und Julia Francks *Mir nichts, dir nichts*', in Karl Heinz Götze and Katja Wimmer, eds, *Liebe in der deutschsprachigen Literatur nach 1945: Festschrift für Ingrid Haag* (Frankfurt am Main: Peter Lang, 2010), 257–65.

—— 'Mythos Berlin: Orte und Nicht-Orte bei Julia Franck, Inka Parei und Judith Hermann', in Christiane Caemmerer, Walter Delabar and Helga Meise, eds, *Fräuleinwunder literarisch: Literatur von Frauen zu Beginn des 21. Jahrhunderts*, Inter-Lit (New York: Peter Lang, 2005), 125–50.

Meyer, Franziska, '"und dabei heißt es immer *aufbruchstimmung*": Das Verschwinden einer Metropole in ihren Texten', in Heike Bartel and Elizabeth Boa, eds, *Pushing at Boundaries: Approaches to Contemporary German Women Writers from Karen Duve to Jenny Erpenbeck*, German Monitor (New York: Rodopi, 2006), 168–84.

Miller, William Ian, *The Anatomy of Disgust* (Cambridge, MA: Harvard University Press, 1997).

Mitchell, Juliet, *Psychoanalysis and Feminism* (New York: Vintage Books, 1975).

Moffit, Gisela, *Bonds and Bondage: Daughter-Father Relationships in the Father Memoirs of German-Speaking Women Writers of the 1970s*, Studies in Modern German Literature (New York: Peter Lang, 1993).

Müller, Heidi, 'Berlins literarisches Quintett', *Welt am Sonntag* (29 October 2000).

Müller, Heidelinde, *Das 'literarische Fräuleinwunder': Inspektion eines Phänomens der deutschen Gegenwartsliteratur in Einzelfallstudien*, Inter-Lit (Frankfurt am Main: Peter Lang, 2004).

Nagelschmidt, Ilse, Lea Müller-Dannhausen and Sandy Feldbacher, eds, *Zwischen Inszenierung und Botschaft: Zur Literatur deutschsprachiger Autorinnen ab Ende des 20. Jahrhunderts* (Berlin: Frank & Timme, 2006).

Nentwich, Andreas, 'Alle Macht geht von den Koerpern aus', *Süddeutsche Zeitung* (25 July 2000).

Nikolchina, Miglena, *Matricide in Language: Writing Theory in Kristeva and Woolf* (New York: Other Press, 2004).

Norman, Beret, 'Social Alienation and Gendered Surveillance: Julia Franck Observes Post-*Wende* Society', in Patricia Herminghouse and Katharina Gerstenberger, eds, *German Literature in the Twenty-First Century: Trends, Traditions, Transformations, Transitions* (New York: Berghahn Books, 2008), 237–52.

Parker, Rozsika, *Mother Love / Mother Hate: The Power of Maternal Ambivalence* (New York: Basic Books, 1995).

Paul, Georgina, *Perspectives on Gender in Post-1945 German Literature* (Rochester, NY: Camden House, 2009).

Pezzei, Kristina, and Philipp Sawallisch, '"Die Grenze hat sich verändert"', *taz.de* [online newspaper] (16 March 2009). <http://www.taz.de/regional/berlin/aktuell/artikel/1/die-grenze-hat-sich-veraendert-in-20-jahren/?type=98> accessed 1 April 2009.

Pohle, Julika, 'Gebranntes Kind zündet ein Feuer an', *Die Welt* (27 September 2007).

Price-Chalita, Patricia, 'Spatial Metaphor and the Politics of Empowerment: Mapping a Place for Feminism and Postmodernism in Geography?', *Antipode* 26/3 (1994), 236–54.

Radisch, Iris, 'Der Preis des Glücks', *Die Zeit* (16 March 2006).

—— *Die Schule der Frauen: wie wir die Familie neu erfinden* (Munich: Deutsche Verlags-Anstalt, 2007).

Rafael, Simone, 'Reich-Ranickis Hoffnung', *Welt am Sonntag* (27 August 2000).

Rauch, Tanja, 'Das Fräuleinwunder', *Emma* (September/October 1999), 104–9.

Reents, Edo, 'Im Westen viel Neues', *Frankfurter Allgemeine Zeitung* (7 October 2003).

Rich, Adrienne, *Of Woman Born: Motherhood as Experience and Institution* (New York: W. W. Norton, 1976).

Riesselmann, Kirsten, 'Alphamädchen: Wir wollen mehr', *Der Tagesspiegel* (15 April 2008).

Rueschmann, Eva, *Sisters on Screen: Siblings in Contemporary Cinema*, Culture and the Moving Image (Philadelphia: Temple University Press, 2000).

Russo, Mary, 'Female Grotesques: Carnival and Theory', in Nadia Medina, Katie Conboy and Sarah Stanbury, eds, *Writing on the Body: Female Embodiment and Feminist Theory* (New York: Columbia University Press, 1997), 318–36.

Rüther, Tobias, 'Komm, lass uns tiefer gelangen!', *Frankfurter Allgemeine Zeitung* (7 October 2007).

Rybczynski, Witold, *Home: A Short History of an Idea* (New York: Viking, 1986).

Salih, Sara, *Judith Butler*, Routledge Critical Thinkers (New York: Routledge, 2002).

Schacht, Steven P. and Lisa Underwood, eds, *The Drag Queen Anthology: The Absolutely Fabulous but Flawlessly Customary World of Female Impersonators* (Binghamton, NY: Harrington Park Press, 2004).

Schafi, Monika, 'Housebound: Selfhood and Domestic Space in Narratives by Judith Hermann and Susanne Fischer', in Norbert Otto Eke and Gerhard P. Knapp, eds, *Neulektüren – New Readings: Festschrift für Gerd Labroisse zum 80. Geburtstag*, Amsterdamer Beiträge zur neueren Germanistik (New York: Rodopi, 2009), 341–58.

Schillinger, Liesl, 'The Life She Fled', *The New York Times* (15 October 2010).

Schlette, Magnus, 'Ästhetische Differenzierung und flüchtiges Glück: Berliner Großstadtleben bei T. Dückers und J. Hermann', in Erhard Schütz and Jörg Döring, eds, *Text der Stadt – Reden von Berlin: Literatur und Metropole seit 1989* (Berlin: Weidler Buchverlag, 1999), 71–94.

Schmelcher, Antje, 'Der Mann im roten Ford', *Die Welt* (23 October 1999).

Schmidt, Ricarda, 'GDR Women Writers: Ways of Writing For, Within and Against Socialism', in Jo Catling, ed., *A History of Women's Writing in Germany, Austria, and Switzerland* (Cambridge: Cambridge University Press, 2000), 190–99.

Schreiber, Matthias, 'Düstere Lichtgestalt', *Der Spiegel* 38 (2007), 196–9.

Schröder, Christoph, 'Das abgestorbene Innenleben', *Frankfurter Rundschau* (18 September 2007).

Schütz, Erhard, 'Text der Stadt – Reden von Berlin', in Erhard Schütz and Jörg Döring, eds, *Text der Stadt – Reden von Berlin: Literatur und Metropole seit 1989* (Berlin: Weidler Buchverlag, 1999), 7–15.

Schwarz, André, 'Das Schweigen im Flachs: Julia Francks Roman *Die Mittagsfrau*', *Literaturkritik* [online journal] 10 (October 2007). <http://www.literaturkritik. de/public/rezension.php?rez_id=11240&ausgabe=200710> accessed 1 February 2012.

Schwarzer, Alice, *Die Antwort* (Cologne: Kiepenheuer & Witsch, 2007).

Seegers, Armgard, 'Julia Franck: "Dieses Buch prägte Deutschland"' *Hamburger Arbendblatt* (14 September 2009).

Sieg, Katrin, *Ethnic Drag: Performing Race, Nation, Sexuality in West Germany*, Social History, Popular Culture and Politics in Germany (Ann Arbor: The University of Michigan Press, 2002).

Stöcker, Mirja, ed., *Das F-Wort: Feminismus ist sexy* (Königstein: Helmer, 2007).

Stockmann, Kristina, 'Erzählungen zwischen Begehren und Scheitern: Julia Francks neues Buch *Bauchlandung*', *Literaturkritik* [online journal] 9 (September 2000). <http://www.literaturkritik.de/public/rezension.php?rez_id=1530&ausgabe=200009> accessed 1 February 2012.

Taberner, Stuart, *German Literature of the 1990s and Beyond: Normalization and the Berlin Republic*, Studies in German Literature, Linguistics and Culture (Rochester, NY: Camden House, 2005).

—— '"West German Writing" in the Berlin Republic', in Stuart Taberner, ed., *Contemporary German Fiction: Writing in the Berlin Republic*, Cambridge Studies in German (Cambridge: Cambridge University Press, 2007), 72–91.

——, ed., *Contemporary German Fiction: Writing in the Berlin Republic*, Cambridge Studies in German (Cambridge: Cambridge University Press, 2007).

——and Frank Finlay, eds, *Recasting German Identity: Culture, Politics, and Literature in the Berlin Republic* (Rochester, NY: Camden House, 2002).

Theweleit, Klaus, *Männerphantasien*, 2 vols (Frankfurt am Main: Verlag Roter Stern, 1977).

Tuan, Yi-Fu, 'Home', in S. Harrison, S. Pile and N. Thrift, eds, *Patterned Ground: The Entanglements of Nature and Culture* (London: Reaktion Books, 2004), 164–5.

Voigt, Claudia, 'Sex ist nur Sex', *Der Spiegel* 14 (2008), 168.

von der Leyen, Ursula, 'Heimchen oder Rabenmutter?', *Cicero* (June 2006), 74–6.

Weedon, Chris, ed., *Post-War Women's Writing in German: Feminist Critical Approaches* (Providence, RI: Berghahn Books, 1997).

—— 'Power and Powerlessness: Mothers and Daughters in Postwar German and Austrian Literature', in Adalgisa Giorgio, ed., *Writing Mothers and Daughters: Renegotiating the Mother in Western European Narratives by Women* (New York: Berghahn Books, 2002), 215–50.

Wehdeking, Volker, and Anne-Marie Corbin, eds, *Deutschsprachige Erzählprosa seit 1990 im europäischen Kontext* (Trier: Wissenschaftlicher Verlag, 2003).

Welldon, Estela V., 'Why Do You Want to Have a Child?', in Alcira Mariam Alizade, ed., *Motherhood in the Twenty-First Century*, Psychoanalysis and Women (New York: Karnac, 2006), 59–71.

Whittmann, Martin, 'Ausgesetzt: Julia Franck liest aus ihrem Buch *Die Mittagsfrau*', *Frankfurter Allgemeine Zeitung* (24 September 2007).

Wild, Inge, 'Die Suche nach dem Vater', in Gertrud Lehnert, ed., *Inszenierungen von Weiblichkeit: Weibliche Kindheit und Adoleszenz in der Literatur des 20. Jahrhunderts* (Opladen: Westdeutscher Verlag, 1996), 137–57.

Wirtz, Christiane, 'Warum reizt Poesie Sie mehr als Paragrafen, Frau Franck? Zwischenfrage', *Süddeutsche Zeitung* (21 March 2000).

Wirtz, Thomas, 'Schmeckt es euch nicht?', *Frankfurter Allgemeine Zeitung* (12 August 2000).

Wolf, Martin, 'Unter Wölfen', *Der Spiegel* 10 (2006), 76–84.

Index

abandonment 6, 66, 143
  of a child 83, 118, 134–5, 147, 155, 156,
    161
abject 93–8
abortion 48, 115, 119
alienation 33–45, 46, 58
  see also Berlin literature; urban life
anger, maternal 118, 126, 130, 139–44, 146
Augé, Marc 11, 37–41
aunts 53–5, 141, 158

Bauchlandung: Geschichten zum Anfassen
    1, 7, 33, 36–7
  see also *individual stories*
'Bäuchlings' 25, 29–30, 78, 159–60
Beauvoir, Simone de 8, 17
Benjamin, Jessica 63, 77, 85, 130
Berlin literature 1–2, 33–7, 41–3, 46
Berlin Wall 5
*Blind Side of the Heart, The see Mittags-
    frau, Die*
*Blindness of the Heart, The see Mittags-
    frau, Die*
bodies 17–19, 24, 28, 67–8, 87–8, 93–8,
    159–60
  see also abject; breastfeeding;
    menstruation
Bovenschen, Silvia 8
breastfeeding 71, 82–3, 136
brothers 24, 58, 81, 114, 149, 156–7, 158
Butler, Judith 10–11, 16–18, 21, 27–8, 29,
    78, 106, 162

Carter, Angela 54
Chodorow, Nancy 12, 63, 75–7, 106
co-housing 13, 162–3
clothing *see* performance and costume

daughters 6, 10, 11–12, 30, 63–109, 130,
    149, 156
  narcissism of 63–4, 82–3, 91, 92, 105,
    109, 126–7, 130
  as performative identity 108–9,
    151
  and psychoanalysis 66–79, 82–3,
    105–6
  relationship with father 12, 150–5,
    161–3
  relationship with mother 63–109
  see also abandonment; gender roles;
    home; intimacy; mothers;
    sexuality
Deutscher Buchpreis 4–5, 15
dogs 79, 152
domestic space *see* home
drag 11, 16, 27–9, 30–1
  see also maternal drag; paternal
    drag
Dückers, Tanja 2, 4, 33, 58, 65
Duve, Karen 4, 42

East Germany 4, 80–1, 101, 133, 156–8
Electra complex 69
Erpenbeck, Jenny 59
ethnic drag 16, 161

fathers 12, 150–5, 161–3
'Female Sobriety' 7–8
feminism 7–10, 112–13, 162–3
Franck, Julia 1–10, 15
    and feminism 7–10
    and the *Fräuleinwunder* 3–4
    and the German past 4–6
Fräuleinwunder 1, 2–4, 42, 53–4
Freie deutsche Jugend (Free German
    Youth) 24, 67, 80
Freud, Sigmund 68–72, 74–5, 100
'Für Sie und für Ihn' 44–5

gender roles 17–22, 64, 97, 106–7, 109,
    141–2, 148–63
    see also Butler, Judith; home and
        gender; performativity
globalisation *see* supermodernity
*Grenzübergänge: Autoren aus Ost und
    West erinnern sich* 5

'Hausfreund, Der' 24–5, 66–8, 72–4,
    85–6, 100, 102, 150
Hermann, Judith 2, 4, 5, 8, 33, 42, 58
heterosexuality 19, 27, 70, 78
historia matria 149
home 34, 57–62, 158–63
    and family 58, 62, 63, 98, 158
    feminist geography and 59–61,
        162
    and gender 62, 141–2, 162
    ideal of 59–62, 158
    and intimacy 43, 62, 63, 162–3
    in literature 58–9
    longing for 11, 43, 57–8, 61, 86–7
    and mothers 11, 62, 89–90
    as place 57–8, 60
    as process 162–3
homely and unhomely 57, 60–1, 162
homosexuality 19, 72, 74, 78

hotel 38, 61, 86–90, 98–9, 102, 105, 108,
    158
    see also neue Koch, Der

incest 19, 25, 69, 78, 159–60
intimacy 6, 13, 57–9, 66
    desire for 42–5, 46, 50–5, 57–9, 107,
        113–16
    through home 43, 57–63, 113–16,
        158–63
    impossibility of 35–7
    with mother 65–6, 92–8, 113–14,
        145–8
    sex as replacement for 33, 35–7, 42,
        54, 58, 107, 130–2
    see also 'Hausfreund, Der'; home;
        Liebediener; neue Koch, Der;
        siblings

Jane Eyre 139–41
jealousy 47–8, 67, 71, 73, 82, 85, 105
Jenny, Zoë 4, 65
Jewishness 117, 139, 144–5

Kristeva, Julia 95–6, 114

Lagerfeuer 4, 116, 121–34
    and fathers 150, 156
    mothers in 99, 116, 121–34
    and prostitution 99, 131–2
    siblings in 160
    and spaces of the camp 61, 122–3,
        128–9, 132–3, 163
Lampl-de Groot, Jeanne 70
Liebediener 1, 7, 21–3, 46–59, 63, 100–1,
    102–4
    and brothers 58, 114, 152, 156, 158
    and childhood 48–9, 57–8
    and clowns 22–3, 25, 104
    and desire for child 113–16

and desire for home 55, 57–8, 158
and desire for sister 159
and father 57, 151–2
and intimacy 47–8, 55, 57–8, 113–14
mothers in 100–1, 102–4
and performance 21–3, 25–7, 49
places and non-places in 46, 48,
   56–9, 158
and prostitution 52–4, 100–1,
   102–4
see also alienation; Berlin literature;
   Fräuleinwunder; observation;
   prostitution; social currency;
   urban life
Little Red Riding Hood 53–4
Lolita 154

madwoman in the attic 139–41
Marienfelde *see* refugee camp
masculine gaze 27
maternal desire *see* mothers, desire to
   become
maternal drag 11, 12, 146–8
matrophobia 64–5, 96
Medea 146
   see also anger, maternal
menstruation 27
   see also bodies
'Mir nichts, dir nichts' 36
Mittagsfrau, Die 4–5, 8, 152–3, 156
   and home 61, 63, 158
   mothers in 117–20, 134–48
   and sisters 120, 144, 161
mothers 12, 111–55, 161–3
   absence of 57, 113–14
   bad 111, 121–34
   break with 71–4, 75, 78, 81
   desire for 65, 66–71, 82–6, 88–90,
      127, 153
   desire to become 47–8, 76, 112–20

as model for daughters 75–7, 78–9,
   105–7, 139–44
as performative identity 80, 115–16,
   124–6, 132–3, 144–8, 161–3
and prostitution 98–107
selfless 134–9
significance for daughter 63–109
see also anger, maternal; breastfeeding; gender roles; home;
   intimacy; maternal drag; pre-
   Oedipal phase; prostitution;
   sexuality
see also under individual works
My Mother, My Self 64, 65

National Socialism 5, 59, 144–5
neue Koch, Der 1, 82–99, 102, 150, 159
   and home 61, 63, 85–90, 102, 105,
      158, 163
   mothers in 63, 82–5, 88–99, 102,
      105–7, 148
   and performance 17–20, 28–9,
      106–7
   see also hotel
non-places *see* places and non-places
nursing *see* breastfeeding

object-relations theory 75
observation 48, 50–1
   see also social currency
Oedipal complex 69–70, 75, 76

parenting 13, 76, 162
parody 17–18, 29–30, 106, 155
   see also drag
paternal drag 155
patriarchy 76, 99
penis envy 69, 72, 119
performance 10, 15, 21–7, 39–40, 49–50,
   130–1, 132

and costume 23–6, 29–30, 104
vs performativity 16, 27, 133
see also under individual works
performativity 10, 16–20, 109, 111, 133,
    141–8
see also under individual works
places and non-places 11, 37–41, 60, 61–2,
    86, 163
see also under individual works
popfeminism 9–10
pregnancy *see* mothers, desire to become
pre-Oedipal phase 68–9, 70–4, 75, 78,
    106
privacy 86
prostitution 52–3, 98–107, 131–3
psychoanalysis 12, 63, 68–79, 91, 100,
    105–6, 108
    feminist responses to 63, 75–9
    see also Benjamin, Jessica; Chodorow,
        Nancy; *Reproduction of
        Mothering, The*

refugee camp 4, 61, 122–3, 128–9,
    132–3
Reproduction of Mothering, The 12, 75–9,
    112
reproduction of mothering *see* mothers,
    as model for daughters
role play *see* performance
Rücken an Rücken 6, 24
    and fathers 153
    mothers in 63, 79–81, 101, 102, 116,
        156, 157
    and place 163
    and siblings 156–7, 158, 160–1
    and sons 156–7

separation anxiety *see* mothers, desire for
sex 80–1, 100–7
    as replacement for intimacy 33, 35–7,
        42, 54, 58
    in supermodernity 35–7
    see also prostitution; sexuality
sexuality
    active 54, 64–5, 71, 108, 142
    passive 12, 64, 70–1, 81, 106
    repressed 71–2, 157
siblings 13, 156, 159–61
    see also brothers; sisters
sisters 4, 19, 25, 72–3, 78, 120, 144, 149,
    157, 159–61
    see also under individual works
social currency 45, 51–2, 53
sons 12, 137–8, 156–7, 160–1
'Strandbad' 25, 41–3, 45, 46
'Streuselschnecke' 153–5
supermodernity 11, 58, 61, 162–3
    see also Augé, Marc; places and
        non-places

Unmöglichkeit der Nähe see intimacy,
    impossibility of
urban life 33–7, 56
    see also alienation; Berlin literature

West Germany 4, 66, 124–9, 131, 133
'Wonder (of) Woman, The' *see* 'Wunder
    Frau, Das'
World War I 152–3
World War II 135, 144, 153, 155
'Wunder Frau, Das' 7–8

'Zugfahrt' 37–41, 43–4, 45

Women in German Literature

Helen Watanabe-O'Kelly, University of Oxford
Series Editor

Women in German Literature is a series of monographs and rigorously edited essay collections focusing on the work of women writers and the representation of women in literature from the Middle Ages to the present day. The series contributes to efforts to broaden the German canon by publishing pioneering studies of work by women as well as cutting-edge assessments of relatively well-known women writers. This includes studies of the participation of women in German intellectual life and in the struggle for rights. The other major concern of the series is the representation of women in literature and media. Studies on this topic offer fresh perspectives on canonical texts and writers and analyse existing tropes that are often still dominant in German cultural life today.

1   Helga S. Madland, *Marianne Ehrmann: Reason and Emotion in Her Life and Works*. 340 pp. 1998. US-ISBN 0-8204-3929-0

2   Ludmila Kaloyanova-Slavova, *Übergangsgeschöpfe: Gabriele Reuter, Hedwig Dohm, Helene Böhlau und Franziska von Reventlow*. 200 pp. 1998. US-ISBN 0-8204-3962-2

3   Forthcoming.

4   Albrecht Classen, *Frauen in der deutschen Literaturgeschichte. Die ersten 800 Jahre. Ein Lesebuch*. 337 pp. 2000. US-ISBN 0-8204-4109-0

5   Luise Büchner (Translated by Susan L. Piepke), *Women and their Vocation: A Nineteenth-Century View*. 127 pp. 1999. US-ISBN 0-8204-4142-2

6   Moira R. Rogers, *Newtonianism for the Ladies and Other Uneducated Souls: The Popularization of Science in Leipzig, 1687–1750*. 183 pp. 2003. US-ISBN 0-8204-5029-4

7   Karin U. Schestokat, *German Women in Cameroon: Travelogues from Colonial Times*. 216 pp. 2003. US-ISBN 0-8204-5538-5

8   Katrin Komm, *Das Kaiserreich in Zeitromanen von Hedwig Dohm und Elizabeth von Arnim*. 267 pp. 2003. ISBN 3-03910-139-0, US-ISBN 0-8204-6899-1

9   Cordelia Scharpf, *Luise Büchner: A Nineteenth-Century Evolutionary Feminist*. 391 pp. 2008. ISBN 978-3-03910-325-6

10 Cecilia Pick, *The Front Matters: Artistic Presentation of Maria Sibylla Merian*. Forthcoming.

11 Traci S. O'Brien, *Enlightened Reactions: Emancipation, Gender, and Race in German Women's Writing*. 351 pp. 2011. ISBN 978-3-03911-568-6

12 Daniela Richter, *Domesticating the Public: Women's Discourse on Gender Roles in Nineteenth-Century Germany*. 205 pp. 2012. ISBN 978-3-0343-0180-0

13 Cordelia Scharpf: *Luise Büchner (1821–1877): Eine evolutionäre Frauenrechtlerin*. Forthcoming.

14 Alexandra Merley Hill, *Playing House: Motherhood, Intimacy, and Domestic Spaces in Julia Franck's Fiction*. 192 pp. 2012. ISBN 978-3-0343-0767-3